MOUNT MAGIA

BY

ERIK P. ANTONI

Proof Editing By
Monica Lamb

Cover Design By
Rimsha Hassan

Noetic Press
Text Copyright © 2018-2026 Erik P. Antoni
Registration: TXu 2-114-016
ISBN: 978-1-7363242-9-5
Third Edition
3.6.9

Please visit the author's webpage at:
www.songoftheimmortalbeloved.com

Other Books Written By Erik P. Antoni:

Concerto of the Rising Sun
The Alchepedia
Anthros Galactica (Book Series)

ACKNOWLEDGEMENT

The people who contributed the most to my alchemical journey and the writing of this book are my beloved family. The way each of them have uniquely reflected the divine love of the Spirit throughout my life has served as a pillar of strength and support on my journey into the Eternal. It is with this same Spirit that I now present to you this book.

CONTENTS

	INTRODUCTION SECTIONS	V1	V2	V3
i.	ACKNOWLEDGMENT	✓	✓	✓
ii.	PREFACE	✓	✓	✓
iii.	ADVENT OF THE VALKYRIE	✓	✓	✓
	CHAPTERS			
1.)	VALLEY OF THE GODS	✓		
2.)	JOURNEY TO THE MOUNTAINS	✓		
3.)	MOUNT SOPHIA	✓		
4.)	MOUNT KABBALAH		✓	
5.)	MOUNT MAGIA			✓
6.)	THE THIRD SANCTUM			✓
7.)	FELLOWSHIP OF THE LOGOS			✓
8.)	SYMPHONY OF THE ECHELONS			✓
	AFTERWORD			
iv.	ECHOES OF THE BELOVED	✓	✓	✓
v.	INDEX OF NOTES	✓	✓	✓
vi.	INDEX OF FIGURES & IMAGES	✓	✓	✓
vii.	BIBLIOGRAPHY	✓	✓	✓

PREFACE

Alchemy is the interaction of matter and consciousness. It occurs at the most fundamental level within all things in an attempt to reunify matter with the source consciousness from which it spontaneously emerges. This source precedes all of creation with an absolute eternal existence. The force exerted by the source to reunify matter is the ultimate driving force of the cosmos. It is slowly elevating all of creation to eventually achieve this unity. All human beings have the ability to tune their minds to this universal alchemical process to quicken their own evolution and transform themselves to a higher level of existence. This is alchemy.

What I attempt with this book is to expand the boundaries of human understanding of the most profound phenomenon of human existence, which is the innate capacity of the human mind to develop a direct experience of the universal intelligence latent within nature, out of which manifests all life-forms of existence, and literally transform itself.

This book explains an ancient alchemical philosophy in a new modern form. This philosophy is based on the teleological premise that there is a higher purpose to the grand order of the cosmos, within which alchemy is playing a key role in leading all things to an ultimate final design. The Human Soul holds a special position in the realization of that final design. Through alchemy, the spiritual mission and divine purpose of the Human Soul is revealed.

Each time the language development of a civilization evolves - due to a revolution in mathematics, physics, music, philosophy, poetry, art, and other fields of human understanding - there is an opportunity for others who are consciously endeavoring upon the alchemical process to build upon and transform the ideas of those who came before them to a more evolved explanation of our ultimate reality.

The alchemy presented to you in this book is the alchemy of the human being. It is not the alchemy of physical substances. Alchemy has a broad and rich history and is the origin of many of humanity's greatest inspirations, philosophies, and fields of study. The European alchemy of medieval history was a cryptographic language encoded with instructions for the alchemical transformation of the human being. This was done to protect alchemists from religious persecution. It was by secondary effect that medieval alchemy compelled the rise of modern chemistry. Alchemy's primary goal has always been spiritual.

Until now, the primary focus of my alchemical study has not been in the academic research on the history of alchemy, the translation of its cryptographic code, or the study of other people's theories of alchemy.

The primary focus of my study has been a lifetime pursuit to directly experience and undergo the transformation process made possible by alchemy. This book is the literary result of that pursuit.

To correctly decode any alchemical cryptography, you must first possess either a cypher, or your own direct experience of the universal alchemical process.

I was initially reluctant to write this book as a book can easily be used to indoctrinate and control others. The purpose of this book is not to indoctrinate people into yet another philosophy or religion, but to do just the opposite. The purpose of this book is to share a process of human liberation where people are no longer bound to any faith, belief system, or system of sociological control, but where each person is free to think, explore, and function as an independent investigator of the mysteries of the universe.

Wherever a person begins the alchemical process, the process is entered upon through the imperfect ideas, concepts, and conclusions others have of the nature of God and the universe. If an alchemist places all his or her faith in such worldly institutions, the alchemical process itself will eventually challenge the alchemist's faith, not to lose the alchemist, but to properly orient the alchemist into a direct relationship with the universe itself, rather than through the imperfect and illusionary mediums of humanity.

Preface

The research of others in the fields of psychology, quantum physics, anthropology, neurology, mythology, religion, and many other fields, provides the language development to make writing a book such as this possible.

Alchemy is a living philosophy. We all contribute to its understanding. No one person will ever be the final authority of its great mystery. The universe makes alchemy available to all human beings and requires no special intercession of select human beings on behalf of other human beings. Human beings do not make alchemy accessible to one another. Human beings only assist other human beings in recognizing the path that the universe has always provided.

This book is my interpretation of my experience of the great mystery. I wrote this book to assist others who may be endeavoring upon the universal alchemical process. It is important to realize, however, that we all interpret our experiences based on our own level of consciousness and our own level of learning, which has no limit. For this reason, there will always be others in the future who achieve a deeper and more profound understanding of the most fundamental reality of the universe and its alchemical process.

Although this book is long, I know of no other book currently in existence that explains the alchemical process so plainly and succinctly. This book was written in a format that conveys the alchemical information in a very concise, sequential, and logical format, and is intended for those who are serious in their study of alchemy. Someone who is serious desires to receive the information absent of fillers, feel-good stories, or non-essential phrases. This book contains densely interconnected information. When explaining a subject containing many interrelated principles, it is best to be as concise as possible.

In my own research throughout my life, I have come across and studied many books claiming to have, but most often did not have, any actionable information regarding the process of spiritual transformation. I chose to write a book I would have wanted to read myself when I first began my alchemical journey.

A philosophical school I attended from the ages of 16 to 25 proclaimed to have a book in its library that offered the road maps of the grand alchemical work, but it was in a language I could not read. I waited many years for the opportunity to study from this book. When it was finally translated, I was disappointed with the lack of detail, practical guidance, and actionable information. The book was mostly just a series of short stories and metaphors. This book you are reading now is my answer to the calling for a book that truly provides the reader with a real-world actionable roadmap to the alchemical work of the legendary *"Three Mountains"* spoken of in hermetic lore.

The Three Mountains are very real.

The logical sequence of this book is to first, in Chapter One, *"The Valley of the Gods,"* paint the landscape of our relationship with the universe and how we all fit within it, so we know where we're starting from relative to the alchemical work.

In Chapter Two, *"Journey to the Mountains,"* I provide a summary outline of the principles of the alchemical work. By the end of chapter two, we know both our current standing in the universe and the philosophical principles involved in accomplishing the work.

In Chapter Three, *"Mount Sophia,"* I take the reader through the process of the First Mountain, where we move into a direct apprenticeship with the universal alchemical process. In Chapter Three, I provide practical explanations with real-life practices of how to implement the work. In Chapter Three, I share with the reader the grand key to the alchemical transformation practice that has been missing from the teachings of countless teachers of the alchemical arts, lost soon after the oral tradition began thousands of years ago.

In Chapter Four, *"Mount Kabbalah,"* I take the reader through the process of the Second Mountain where we deconstruct the compensating mechanisms of the human ego and the adaptive instincts of our animal nature which prevent the authentic-self within us from integrating into a cohesive individuated whole. By going through this deconstruction process, we are at the same time allowing a fragmented-self to self-assemble into an individuated-self – which, when achieved - liberates our true authentic nature.

Finally - In a four-part series - I take the reader through the alchemical process of the Third Mountain known as *"Mount Magia"* where we harmonize our individuated-self with the Cosmic Consciousness, the Cosmic Mind, and Creation thereby accomplishing the Great Work. This four-part series includes chapters:

- Five: *"Mount Magia"*

- Six: *"The Third Sanctum"*

- Seven: *"Fellowship of the Logos"*

- Eight: *"Symphony of the Echelons"*

Beyond chapter eight (the book's conclusion), is a procession of short writings and imagery called "*Echoes of the Beloved.*"

ADVENT OF THE VALKYRIE
INTRODUCTION

<u>My Way Into The Path</u>

I did not find alchemy. Alchemy found me. My alchemical journey began in early childhood in a way that was spontaneous, natural, and undefined by others. It was not until many years later in my journey that I would realize the journey of transformation I was on was indeed alchemy.

Rather than beginning my journey through a philosophical school, religion, or intercession of another human being, my process was seeded and started through a series of profound spiritual experiences early in my childhood.

Later, beginning in my teenage years into my mid-20s, I studied in a philosophical school that taught its own version of hermetic philosophy. This school's philosophy was greatly influenced by Gurdjieff, Rudolf Steiner, Blavatsky, Krumm-Heller, Eliphas Levi, Charles Leadbetter, among others.

Toward the end of my time with the philosophical school, I realized through my own process, that the school itself had stumbled upon some core principles of spiritual transformation but lacked a depth of understanding of the core principles involved or how to correctly work with them. It was only through my own solitude and perseverance in the alchemical process that I was able to delve deeply into, discover, and explain its mysteries.

Witnessing the universal principles at work, unfiltered by the preconditioning of others, became essential to achieving a deeper understanding of what was being missed by the school. It was initially difficult to untangle my thought processes from those taught in the school, but this untangling process was in itself a catalyst that brought me closer to the Spirit of God, within which, I would come to discover the grand key to the alchemical transformation process.

My solitude coupled with my early childhood experiences led me to a realization of the existence of the Divine Spirit and how to include it as part of the alchemical transformation process. The profound result of this cooperation, accumulated over many years of continuous application, has proven beyond all doubt to be the grand alchemical formula - lost in the Dark Ages - and long sought ever since.

I do not see myself as a spiritual teacher, nor do I wish to be. I am just a man living an ordinary life, but my inner life's journey has been exceptional and extraordinary. Before writing this book, I was content with keeping my spiritual life to myself. I shared it with people only when I felt compelled to, which wasn't very often. Revealing my spiritual perspective happened rarely and only in small doses. It was only with a few people in my life that I would come to share much on the subject of alchemy. I shared mostly with just close friends and family members. Even until this day – I haven't shared everything.

The reason I have been so reserved on the subject is that alchemy can be explained simply on a high level, but to convey its true depth requires a serious, structured discourse, which very few people ever seem willing to engage in. I always found most people to be more interested in the trivialities of their lives than in the more profound subjects of human existence.

I also found entering into a direct alchemical dialogue with most people served only to disrupt the natural chemistry between people, which in turn, compromised opportunities for self-discovery. I learned to conceal my alchemy and live life naturally in the most unassuming manner possible. In this way, whatever gifts were meant to be shared between myself and others would be shared through an indirect, spontaneous, and unintentional manner. This approach proved to be the most powerful and most harmonious.

One evening, while having dinner with a friend, I felt compelled to share a bit on the subject of alchemy. This friend asked if I would write down the process for her, and I felt obligated to do so. What started out as a series of notes eventually evolved into this book. During the process of writing this book, I also found the writing to be a catharsis, as I was finally letting go of something I had secretly carried inside of me my whole life.

As noted earlier, my alchemical journey was initially seeded through a series of transcendental experiences in my early childhood. As I grew up, and as I spoke of these experiences with my family, I realized these experiences were not normal, and I quickly became quiet about them. These experiences eventually subsided as I approached puberty.

As a young child having these experiences, I never contemplated their significance because I did not have the life experiences yet to place them in a proper context. My life, however, would come to be guided by these experiences for many years to come. Even until this day - in my mid-40s - I am still reeling from these experiences and find them difficult to speak of. There is no adequate language.

As I attempt to share a few of these experiences, keep in mind that I had no formal training at this stage in my life regarding meditation, or any form of metaphysics for that matter. In the first experience, I was only seven years old. I would not even come to learn of such things until a few years later.

<u>The Emerald Green Valley</u>

One night, as I went to bed, when I closed my eyes to sleep, something other than sleep occurred. I do not remember falling asleep. My mind suddenly entered a completely different state of reality. This state of reality was as different from a dream as night is from day. As a matter of fact, this state was dramatically more real than even my waking life in the physical world. It was a state of ultra-reality.

I found myself floating over a paradisiacal emerald green valley surrounded by magnificent velvet green mountains, which folded into each other like pillows, with a crystal royal blue sky above. The valley below me was beautifully manicured, and the sun was warm and soothing as it glistened across everything. The scene was so surreal, and the colors so vibrant, I would qualify the environment as animated or magical. As amazing and stunningly beautiful as this scene was, it could not even compare to the state of mind running through me in that moment. I was filled with a total state of complete and utter ecstasy, bliss, and euphoria, which was so intense and profound, that when I attempt to speak of it, I'm rendered speechless.

The ecstasy in that moment was accompanied by a profound realization that was absolutely astonishing. I remembered this place! How could I even forget! This is where we all come from before being born, and it is where we all go back to after we die. See Figure [B]

This place is a manifestation of Earth in a parallel universe I refer to as the "*Primordial Universe*." The bliss came from the Divine Spirit (Spirit). When an individual's conscious awareness is fully aware of the primordial universe, the Spirit is easily felt. The bliss I felt was emerging from a deep internal interaction with what I refer to as the "*Spiritual Group Mind*," which completely envelopes the Earth in the primordial universe. The spiritual group mind is the illuminated planetary mind of the Earth. It has its own highly developed awareness of the Cosmic Consciousness. *"Spirit"* and *"Divine Spirit"* are used interchangeably and mean the same thing. See Note [A]

I remembered in this moment, our lifetimes on Earth in the physical universe are but brief voyages into a different universal reality to participate in a cosmic agenda to awaken the planetary soul of the physical Earth, which I refer to as the "*Temporal Group Mind*," and to deepen our own conscious awareness of the Cosmic Consciousness.

The temporal group mind envelopes the Earth in the physical universe and is what others call the Collective Unconscious, Noosphere[1], Lower Astral, or Lunar Astral, etc. The temporal group mind of the Earth is not yet fully aware of the Cosmic Consciousness. The spiritual group mind is what others call the Upper Astral or Solar Astral and is also part of the Collective Unconscious.

---

[1] **The Phenomenon of Man** – By Pierre Teilhard de Chardin, 1955 – In the book, Teilhard describes the *"Noosphere."*

In that moment, I remembered that our individual realizations of the Cosmic Consciousness are consummated at the end of each physical lifetime after we die and we return to our higher eternal reality within the primordial realm of the Earth. These realizations are set up by the life experiences we had while alive within the physical realm of the Earth.

We keep returning to the physical Earth to set up new realizations of the Cosmic Consciousness within us - each time gaining a deeper realization of it - and that somehow, our own individual realizations don't just serve us, they serve all of us in the awakening of our planet's planetary soul (Temporal Group Mind).

I awoke with tears already on my face. My reaction as a 7-year-old little boy was more of bewilderment. When I first awoke in my physical body, I was grasping onto the blissful feeling, trying not to lose it. I would later in life come to realize that the magical feeling was the Spirit, whose very nature I would come to define as the love of God.

I spent the rest of my life trying to figure out how to return to that heavenly realm. The alchemical process shared with you in this book eventually took me back.

The Primordial Earth

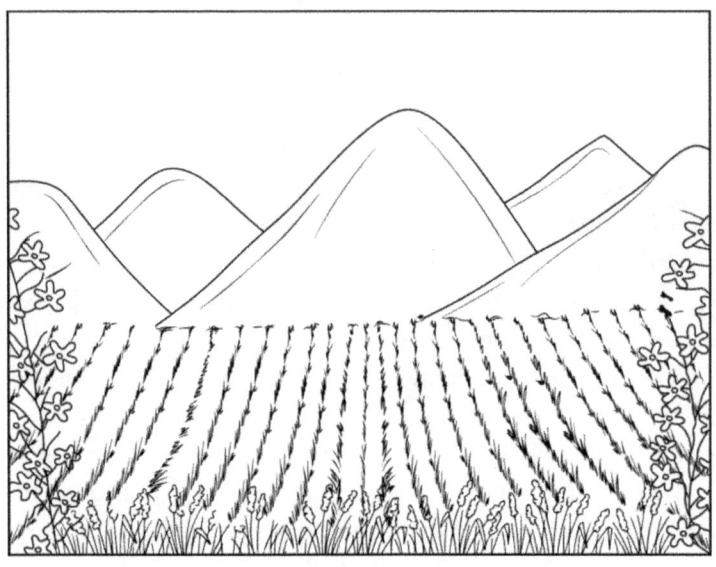

Figure [B]

An artistic impression of a view of the Emerald Green Valley located on Earth in the Primordial Universe. It is an image of Heaven. This place is very real. It actually exists. This image comes from my memory of this heavenly realm. The Emerald Green Valley is the other side of a portal between the physical Earth and the Primordial Earth. The Primordial Earth is the Celestial Jerusalem, Hyperborea, and Shambhala.

> **Note: A**
> **Definitions**

Divinity: That which was never born, and always was, and always will be. It precedes creation with an absolute eternal existence. There are only three divine forces. They are the three forces of the Cosmic Consciousness, which are: Awareness (Father), Life (Divine Soul), and Love (Spirit). The three original divine forces expressed in unity is *"Ain Soph."* Ain Soph is the *"God Particle," "Source,"* and original *"Monad."* All other forces are permutations of the three original divine forces.

Father: The trinity Godhead within the unity of Ain Soph and the universal awareness within the Cosmic Consciousness.

Divine Soul: The absolute, infinite, and eternal life force of the Father expressed universally within the Cosmic Consciousness.

Spirit: The infinite energy of the Father's love irradiating the Cosmic Consciousness. It is the Holy Spirit.

God: There is a *"God"* and there is a *"God-Above-God."* The God-Above-God is *"Ain Soph,"* the original Monad. Creation and its matter spontaneously arise from the infinite love generated by Ain Soph. A will emerges to reunify creation with Ain Soph and form a new Monad. The new Monad brings a new order to creation under the umbrella of a harmonized Cosmic Mind. This is God, otherwise known as the *"Immortal Beloved."*

Alchemy: The interaction of matter and consciousness forever driven by the relationship divinity has with itself and its creation. Its story is known as the *"Song of the Immortal Beloved."*

- End Note -

At the age of 7, I had no preconceived idea of what God was - or what Heaven was - but I sensed it might have something to do with the terms I occasionally heard.

I went to the kitchen that morning and found my father preparing breakfast. My father was a highly educated psychotherapist and social worker. At this stage in his life, he sought a mainstream explanation for things. I had no vocabulary or any capacity to attempt to explain what I had just experienced.

I just asked: "Dad, what is Heaven?"

He replied: "Heaven is a state of mind."

His answer was exactly what I needed to hear, for I would attempt to reconcile his answer with my experience for many years to come, ultimately launching me into a spectacular journey of the mind. Only now, at this stage in my life, can I appreciate the true brilliance of that answer. As a young boy, the answer just settled in the back of my mind to ponder later in life.

The Broken Helmet, Something Lost

A few months later, I'm asleep. That overwhelming sense of bliss and euphoria has returned (Spirit). I'm full of nostalgia, as I feel I'm being reacquainted with a part of myself I had forgotten long ago (yet I was only 7 or 8 years of age). There was something different about this experience than the green valley experience. That sense of ultra-reality was not present in this second experience. This second experience was more like a cross between a dream and the green valley experience.

Looking back on the emerald green valley experience after many years of practicing alchemy, I have since come to the realization that this experience was a full re-manifestation of my focus of conscious awareness within my primordial body. The primordial body will soon be explained.

Advent of the Valkyrie

I was experiencing the primordial Earth in the primordial universe. The sense of ultra-reality emerged because in that moment I was fully present within the totality of my being. For a brief moment, my temporal-physical being and my eternal-primordial being had become one. In the physical universe, a person manifests only a fraction of his or her total being. This suppresses and distorts his or her experience of reality.

In the emerald green valley experience, the bliss and euphoria arose from the Spirit, as well as from a deep interaction with the spiritual group mind enveloping the primordial Earth.

I was not in my primordial body in this second experience. In the second experience, my focus of conscious awareness went only as deep as my spiritual ethereal bodies that communicate with the spiritual group mind. I was having a virtual interactive experience with the spiritual group mind enveloping the primordial Earth. When our focus of conscious awareness is fully embedded in the spiritual group mind, the environment is dreamlike, yet different from a dream; it is full of Spirit.

In this second experience, while full of Spirit, I walked out the back door of my childhood home. I looked to the left and gazed off into the distance. The scenery was different. Instead of seeing my neighbor's house, there was a tall metal structure which looked almost like a water tower. It was very advanced or super-modern looking. It made a humming sound that pulsed and vibrated like a power station. The scenery was oddly familiar.

Then, above me, an aerial craft quietly descended and landed. The silhouette of a man emerged from the craft. The man handed me a brown and white helmet that was also very familiar. It provoked feelings of nostalgia. I was so happy to hold it in my hands once again. I held it for only a brief second when the helmet slipped from my hands and broke into pieces on the ground. My heart sank. I ran into my home to find an older adult relative to whom I attempted to explain what just happened. I was brushed aside as a nonsensical little child. That was the whole experience.

Because this second experience was a virtual interactive experience within the spiritual group mind, and not a fully embedded experience in the primordial universe, like that of a dream, the experience needs to be analyzed for its symbolic meaning. The planetary group mind speaks to us with a metaphorical and archaic language, reflecting back to us knowledge of ourselves and the universe.

As a child, I was not yet mindful of this dynamic. For a child, the message was clear and simple. I was left with the impression I had lost something special. However, it is important to note that at this point in my childhood; I had lost nothing in my waking physical life special or dear to me. This experience was referencing an artifact of my unconscious mind, of which I was unaware. Between the blissful state of mind returning to me once again (Spirit) coupled with the message of having lost something, the universe was preparing me for something I would not come to realize until many years later.

Precipice in Paradise

I am now 11 years old. I'm having a common dream (temporal group mind experience). In this dream, I'm riding my bicycle down a road in my hometown leading to the middle school I used to attend. While riding, I decided to veer off course and ride behind a building I had never explored before, when suddenly everything changed. The presence of the Spirit is back. I'm in a state of ecstasy. (I transitioned from the temporal group mind to the spiritual group mind)

The scenery is familiar to me. It is reminiscent of the primordial Earth. I'm standing at the edge of a precipice, staring down through a mist. Through the mist, I see my childhood town. Suddenly, I find myself hanging from the edge of the precipice. I look up to find my physical twin brother reaching down to grab my hand to help me back up. I'm struggling and then, at the last moment before falling, I finally reach safety. The experience ends, and I wake up from my sleep.

As with the last experience, it was not until many years later in my alchemical work that I would realize the profound meaning of this experience. At the early age of 11, I had not yet grasped the full reality of the temporal group mind and the spiritual group mind, and I was not yet fully cognizant of the existence of the Divine Soul or my primordial being. Your primordial being is a parallel manifestation of your physical being whose existence precedes the existence of your physical being. Your primordial being is immortal and lives inside eternity. When your physical body dies, you eventually re-awaken in your primordial body in the primordial universe. You have only one primordial existence and many physical existences.

Reflecting many years later, the meaning of this experience is obvious. My physical twin brother symbolized the twin relationship between the Human Soul and Divine Soul as well as the twin relationship between my physical being and my primordial being.

My primordial being was sending me a message that he was attempting to lift my physical being up to the same paradisiacal state as my primordial being. I would ponder this profound experience for many years to come until its meaning was finally realized.

The Dead Sea of the Ein Gedi

I am now 12 years old. My mind is fully submerged in the temporal group mind while I lie asleep. I am standing at the shoreline of a desert seaside. The sky is overcast. The sea is silvery gray. The environment is serene and mystical. An eeriness pervades. I look to my right and see two tall middle-aged men with long, straight hair falling past their shoulders. They're wearing pristine white tunics that extend to their feet. One man's hair is auburn red and the other man's hair is brown. They're both standing at the water's edge. The red-haired man is standing about 20 feet from me, and the other man is about 40 feet away. I look down to see the water washing up on my feet and, to my amazement, I see human hair in the water. I then look up to see rising up on the horizon a large wave forming. I turn and start running for higher ground. I reach a rocky embankment and begin to climb. My twin brother is there again at the top, helping me. Just before the wave hits, I make it to safety.

This experience was not well understood until later in my adult life, but it was one of those experiences that stayed with me all the years of my life. It was significant, and I understood that, even at the young age of 12. In the chapter on the Second Mountain (Mount Kabbalah), in the section on Uranus, I explain how the alchemist is working to free the emergent forces of the Cosmic Consciousness which seek to rise to the level of our conscious mind, but the suppressive forces of the mind - including our ego defense mechanisms and auto-cognitive programs - keep the emergent forces mostly at the level of our unconscious mind. I explain that there is an emergent force that is the fourth in a series called Eros. Eros is our creative life force. At its cosmic inception point within our mind-body system, Eros is perfect, but as it rises through the 13 layers of our mind, it becomes progressively distorted and disfigured. In its distorted state, it brings about much conflict within the mind.

At the age of 12 I was going through puberty, and more auto-cognitive programs of my instinctive nature were switching on. Although our auto-cognitive programs are natural, they're coded with genetic instruction to follow the evolutionary program of nature. When the conscious mind of a human being is seeking to rise up and take control of the very same system of nature which brought it into existence, it creates a conflict between the conscious mind and the evolutionary auto-cognitive programs of nature. The alchemist wins this great battle. Nature cannot automate a human being into self-actualization. It is a contradiction. At some point, the conscious mind must stand up and take control rather than be controlled.

This experience was showing me the twin primordial and physical dimensions of my total being (the two men standing along the shoreline) and that my instinctive nature was rising up and taking control (the rising sea). Eros was losing its perfect nature within me (the hair in the sea). However, before being subdued, I would eventually rise up and free myself with the help of my primordial twin being, who like all primordial beings, lives in the eternal realm in a highly developed sympathetic resonance with the Divine Soul - the life force of the Cosmic Consciousness.

The Grand Alchemical Key

The transcendental nature of my early life experiences was instrumental in leading me to the realization of the Grand Alchemical Key of the Great Work. These childhood experiences awoke within me an awareness of the Spirit I would not come to formally recognize as the Spirit until many years later in my life. Along with this recognition would also come a profound realization of the power latent within the Spirit in its ability to transform the mind.

The hermetic school I had studied at from the ages of 16 to 25 had an elementary understanding of the Three Factors, which I was still fortunate enough to learn. I struggled intensely during those ten years applying the school's meditation practices to break down the contents of my mind, but the school's practices missed the key element of transformation, which I would later come to realize and complete on my own. If I had lacked these childhood experiences, I would have never been able to complete the alchemical puzzle.

What led me finally to discover and realize the profound transformative power of the Spirit and its connection to my childhood experiences was an experience I had one morning in my mid-20s while in deep meditation. During my meditation, the Spirit spontaneously emerged within me while I was praying for the transformation of an element of my mind. The Spirit emerged in such a subtle form that if I had lacked the spiritual experiences of my childhood, I would have missed it. The Spirit caught my attention.

I focused on the Spirit, and while doing so, the Spirit emerged even brighter within me in contrast to what I was seeking to transform. Once the Spirit was held in contrast to what I was seeking to transform, the target element of my mind instantly transformed.

I would come to refine this method of meditation over the full course of my alchemical journey. I went through many years of intensive alchemical self-experimentation to finally deliver to you in this book the results of these alchemical labors.

In Chapter Three, *"Mount Sophia,"* I share precise step-by-step instructions on how to compel the alchemical transformation of your mind. On a higher level, I will share with you now - in very simple terms - the key to alchemical transformation is the realization of the light of God within you relative to the darkness of what is false within you. By false, I mean that which is outside the core essence of your Human Soul.

MOUNT MAGIA

THE THIRD MOUNTAIN

CHAPTER 5
MOUNT MAGIA

<u>Sunrise of The Beloved</u>

The wind ushers in the season's change. Darkness bellows fires of tempest soul. The horizon glows burning embers of orange rose. The Father calls deep, and the hero rises for the Immortal Beloved to sing and be known.

The darkest hour of night is the hour just before sunrise. It was mid-summer in the early morning hours of July 17, 2011, just before sunrise, while my physical body was asleep, and my focus of conscious awareness was fully submerged within the Void, that I found myself kneeling in a pitch-dark room, tired in my soul from all the toils of my alchemical labors, waiting for something which I did not know.

As I waited with my head down, from the corner of my left eye, a light appeared. I lifted my head. In the light I was being shown a staircase. It was the staircase I had descended in the Second Mountain while unravelling all the layers of my temporal mind. Each riser of the staircase was both a level within my mind and a level within the temporal group mind. After realizing the meaning of this apparition, from the corner of my right eye, a second light appeared. I turned my head to look into the light. In this light, a new staircase emerged. I realized in this moment I was being shown the staircase I would have to ascend in the Third Mountain.

Ah, but what was this? Unexpectedly, the second staircase was unlike the first staircase I had descended in the Second Mountain. The Second Mountain staircase was straight. The Third Mountain staircase had a beautiful geometry with two sets of stringers spiraling upward and downward like a double helix. I knew there was a special meaning here I would soon understand as I began climbing. Then suddenly, from a force beyond myself, I felt compelled to stand and begin my new journey. With renewed energy and a strengthened fortitude, I stood up and headed straight for Mount Magia and began climbing the Third Mountain.

Chapter 5

After many long hard-fought labors in the process of deconstructing the temporal sphere of the human mind, the Journeyman finally reaches the summit of Mount Kabbalah. After completing all the alchemical labors of the Second Mountain, the temporal sphere of our mind has coalesced into an individuated whole, however, our mind remains in a state of illusion.

At this stage, our state of illusion remains due to the temporal-physical hemisphere of our being remaining cognitively unaware of our eternal-primordial being. In the Third Mountain, we must integrate our temporal individuated being with our eternal-primordial being.

After achieving the individuation of our temporal cosmos in the Second Mountain, and while our Human Soul continues to animate the life of our temporal-physical existence in the Third Mountain, if our Human Soul further escalates its resonance with the Divine Soul from within our temporal-physical body, the self-organizing forces of Alpha will begin compelling the integration of our temporal-physical being with our eternal-primordial being. This is made possible due to our eternal-primordial being existing in full resonance with the Divine Soul well before our temporal-physical being ever attempts to establish resonance with the Divine Soul.

The escalating resonance between the Human Soul and Divine Soul serves as a bridge between the temporal and the eternal, between the physical and the primordial. When the temporal and the eternal resonate as one, the world of illusion is transcended.

Beyond the world of illusion, we enter into the noumenal realm of the cosmic quanta. It is the ultimate reality within all things.

It is a spectacular moment when our primordial being arrives inside the Void to lead our Human Soul into the Eternal and begin our journey of integration.

The geometric self-organizing patterns of Alpha immediately change their directional configuration to compel our journey upward in a continuous escalating resonance with the Father. In this moment, the Journeyman becomes a Foreman. This is how we complete Mount Kabbalah and begin Mount Magia.

Mount Magia

The alchemical period between the time the Journeyman regains conscious awareness of his or her primordial being upon reaching the summit of Mount Kabbalah, to when the Foreman begins Mount Magia, I call the *"Reclamation Period."*

It is during our reclamation period that the self-organizing forces of Alpha respond to our level of resonance with the Divine Soul by either compelling our alchemical process to proceed immediately onward to Mount Magia or compelling us to enter an *"Erodao"* cycle.

Erodao is a geometric Alpha pattern which spans lifetimes. Its sole purpose is to prepare us for the Third Mountain. Erodao emerges as a pathway at the end of the Second Mountain when it's been detected by the self-organizing forces of Alpha that the temporal dimensions of our mind are not reaching critical mass in resonance with the Divine Soul. Alpha does not give up on the alchemist. Instead, Alpha intervenes with its own organizational pattern and charts out a new course to the Third Mountain.

I had undergone my own Erodao cycle. This cycle began at the end of my prior physical existence and reached its peak between lifetimes in the heavenly realm of the primordial Earth. I was eventually reborn into my current physical existence and quickly retraced Mount Sophia and Mount Kabbalah.

Thanks to Erodao, and the time allotted to me in the heavenly realm of the primordial Earth prior to my current physical existence, after reaching the end of the Second Mountain for a second time in back-to-back lifetimes here on Earth, I finally achieved the prerequisite level of resonance with the Divine Soul to begin my journey of the legendary Third Mountain.

Erodao redirects our alchemical process starting in either our current life or in our previous life. However, after a period of cognitive conditioning in the primordial, Erodao fast tracks our alchemical process in our next life. As such, in my current physical life, which is the next life after the lifetime when I started my Erodao cycle, I reached the base of Mount Magia at the youthful age of 39.

I began writing this book only four months after beginning my journey and ascent of Mount Magia. I began writing November 4, 2011. The book itself became part of my journey of integration. I would come to learn that expression completes the cycle of realization and comprehension. From the very moment I started writing this book, my alchemical integration process, and my writing of the same process, would unfold together in tandem and become mutually supportive.

All the chapters up to and including Mount Sophia and Mount Kabbalah were written mostly in retrospect. All four chapters of Mount Magia were written as I climbed Mount Magia. For this reason, all the chapters leading up to Mount Magia read more like a dissertation on alchemy, while the four chapters on Mount Magia read more like a diary. After completing Mount Magia, I revisited the earlier chapters and synchronized the whole book.

It was in the evening hours of October 17, 2009 when I was reunited with my primordial being. I had regained a degree of super cognitive awareness of my primordial being which was transmitting through the dense psycho-neurological constructs of my temporal mind. The mystical event marked my completion of Mount Kabbalah and the beginning of my reclamation period in the Void. My reclamation period began on October 17, 2009 with my completion of Mount Kabbalah and ended with my start of Mount Magia on July 17, 2011.

In temporal time measured on the physical Earth, my reclamation period was 21 months. I was in the Void for 3 months prior to starting my reclamation period. In total, I was in the Void for 24 months before beginning my ascent of Mount Magia. I mention this time period only to demonstrate that the reclamation period is not short but requires a sustained period of cultivation of resonance with the Divine Soul. Even with the cognitive support of my own Erodao cycle, the process still took many months.

On October 17, 2009, the primordial twin being of my physical being arrived radiating with all the majestic energy of the Divine Soul. He appeared as an exalted young child of about 18 months in age. His aura was otherworldly. A sense of divinity, power, and royalty pervaded his aura. Other than recognizing the symbolic meaning, my focus was not so much on the appearance of my primordial being. Most importantly, I immediately recognized the radiant energy of the Divine Soul in his aura with the faculties of my super cognitive emotional awareness. Utilizing my super cognitive awareness of the Divine Soul, I began the process of integrating my eternal-primordial being with my temporal-physical being.

The integration would require higher and higher degrees of resonance. The escalating resonance would become the ladder upon which I would climb Mount Magia.

Our super cognitive faculties stem from our primordial body, and as such, the emergence of our conscious awareness of the Divine Soul via our primordial being is a spiritual event of paramount importance. The conscious mind of the alchemist expands into his or her own unconscious mind to allow for a conscious awareness of the Divine Soul to emerge.

The majestic quality of the energy of the Divine Soul is a super cognitive marker. Take notice of it and allow it to guide your developing awareness.

The moment I became aware of the Divine Soul within the depths of my being, my level of Q advanced from $Q3$ to $Q2$. Over time $Q2$ would become brighter and brighter. With $Q2$, I gained the ability to use my combined super cognitive awareness of the Divine Soul and Spirit as the fulcrum of differentiation within my internal alchemy.

My awareness of the divine source was becoming less and less filtered and refracted by my temporal mind. Its rays of light were gradually merging into one.

The individual mind always has a cognitive base (psychic cognitive background or bandwidth) which transcends the individual mind itself. Your cognitive base is the bandwidth of the planetary group mind with which your individual mind is most resonate - either unconsciously or consciously.

The planetary group mind functions as a cognitive base to our individual mind. However, the ultimate cognitive base is the Cosmic Consciousness. The Cosmic Consciousness is the source bandwidth. It is the ultimate vibrating string from which all other vibrating strings emerge. In the final analysis, it is the only thing that is truly real.

As a fundamental rule, any cognitive base always has a collective nature. By *"collective"* I mean, it either exists by resonate effect of many minds co-animating its very existence (planetary group mind) or it includes the Cosmic Consciousness from which all life and all things come forth. The temporal group mind, the spiritual group mind, and the Cosmic Consciousness, are all collectives at some level, or by some degree.

Alpha is steering the evolution of all life to become self-aware of the ultimate cognitive base of the Cosmic Consciousness which exists as the most fundamental level of reality underlying all creation. The steering of all life to become self-aware of the cognitive base of the Cosmic Consciousness is a function I call *"The Alpha Principle."*

The self-organizing forces of Alpha first steer our Human Soul to form the individuated mind of our temporal being over the course of the First and Second Mountains. In the Third Mountain, Alpha leads our Human Soul in achieving the integration between our primordial being and our physical being, and by way of our primordial being, we ultimately achieve a new level of conscious awareness of the divine source, the Cosmic Consciousness.

The progressive escalation of resonance between our conscious mind and the Divine Soul continuously retunes our psycho-cognitive faculties, transitioning our focus of conscious awareness to beyond the temporal group mind, up the ladder of resonance of the spiritual group mind, and then finally delivering us into the hands of the Father.

In Mount Kabbalah, Alpha moves the Human Soul of the Journeyman from one planetary group mind bandwidth to the next within the temporal group mind of the Earth. It is a simple geometry.

Mount Magia

In Mount Magia, in response to the Foreman's escalating resonance with the Divine Soul, Alpha adjusts the frequency of the Foreman's temporal bodies to achieve a deeper sympathetic resonance with the Foreman's spiritual bodies. As this process unfolds, the Foreman experiences a lifting of his or her temporal bodies from the temporal group mind of the Earth into the spiritual group mind of the Earth.

This is how we ascend and come to know the heavenly realms enveloping and enshrining the Earth in the primordial universe.

As the Foreman lifts the vibrational resonance of his or her temporal bodies, he or she is also pulling the temporal group mind into the spiritual group mind at the intersection point of his or her being.

Step by step, this process integrates our physical being with our primordial being, and it also partially brings into resonance the two halves of the planetary group mind of the Earth.

As we climb Mount Magia, Alpha compels our Human Soul to repeatedly cycle through each bandwidth of the temporal group mind. This is to lift the frequency of each of our temporal bodies and their corresponding temporal bandwidths to increasingly higher degrees of resonance with each of our spiritual bodies and their corresponding spiritual group mind bandwidths.

All six of our temporal bodies must rise to the same new spiritual frequency before the cycle starts again to the next higher spiritual frequency. Each higher interval brings our entire temporal-physical being into a higher level of resonance with the Divine Soul and our eternal-primordial being.

It all builds to a crescendo at which time something extraordinary happens. What ultimately happens, along with each interval step, is all revealed as we take this journey together through the forthcoming pages of this book. The geometry of the stairway of Mount Magia has a beautiful complexity.

As previously explained, all the psychic activity generated by all life on Earth co-animates the two halves of the planetary group mind. Life on Earth in the physical universe generates the temporal group mind. Life on Earth in the primordial universe generates the spiritual group mind.

The physical Earth, the primordial Earth, the temporal group mind, and the spiritual group mind, all co-exist in the same locality of space, just at different frequencies of space-time. Our temporal-physical being corresponds to the physical Earth and the temporal group mind. Our eternal-primordial being corresponds to the primordial Earth and the spiritual group mind.

The journey of our Human Soul through the temporal group mind of the Earth in the Second Mountain resolves the fractured dissociative nature of our psyche within the temporal sphere of our being.

The Human Soul's journey through the spiritual group mind in the Third Mountain integrates the physical side of its being with the primordial side of its being, and by way of this integration, the Human Soul enters a profound resonance with the Divine Soul - all while maintaining a living physical body. Typically, such levels of resonance are experienced only after death of the physical body.

The cultivated resonance between our Human Soul and the Divine Soul leads our total being into a deeply profound resonance with the Cosmic Consciousness. This is how we become reflectively aware of the Cosmic Consciousness while in physical form. The Divine Soul is *"the way, the truth, and the life."* The Divine Soul lives in the center of all life and in the center of all things.

> *"I am the light that is over all things. I am all.*
> *From me all came forth, and to me all attained.*
> *Split a piece of wood, I am there.*
> *Lift up the stone, and you will find me there."*
> *... Gospel of Thomas*

Mount Magia

Just as there is an ordered unfoldment of Alpha as we progress through the temporal group mind of the Earth in the Second Mountain, there is also an ordered unfoldment of Alpha as we progress through the spiritual group mind of the Earth in the Third Mountain. Progressing through an ordered system which is *"awake"* (spiritual group mind) versus one which is *"asleep"* (temporal group mind) as well as integrating with a life force beyond our physical being (our primordial being) versus integrating all the fractured elements within the psyche of our temporal mind (Second Mountain), creates a very different geometry and pathway in the Third Mountain versus the Second Mountain.

In the Second Mountain (Mount Kabbalah) we experience how each level of our individual mind corresponds to a different bandwidth within the temporal group mind. Each alchemical planet (level of our individual mind) has its own frequency of resonance within the temporal group mind. In this way, for example, when in the Second Mountain, we speak of Jupiter, or any of the alchemical planets, we are speaking about both the level of mind within us, and the temporal group mind bandwidth that the level of mind within us is resonant.

Each level of mind also corresponds to one of the 12 bodies of our being. Jupiter corresponds to our emotional body. Just as we have a temporal ethereal emotional body, we also have a spiritual ethereal emotional body. The temporal emotional body is our temporal Jupiter. The spiritual emotional body is our spiritual Jupiter. See Figure [2.4] When we work with each temporal body, we are lifting its vibrational resonance to be closer and closer in harmony with its spiritual twin body. This is called *"Planet Lifting."* Each alchemical planet is revisited 17 times in the Third Mountain - each time lifting its vibrational resonance to a higher harmony with its spiritual twin.

Chapter 5

The Trans-Dimensional Anatomy of the Human Being
The Twelve Bodies

Figure [2.4]

The hourglass figure in the center is composed of the primordial body (7) on top and the physical body (1) on the bottom. The upper lighter hemisphere is the primordial universe. The lower darker hemisphere is the physical universe. The five upper rays represent one of the five spiritual ethereal bodies surrounding the primordial body. The five lower rays represent one of the five temporal ethereal bodies surrounding the physical body. Each gradient within each ray represents the stages of alchemical transformation (Dark, Fire, Gold, Light). The inner circle around the hourglass represents the celestial body of light which forms when all the bodies come to resonate as one.

Mount Magia

In the Third Mountain (Mount Magia), we must lift the resonant frequency of each alchemical planet (level of temporal individual mind; temporal body) to increasingly higher levels of harmony with each successive bandwidth of the spiritual group mind.

When we do this, we are bringing the temporal levels of our being into harmony with the spiritual levels of our being. This is how we progressively become one integrated being. This is how we form our grand unified celestial body of light.

This may sound complicated, but it's not, because all we need do is practice the Three Factors. Alpha takes care of all the mechanics and all the changing in frequencies and bandwidths. Alpha leads us and directs us through the process.

However, we have the super cognitive ability to witness Alpha in action. Most of the content of this book is me charting and mapping the natural unfoldment of Alpha during the alchemical transformation and integration process. You do not need to pay close attention to Alpha if you do not wish to. Simply applying the Three Factors is enough. However, paying attention to Alpha brings about tremendous knowledge and profound understanding. It is just a matter of how much you want to know.

The alchemical process of integrating the twin spheres of our individual being involves the twin spheres of the planetary group mind of the Earth.

The lifting of the alchemical planets happens in stages in accordance with the number of bandwidths within the spiritual group mind for which there are 17.

We must lift all 13 levels of our individual temporal mind 17 times through the spiritual group mind during the integration between the physical and primordial hemispheres of our being. This means the Foreman has 221 planetary lifts which he or she must accomplish. ($17 \times 13 = 221$).

First, we must lift all 13 levels of our individual mind, one after another, to the 1st spiritual group mind bandwidth of *"Bardo"* before moving onto each successive spiritual group mind bandwidth.

Once all 13 levels of our temporal mind have been moved up one level of resonance to Bardo, we repeat the cycle of 13 again for *"Eroplatia"* by individually lifting all 13 levels of our individual mind one more notch up the ladder of resonance.

We repeat the cycle of 13 for each one of the 17 spiritual group mind bandwidths. This creates 221 steps, or 221 degrees of approach, upward through the entire spiritual group mind of the Earth.

Although the Third Mountain geometric cycles of Alpha may seem complex to the reader, all the Foreman really needs to do during the planet lifting process is to stay focused on both the resonance of the Divine Soul and the temporal body which Alpha is focusing his or her conscious awareness upon and allow Alpha to do all the work of the alchemical integration.

It is beneficial for the Foreman to direct his or her focus of awareness upon the energy of the spiritual group mind bandwidths which Alpha is shifting the Foreman between during the ascension process. Information is passed to us from the bandwidths directly into our soul while we concentrate upon them. The transmission is subtle and delicate, but the information is deep and profound.

Each degree of approach corresponds to one of the 13 levels within the mind encompassing our temporal-physical being, and to one of the 13 levels within the mind encompassing our eternal-primordial being.

Each time the Foreman completes one degree of the 221 degrees, this sews together, one degree closer, our temporal-physical being with our eternal-primordial being, as well as sewing together the temporal group mind with the spiritual group mind within the center of our celestial being.

The Foreman becomes a supercharged cosmic intersection between the two hemispheres of the planetary group mind of the Earth. The union of the two halves of the planetary group mind within the center of the Foreman forms a quantum gateway between the physical and primordial universes within the core of the mind-body system of the Foreman. Once this quantum gateway has fully synchronized, the temporal side of the human being can cross into the eternal side at will. This ability emerges within the unified celestial body.

The supercharged inner quantum gateway sets up and makes possible an entire new level of alchemy beyond the Third Mountain where the focus is no longer just the liberation and integration of our human being. The focus becomes the liberation and integration of the temporal group mind with the spiritual group mind of the planet.

Any alchemist who completes the Third Mountain participates in this very high order of planetary alchemy. It is a grand alchemical symphony of celestial beings who live beyond Mount Magia.
It is a cosmic symphony of light.

Some may ask why the inner quantum gateway is not easily accessible before completing the process.

The answer is: there are ways to experience the primordial (eternal) while leaving behind the physical (temporal) before completing the integration process. However, to truly become a trans-dimensional being - where nothing is left behind - we must complete the integration of the eternal dimensions of our being with the temporal dimensions of our being. The key is allowing our conscious mind to become aware of our eternal nature from within the matrix of our temporal nature. When all dimensions of our total being enter into resonance with each other via the conscious mind, all the dimensions come to function together as one. This is the unified mind.

A guitar does not play correctly until every string has been properly pulled and tuned. A lock does not open until every pin is in the correct position. Such is the way of the universe. Resonance unlocks all locks and opens all doors.

During the journey of the Third Mountain, Alpha leads the conscious mind of the Foreman through two great integration periods. Mythologically speaking – and in tradition of the ancients - the two great integration periods are represented as *"Purgatory"* and *"Heaven."*

Chapter 5

Purgatory is the Third Mountain ascension period where the Foreman is under a greater influence of the temporal group mind than the spiritual group mind, with the influence of the temporal group mind slowly subsiding and giving way to the rising influence of the spiritual group mind.

This gradual progressive shifting of influence is due to the bodies of our temporal being shifting closer and closer in resonance incrementally with the bodies of our primordial being during the Foreman's ascension of the Third Mountain.

As our temporal ethereal bodies enter higher degrees of sympathetic resonance with our spiritual ethereal bodies, the spiritual group mind bandwidths emerge within our psycho-cognitive background and are transversed by effect of our escalating resonance. Once the rising influence of the spiritual group mind reaches parity with the subsiding influence of the temporal group mind, the Foreman enters the spectrum of heaven and transverses each heavenly realm of the spiritual group mind on his or her way to the source bandwidth of the Cosmic Consciousness.

The names of the spiritual group mind bandwidths were arrived at during moments of deep meditation while fully immersed within and sojourning each bandwidth of purgatory and heaven. The names arose out of the resonance with the cosmic quanta. The "cosmic quanta" pairs our vocabulary to the resonance arising out of the underlying phenomena to formulate the language. It's the resonance of the words which is important, not the words themselves.

We are always submerged within a planetary group mind bandwidth even while our focus of conscious awareness is focused purely upon the physical world. We are considered "fully immersed" in our underlying bandwidth when our focus of conscious awareness shifts its attention away from the physical to focus exclusively on its underlying bandwidth. While fully immersed within each bandwidth, and in cooperation with the intelligence operating within the spiritual group mind, I translated the information flowing from the super cognitive resonance with each bandwidth.

The frequency of the bandwidth itself can be translated into a name. I translated the frequency of each bandwidth into a name using the phonetic pronunciation of the English language. When the resonant tones were very close in pronunciation to already well-known names, I felt compelled to select these names such as Bardo, Nirvana, and Valhalla.

I later realized during my alchemical progression through the spheres that I was being inspired and steered by the planetary intelligence operating within the spiritual group mind of the Earth to access the information held within the collective unconscious of our humanity and utilize its language. Its language is the language of mythology.

Although the popular names Bardo, Nirvana, and Valhalla manifest mythologically within the writings of our humanity, they represent very real frequencies of the planetary consciousness.

Granted these realms are not natural universes created through celestial mechanics in the way we know the physical universe, or in a way they may be mythologically portrayed. They are simple frequencies of planetary consciousness. Each contain a vast reservoir of information within the noumenal realm.

The planetary frequencies of consciousness, or in other words, the bandwidths of the planetary group mind, have been repeatedly experienced by many individuals within our humanity for eons of time and written so much about in our literature.

I was inspired and guided by the Earth's planetary intelligence to revisit and re-examine - at its source - the cosmological structure of the Earth's planetary group mind. In the midst of that pursuit, I wrote down what I was learning and re-casted the information within a new re-organized architecture - organized in relation to the unfoldment of the alchemical process.

Metaphorically, the realms of hell, purgatory, and heaven all represent ranges within a spectrum of resonance between the mind and the Divine Soul. The closer in resonance to the frequency of the Divine Soul the mind becomes, the more we experience with the metaphysical faculty of our super cognitive emotional awareness, the spectrums of heaven. The less resonant the human mind is with the Divine Soul, the more in darkness our mind becomes. This is Hell.

In the spectrum of hell, the conscious mind is resonant with only the temporal group mind.

In the spectrum of heaven, the conscious mind has a profound resonance with the spiritual group mind free of the suppression of the temporal group mind.

In the spectrum of purgatory, the conscious mind has a resonance with both spheres of the planetary group mind, but the temporal group mind dampens the mind's resonance with the spiritual group mind.

Most people in their physical life on Earth are resonate with only the temporal group mind and experience the spiritual group mind only after physical death.

The alchemist experiences every level of every sphere during his or her alchemical transformation process while in physical life.

The experience of purgatory begins with the 1st bandwidth of the spiritual group mind called *"Bardo,"* and ends with the 8th bandwidth of the spiritual group mind called *"Parabinlaya."*

The Foreman reaches the first firm footing within the spectrum of heaven with the beginning of the 9th bandwidth of the spiritual group mind which I realized to be the Buddhist heaven, *"Nirvana."*

The Third Mountain ladder of ascension is as follows: Sorted first by the spiritual group mind bandwidth order of succession, next by degree, and then finally by the associated level within the individual human mind.

The hierarchy of angels is a mythological designation for the levels of resonance between the temporal sphere of the human mind and the Father. I make the cognitive association here to explain the historical references and to make way for a new vocabulary.

Mount Magia

<u>Lower Kingdom - Individual Integration</u>
<u>Bandwidth (1) Purgatory (1) - Bardo - 5th A.P.</u>

- (1) Moon (1) High Cog Emotions
- (2) Mercury (2) High Cog Thinking
- (3) Venus (3) High Cog Instincts
- (4) Mars (4) High Cog Perception
- (5) Trans-Jupiter (5) Trans Cog Emotion
- (6) Trans-Saturn (6) Trans Cog Thinking
- (7) Trans-Uranus (7) Trans Cog Instincts
- (8) Trans-Neptune (8) Trans Cog Perception
- (9) Jupiter (9) Deep Cog Emotions
- (10) Saturn (10) Deep Cog Thinking
- (11) Uranus (11) Deep Cog Instincts
- (12) Neptune (12) Deep Cog Perception
- (13) Void (13) Center of Temporal Mind

<u>Bandwidth (2) - Purgatory (2) – Eroplatia</u>

- (14) Moon (1) High Cog Emotions
- (15) Mercury (2) High Cog Thinking
- (16) Venus (3) High Cog Instincts
- (17) Mars (4) High Cog Perception
- (18) Trans-Jupiter (5) Trans Cog Emotion
- (19) Trans-Saturn (6) Trans Cog Thinking
- (20) Trans-Uranus (7) Trans Cog Instincts
- (21) Trans-Neptune (8) Trans Cog Perception
- (22) Jupiter (9) Deep Cog Emotions
- (23) Saturn (10) Deep Cog Thinking
- (24) Uranus (11) Deep Cog Instincts
- (25) Neptune (12) Deep Cog Perception
- (26) Void (13) Center of Temporal Mind

Bandwidth (3) Purgatory (3) – Gerishan

- (27) Moon (1) High Cog Emotions
- (28) Mercury (2) High Cog Thinking
- (29) Venus (3) High Cog Instincts
- (30) Mars (4) High Cog Perception
- (31) Trans-Jupiter (5) Trans Cog Emotion
- (32) Trans-Saturn (6) Trans Cog Thinking
- (33) Trans-Uranus (7) Trans Cog Instincts
- (34) Trans-Neptune (8) Trans Cog Perception
- (35) Jupiter (9) Deep Cog Emotions
- (36) Saturn (10) Deep Cog Thinking
- (37) Uranus (11) Deep Cog Instincts
- (38) Neptune (12) Deep Cog Perception
- (39) Void (13) Center of Temporal Mind

Bandwidth (4) Purgatory (4) – Ferris

- (40) Moon (1) High Cog Emotions
- (41) Mercury (2) High Cog Thinking
- (42) Venus (3) High Cog Instincts
- (43) Mars (4) High Cog Perception
- (44) Trans-Jupiter (5) Trans Cog Emotion
- (45) Trans-Saturn (6) Trans Cog Thinking
- (46) Trans-Uranus (7) Trans Cog Instincts
- (47) Trans-Neptune (8) Trans Cog Perception
- (48) Jupiter (9) Deep Cog Emotions
- (49) Saturn (10) Deep Cog Thinking
- (50 Uranus (11) Deep Cog Instincts
- (51) Neptune (12) Deep Cog Perception
- (52) Void (13) Center of Temporal Mind

Mount Magia 49

Bandwidth (5) Purgatory (5) - Vishu - 6th A.P.

- (53) Moon (1) High Cog Emotions
- (54) Mercury (2) High Cog Thinking
- (55) Venus (3) High Cog Instincts
- (56) Mars (4) High Cog Perception
- (57) Trans-Jupiter (5) Trans Cog Emotion
- (58) Trans-Saturn (6) Trans Cog Thinking
- (59) Trans-Uranus (7) Trans Cog Instincts
- (60) Trans-Neptune (8) Trans Cog Perception
- (61) Jupiter (9) Deep Cog Emotions
- (62) Saturn (10) Deep Cog Thinking
- (63) Uranus (11) Deep Cog Instincts
- (64) Neptune (12) Deep Cog Perception
- (65) Void (13) Center of Temporal Mind

Bandwidth (6) Purgatory (6) – Orial

- (66) Moon (1) High Cog Emotions
- (67) Mercury (2) High Cog Thinking
- (68) Venus (3) High Cog Instincts
- (69) Mars (4) High Cog Perception
- (70) Trans-Jupiter (5) Trans Cog Emotion
- (71) Trans-Saturn (6) Trans Cog Thinking
- (72) Trans-Uranus (7) Trans Cog Instincts
- (73) Trans-Neptune (8) Trans Cog Perception

Middle Kingdom Transition Zone

- (74) Jupiter (9) Deep Cog Emotions
- (75) Saturn (10) Deep Cog Thinking
- (76) Uranus (11) Deep Cog Instincts
- (77) Neptune (12) Deep Cog Perception
- (78) Void (13) Center of Temporal Mind

Middle Kingdom - Planetary Integration
Bandwidth (7) Purgatory (7) - Seraphina

- (79) Moon (1) High Cog Emotions
- (80) Mercury (2) High Cog Thinking
- (81) Venus (3) High Cog Instincts
- (82) Mars (4) High Cog Perception
- (83) Trans-Jupiter (5) Trans Cog Emotion
- (84) Trans-Saturn (6) Trans Cog Thinking
- (85) Trans-Uranus (7) Trans Cog Instincts
- (86) Trans-Neptune (8) Trans Cog Perception
- (87) Jupiter (9) Deep Cog Emotions
- (88) Saturn (10) Deep Cog Thinking
- (89) Uranus (11) Deep Cog Instincts
- (90) Neptune (12) Deep Cog Perception
- (91) Void (13) Center of Temporal Mind

Bandwidth (8) Purgatory (8) - Parabinlaya

- (92) Moon (1) High Cog Emotions
- (93) Mercury (2) High Cog Thinking
- (94) Venus (3) High Cog Instincts
- (95) Mars (4) High Cog Perception
- (96) Trans-Jupiter (5) Trans Cog Emotion
- (97) Trans-Saturn (6) Trans Cog Thinking
- (98) Trans-Uranus (7) Trans Cog Instincts
- (99) Trans-Neptune (8) Trans Cog Percept.

Heaven Transition Zone - Begin Q1

- (100) Jupiter (9) Deep Cog Emotions
- (101) Saturn (10) Deep Cog Thinking
- (102) Uranus (11) Deep Cog Instincts
- (103) Neptune (12) Deep Cog Perception
- (104) Void (13) Center of Temporal Mind

Mount Magia

<u>Bandwidth (9) Heaven (1) - Nirvana 7th A.P.</u>
<u>Divine Soul Resonance: Angel</u>

- (105) Moon (1) High Cog Emotions
- (106) Mercury (2) High Cog Thinking
- (107) Venus (3) High Cog Instincts
- (108) Mars (4) High Cog Perception
- (109) Trans-Jupiter (5) Trans Cog Emotion
- (110) Trans-Saturn (6) Trans Cog Thinking
- (111) Trans-Uranus (7) Trans Cog Instincts
- (112) Trans-Neptune (8) Trans Cog Percept.
- (113) Jupiter (9) Deep Cog Emotions
- (114) Saturn (10) Deep Cog Thinking
- (115) Uranus (11) Deep Cog Instincts
- (116) Neptune (12) Deep Cog Perception
- (117) Void (13) Center of Temporal Mind

<u>Bandwidth (10) Heaven (2) - Simmatuu</u>
<u>Divine Soul Resonance: Archangel</u>

- (118) Moon (1) High Cog Emotions
- (119) Mercury (2) High Cog Thinking
- (120) Venus (3) High Cog Instincts
- (121) Mars (4) High Cog Perception
- (122) Trans-Jupiter (5) Trans Cog Emotion
- (123) Trans-Saturn (6) Trans Cog Thinking
- (124) Trans-Uranus (7) Trans Cog Instincts
- (125) Trans-Neptune (8) Trans Cog Percept.
- (126) Jupiter (9) Deep Cog Emotions
- (127) Saturn (10) Deep Cog Thinking
- (128) Uranus (11) Deep Cog Instincts
- (129) Neptune (12) Deep Cog Perception
- (130) Void (13) Center of Temporal Mind

Chapter 5

<u>Bandwidth (11) Heaven (3) - Khimmadooree</u>
<u>Divine Soul Resonance: Principalities or Rulers</u>

- (131) Moon (1) High Cog Emotions
- (132) Mercury (2) High Cog Thinking
- (133) Venus (3) High Cog Instincts
- (134) Mars (4) High Cog Perception
- (135) Trans-Jupiter (5) Trans Cog Emotion
- (136) Trans-Saturn (6) Trans Cog Thinking
- (137) Trans-Uranus (7) Trans Cog Instincts
- (138) Trans-Neptune (8) Trans Cog Percept.
- (139) Jupiter (9) Deep Cog Emotions
- (140) Saturn (10) Deep Cog Thinking
- (141) Uranus (11) Deep Cog Instincts
- (142) Neptune (12) Deep Cog Perception
- (143) Void (13) Center of Temporal Mind

<u>Bandwidth (12) Heaven (4) - Valhalla</u>
<u>Divine Soul Resonance: Powers or Authorities</u>

- (144) Moon (1) High Cog Emotions
- (145) Mercury (2) High Cog Thinking
- (146) Venus (3) High Cog Instincts
- (147) Mars (4) High Cog Perception

<u>Upper Kingdom Transition Zone</u>

- (148) Trans-Jupiter (5) Trans Cog Emotion
- (149) Trans-Saturn (6) Trans Cog Thinking
- (150) Trans-Uranus (7) Trans Cog Instincts
- (151) Trans-Neptune (8) Trans Cog Percept.
- (152) Jupiter (9) Deep Cog Emotions
- (153) Saturn (10) Deep Cog Thinking
- (154) Uranus (11) Deep Cog Instincts
- (155) Neptune (12) Deep Cog Perception
- (156) Void (13) Center of Temporal Mind

Upper Kingdom - Cosmic Integration
Bandwidth (13) Heaven (5) - Elysium
Divine Soul Resonance: Virtues or Strongholds

- (157) Moon (1) High Cog Emotions
- (158) Mercury (2) High Cog Thinking
- (159) Venus (3) High Cog Instincts
- (160) Mars (4) High Cog Perception
- (161) Trans-Jupiter (5) Trans Cog Emotion
- (162) Trans-Saturn (6) Trans Cog Thinking
- (163) Trans-Uranus (7) Trans Cog Instincts
- (164) Trans-Neptune (8) Trans Cog Percept.
- (165) Jupiter (9) Deep Cog Emotions
- (166) Saturn (10) Deep Cog Thinking
- (167) Uranus (11) Deep Cog Instincts
- (168) Neptune (12) Deep Cog Perception
- (169) Void (13) Center of Temporal Mind

Bandwidth (14) Heaven (6) - Terrasumna
Divine Soul Resonance: Dominions or Lordships

- (170) Moon (1) High Cog Emotions
- (171) Mercury (2) High Cog Thinking
- (172) Venus (3) High Cog Instincts
- (173) Mars (4) High Cog Perception
- (174) Trans-Jupiter (5) Trans Cog Emotion
- (175) Trans-Saturn (6) Trans Cog Thinking
- (176) Trans-Uranus (7) Trans Cog Instincts
- (177) Trans-Neptune (8) Trans Cog Percept.
- (178) Jupiter (9) Deep Cog Emotions
- (179) Saturn (10) Deep Cog Thinking
- (180) Uranus (11) Deep Cog Instincts
- (181) Neptune (12) Deep Cog Perception
- (182) Void (13) Center of Temporal Mind

Chapter 5

<u>Bandwidth (15) Heaven (7) - Barstow</u>
<u>Divine Soul Resonance: Thrones or Ophanim</u>

- (183) Moon (1) High Cog Emotions
- (184) Mercury (2) High Cog Thinking
- (185) Venus (3) High Cog Instincts
- (186) Mars (4) High Cog Perception
- (187) Trans-Jupiter (5) Trans Cog Emotion
- (188) Trans-Saturn (6) Trans Cog Thinking
- (189) Trans-Uranus (7) Trans Cog Instincts
- (190) Trans-Neptune (8) Trans Cog Percept.
- (191) Jupiter (9) Deep Cog Emotions
- (192) Saturn (10) Deep Cog Thinking
- (193) Uranus (11) Deep Cog Instincts
- (194) Neptune (12) Deep Cog Perception
- (195) Void (13) Center of Temporal Mind

<u>Bandwidth (16) Heaven (8) - Jenesis</u>
<u>Divine Soul Resonance: Cherubim</u>

- (196) Moon (1) High Cog Emotions
- (197)) Mercury (2) High Cog Thinking
- (198) Venus (3) High Cog Instincts
- (199) Mars (4) High Cog Perception
- (200) Trans-Jupiter (5) Trans Cog Emotion
- (201) Trans-Saturn (6) Trans Cog Thinking
- (202) Trans-Uranus (7) Trans Cog Instincts
- (203) Trans-Neptune (8) Trans Cog Percept.
- (204) Jupiter (9) Deep Cog Emotions
- (205) Saturn (10) Deep Cog Thinking
- (206) Uranus (11) Deep Cog Instincts
- (207) Neptune (12) Deep Cog Perception
- (208) Void (13) Center of Temporal Mind

Mount Magia 55

<u>Bandwidth (17) Heaven (9) - Erawan</u>
<u>Divine Soul Resonance: Seraphim</u>

- (209) Moon (1) High Cog Emotions
- (210) Mercury (2) High Cog Thinking
- (211) Venus (3) High Cog Instincts
- (212) Mars (4) High Cog Perception
- (213) Trans-Jupiter (5) Trans Cog Emotion
- (214) Trans-Saturn (6) Trans Cog Thinking
- (215) Trans-Uranus (7) Trans Cog Instincts
- (216) Trans-Neptune (8) Trans Cog Percept.
- (217) Jupiter (9) Deep Cog Emotions
- (218) Saturn (10) Deep Cog Thinking
- (219) Uranus (11) Deep Cog Instincts
- (220) Neptune (12) Deep Cog Perception
- (221) Void (13) Center of Temporal Mind

Although this order reads downward, the order is actually an upward ladder of ascension from the 1st degree to the 221st degree. The above listing corresponds to both your physical being and your primordial being. Your primordial being has the same 13 levels of mind. The only difference is within the centers of gravity.

The center of gravity of everyone's physical being is the "*Void.*" The Void exists both at the center of your physical being and at the center of the temporal group mind of the Earth. The center of gravity of your primordial being is the *"Nexus."* The Nexus exists both at the center of your primordial being and at the center of the spiritual group mind of the Earth. The locations of each center of gravity (Void and Nexus) are found in the same place at different frequencies inside the center of the human being and inside the very center of the Earth itself.

The reader may have noticed an asymmetry between the number of heavenly bandwidths versus the number of purgatory bandwidths. In Mount Magia we experience 8 levels of purgatory and 9 levels of heaven due to a greater influence of the spiritual group mind over the temporal group mind.

Many would expect an equal number of bandwidths between the bandwidths of light and darkness, but I did not experience it that way. The asymmetry favors the power of the Cosmic Consciousness to bring creation into resonance with the divine source. Something is causing this dynamic. It is not by chance. The cause of this dynamic is revealed in chapters six through eight.

Whereas some physicists currently believe that all things are headed toward disordered states through the law of entropy, the law of sympathetic vibrations counters the law of entropy, and ultimately wins over it. Entropy is always the first out of the gate when for example, through the process of creative destruction, stars explode into supernova to create new solar systems, but Alpha always wins in the end precisely because of this dynamic. Chaos is always brought back into harmony.

With each degree of resonance we pass through, our physical being and our primordial being become increasingly resonate with each other at each corresponding level of the mind.

All 13 levels of mind are cycled through 17 times, with each cycle further integrating the two hemispheres of our being, until the two centers of gravity are unified.

The center of gravity of our eternal-primordial being (Nexus) does not change. Our temporal-physical being and its center of gravity (Void) keep adjusting closer and closer in frequency to the Nexus - with each degree of 221 - within each cycle of 17.

The 17 bandwidths of the spiritual group mind are only experienced as separate distinct bandwidths from the perspective of the mind of our temporal being. From the perspective of the mind of our primordial being, there is only one bandwidth, the Cosmic Consciousness.

From the perspective of the mind of our primordial being, all the gradient bandwidths of the spiritual group mind are nothing more than refracted rays of light emerging out of the one true bandwidth which is the Cosmic Consciousness.

As we ascend and become aware of these bandwidths with the developing faculty of our super cognitive awareness - and while the two hemispheres of our being are integrating into one unified celestial being - from the perspective of the mind of our temporal being, each bandwidth of the spiritual group mind collapses into a continuing and ever-expanding single ray of light in successive order within the unifying mind of the Foreman.

When the Foreman collapses the 17th final bandwidth of the spiritual group mind, his or her focus of conscious awareness rises above the entire sphere of the spiritual group mind and enters into resonance with a hidden 18th bandwidth.

The 18th bandwidth of our ascension is the unified source bandwidth from which all other bandwidths of consciousness emerge and radiate into a varied colored spectrum of consciousness. The temporal dimensions of the human mind filter the light of the Cosmic Consciousness like a prism refracting light into a rainbow of colors with each color being a bandwidth of consciousness passing through the mind. When the rainbow of light collapses into one white light, something wonderful comes forth. What comes forth is revealed in the pages ahead.

The center of gravity of both our primordial being and the spiritual group mind of the Earth (Nexus) is already in full resonance with the divine source. When the final 17th bandwidth of the spiritual group mind collapses, the conscious mind of the Foreman passes through the central Nexus and enters into a profound resonance with the full breadth of the Cosmic Consciousness. This is *"Source Resonance."*

Source resonance has a cascading effect on the atomic structure of the physical body and its temporal ethereal bodies. What this cascading effect has on the physical body greatly depends on the latent capacity within the physical body itself. The physical body cannot rise above its own potential. However, source resonance continuously tests the limits of this potential. What your limits are, you can only find out by accomplishing the integration process.

Source resonance is the master key which unlocks all locks, opens all doors, and answers all secrets. It is not the divine source which comes closer to us. It is we who go closer. Its position never moves. If you wish to be close to the divine source, all you need do is go to it. To go to it, is simply a matter of resonance.

Once our conscious mind re-establishes an initial base chord of resonance with the Divine Soul while in the Void at the end of Mount Kabbalah, we complete the 4th alchemical process and begin ascending the ladder of resonance in Mount Magia.

Mount Magia culminates as we enter resonance with the original vibrating string at the center of all things. Mount Magia is a measurement of our ascension of resonance. This is how the next alchemical process unfolds as we begin our ascent.

Alchemical Process 5

The legendary mountain of ascension begins with the Foreman's battle-hardened return to the Moon. The self-organizing force of the universe responds to the Foreman's internal state and continued application of the Three Factors by beginning to cycle his or her focus of conscious awareness from one sphere of the mind to the next. The cycling among spheres occurs at a much faster rate than in the Second Mountain. The elevated rate is a function of Alpha compelling the integration of the Forman's temporal-physical being with the source. This is made possible by having already achieved the alchemical individuation of self within the temporal sphere of the mind.

The last time the Foreman visited the Moon, the Foreman was a young Journeyman. Now many years later, the alchemist returns to the Moon as a powerful young Foreman with a whole new set of super cognitive abilities. The level of mind within the human psyche I call the Moon, joins its psychic energy with the same level within all other life on Earth to form the temporal group mind bandwidth of the Earth called the Moon. The bandwidth of the Moon exists both within us and all around us. The same is true for all other bandwidths of the planetary group mind. The temporal group mind bandwidth of the Moon is a bandwidth of the lower astral world enveloping the Earth in the physical universe. The lower astral world is a psychokinetic realm we all virtually experience while dreaming and continue to interact with subconsciously even while physically awake.

When I first returned to the celestial sphere of the Moon, I was surprised to see a barren wasteland. The barren wasteland reflected my inner state of being at the lunar level of my mind being projected upon the movie screen of the astral world.

The temporal group mind - the lower astral world - is a mirror which constantly reflects our inner self. The Moon was abandoned within me and it needed to be re-engaged and lifted-up in harmony amidst my escalating resonance with the Divine Soul.

In the 5th alchemical process, Alpha re-directs the Foreman's focus of conscious awareness to return to each planet (level of mind) the Foreman had visited during the second mountain as a Journeyman. When we return to each planet in the 5th alchemical process, instead of transforming a class of false-selves or silencing a set of auto-cognitive programs embedded within each temporal ethereal body like in the second mountain, the Foreman is tasked by Alpha to tune into the underlying resonance supporting each planet upon which all previously transformed psychic constructs of the mind had once fashioned themselves upon (psychic cognitive background).

This process brings each planet's underlying temporal resonance into a differential contrast with the resonance of the Divine Soul thereby compelling each planet (level of mind) to be lifted-up to a higher order of resonance with the divine source. I call this alchemical process, *"Planet Lifting."* Each planet that we are lifting is a level of the temporal mind of the alchemist. The mythological hero Atlas symbolizes the Foreman of the Third Mountain. See Figure [6]

This process slowly integrates all 12 bodies of the Foreman into a grand unified celestial body and grants the Foreman entry into each heavenly realm of the spiritual group mind of the Earth.

Chapter 5

Atlas

Figure [6]

Atlas symbolizes the Foreman performing the Great Work of the Third Mountain. Atlas is the Foreman "Planet Lifting." Planet lifting is the alchemical process of lifting one's levels of mind to higher orders of resonance with Ain Soph. The three dimensions of consciousness of Ain Soph are the Father, the Divine Soul, and the Spirit.

The Three Factors must continue to be practiced in support of the alchemical planet lifting process.

Each planet is not brought into harmony all in one cycle. Each planet must be revisited, and its vibrational resonance lifted 17 times before all the planets join in a grand symphony within the 18th unified bandwidth of the Cosmic Consciousness.

Bardo is the 1st bandwidth of the spiritual group mind of the Earth. Mythologically speaking, Bardo is the 1st level of Purgatory, and therefore Bardo is the 1st cycle of planet lifting.

When all 13 levels of our temporal mind have been lifted one notch higher along the ladder of vibrational resonance, our physical being achieves a new degree of integration with our primordial being as well as a new higher degree of resonance with the Divine Soul.

The new level of resonance between the following dimensions of the human being becomes the Foreman's new psychic cognitive background and new vibrational base chord from which the Foreman's alchemy consolidates and begins its next geometric move upward into a higher more unified resonance with his or her primordial being and the Divine Soul:

1.) The Foreman's Temporal-Physical Being

2.) The Foreman's Eternal-Primordial Being

3.) The Divine Soul

4.) The Spiritual Group Mind Bandwidth of Bardo

The conscious mind engages the planetary group mind bandwidths differently in the Third Mountain than in the Second Mountain. In the Second Mountain, when we begin a new bandwidth, our focus of conscious awareness begins fully submerged within the new bandwidth while we climb downward inside the mind and work our way deeper into the next denser psychic bandwidth. In the Third Mountain, our conscious mind begins a new spiritual bandwidth barely resonating with it while we climb upward into the new spiritual bandwidth to fully resonate with it.

With our entrance into the Third Mountain - and our Alpha-compelled drive to ascend the vibrational resonance of Bardo - our focus of conscious awareness is thrust back to where it began the Second Mountain - The Moon.

When we return to the Moon in Bardo, the energy of the psychic cognitive background in our mind is very familiar to us, however it lacks all the false-selves we transformed in the Moon in the Second Mountain.

Remember, the psychic background energy within us is the planetary group mind bandwidth energy which our conscious mind is currently resonate with. It runs through us and through all life on Earth. It is the psychic cognitive base of our mind.

This is the first time the alchemist is able to become intimate with the temporal cognitive bandwidth of the Moon absent of false-selves. This new experience is very enlightening.

In Bardo Moon, the Foreman must become deeply familiar with the temporal bandwidth energy of the lunar sphere of the mind and how this bandwidth attempts to influence his or her emotions.

The 5th alchemical process involves transforming the way in which our mind automatically responds to the temporal group mind bandwidth energy which floods our individual mind and creates our psychic cognitive background states (our cognitive base). Imagine this being like an ocean we are swimming inside.

In the Second Mountain, the Journeyman explored that ocean and transformed every level of life he or she found swimming in that ocean. As a Foreman, we return to that ocean to descend into its depths once again. Only this time we focus on the water of the ocean, not the fish. We transform the way the water of that ocean interacts with our mind. In other words, we transform the relationship between our temporal ethereal bodies and the psychic cognitive base of the temporal group mind of our planet. We transform the way they exchange energy.

As Foremen in the Third Mountain, when we transform the relationship between our temporal bodies and our psychic cognitive base within the temporal group mind, we remove the ability of our temporal mind to reanimate the life which used to live in the depths of the ocean. In this case, this constitutes all the false-selves and auto-cognitive programs we had previously transformed as Journeymen in the Second Mountain.

Each time the Foreman transforms an interaction between his or her mind and the temporal group mind, or in other words, each time the Foreman lifts a planet to a higher level of resonance with the Divine Soul, the next planet rises on the horizon for the Foreman to begin lifting to the next level of vibrational resonance.

Alpha compels the Foreman to keep cycling back to each of the 13 levels of his or her individual mind (to each alchemical planet within them), to lift each planet (level of mind) to a higher level of vibrational resonance within the spiritual group mind of the Earth. A new level of resonance can only be sustained when it occurs across all planets (all levels of mind).

There are 17 cycles and 13 planets including the Void. 13 times 17 equals 221 lifts. Each cycle lifts each planet within us to a new level of purgatory, or new level of heaven, within the spiritual group mind of the Earth. The 5th alchemical process includes only the first four cycles which are:

1.) Bardo
2.) Eroplatia
3.) Gerishan
4.) Ferris

Because the Foreman returns to each planet 17 times in the Third Mountain versus only once in the Second Mountain, the Foreman begins to develop a very deep and profound understanding of how the various levels of the mind work on both a broader and deeper level. I could not have written this book while in the Second Mountain, as I did not have yet this broader and deeper perspective.

In the Second Mountain, the Journeyman's focus of conscious awareness can only focus on and discern the false-selves and the temporal bodies. The Journeyman cannot see beyond the content of his or her mind to the underlying vessels of the mind which supports its psychic content. In the 5th alchemical process, we work with the vessels of the mind, or in other words, the cognitive base of the mind.

In the 5th alchemical process, from Bardo to Ferris, the Foreman's focus is on how each bandwidth of the temporal group mind works to maintain each planet (level of mind) within us at its current level of resonance. The Foreman focuses on the temporal group mind bandwidths in contrast to his or her awareness of the Divine Soul. This raises the planets (levels of mind) to their next subsequent levels of resonance within the spiritual group mind.

Much of the psychic energy we felt concentrated within our temporal bodies prior to the alchemical process of rendering them silent in the Second Mountain, is felt again - not within our bodies - but within the temporal group mind bandwidths. It is a distinctly different experience. We begin to feel and realize that we are an extension of - and part and parcel to - the planetary group mind of the Earth.

We come to realize that the energy in the planetary group mind feeds and cultivates the psychic condition within each individual person living within its realm of influence. The alchemist ultimately comes to flip this dynamic and becomes a master of the planetary group mind rather than being mastered by it.

If you wish to influence all the fish swimming in a large pool of water, do not focus on the fish. That is very inefficient. Instead, just focus on the water. This is how we are able to elevate humanity's entire level of existence. If we can learn to positively transform the gross psychic mass of the temporal group mind of the Earth, we can literally lift all of humanity. Alpha is already doing this. It unfolds as the spiral path. The straight path - explained in this book - provides momentum to the spiral path of humanity.

My Return To The Moon

When I first returned to the Moon in Bardo, I had a lower astral experience with my focus of conscious awareness fully submerged in the temporal group mind of the Earth while my physical body was asleep. I found myself completely alone and isolated on the far side of the Moon, totally removed from humanity, with no apparent method of return or communication with Earth. I was walking on the far side of the Moon trying to find a spaceship on the surface which could take me back to Earth (back to humanity). In that cold, dark, isolated state, I could see the Earth on the Moon's horizon gleaming beautifully. How I so longed to return, but the return seemed impossible.

In this experience, the Moon symbolized where I was within my mind (High Cognitive Emotions). My isolation on the Moon, far away from Earth, symbolized the temporary dissociative state I had developed as a Journeyman while silencing each of my temporal ethereal bodies. Due to this silencing of our temporal ethereal bodies, for a brief period of time in the alchemical process, we feel detached and removed from our humanity.

> *"Step away from the others, and I shall tell you*
> *the mysteries of the kingdom."*
> *... Gospel of Judas*

The Earth in this experience symbolized my human family, which is all of humanity, and my inner calling to rediscover it, but this time I would rediscover it in a new context with the Divine Soul. This is an example of how the planetary group mind reflects back to us what is happening in our alchemical journey.

Each alchemical planet in an ascension cycle of the Third Mountain moves very quickly. In the Second Mountain, the Moon can take a year or longer, but in Bardo, the Moon might take only a few weeks. The whole Bardo cycle of 13 planetary lifts (13 degrees), from the Moon to the Void, can pass in as little as a few months.

Once we have completed all 13 degrees of Bardo, we have raised the vibrational resonance of our entire temporal system one notch up the ladder of ascension. This includes all our temporal ethereal bodies. Our level of Q remains at Q2. Q2 includes our awareness of the Divine Soul, the Spirit, and our authentic-self, but Q2 grows brighter and brighter as we move toward Q1.

Once we complete Bardo Void, Alpha loops us back around again to the Moon to begin Eroplatia Moon, and repeats the entire planet lifting cycle, but this time an even higher vibrational resonance.

The main alchemical methodology does not change. We continue to apply the Three Factors. Transformation (First Factor) is almost always *"On-The-Go,"* meaning, very little seated meditation.

When we seek to transform our temporal mind relative to the energy of the temporal bandwidth in which we find ourselves, we apply the practice of differential resonance between the temporal bandwidth energy we feel in our mind-body system in contrast to the Divine Soul and the Spirit. This practice can be done in seated meditation, but you will find it most efficient to do this *"On-The-Go"* as you go about your day in small pauses and quick inner focuses.

Alpha and the Divine Soul are doing most of the work. The Foreman only needs to differentiate and become aware. This awareness brings about a transformation and an elevated resonance. While our resonance ascends through the bandwidths, we can feel each bandwidth collapsing relative to our conscious mind. Each time we collapse a bandwidth we move one degree closer in resonance to the Divine Soul. Once we collapse all 13 temporal bandwidths in a cycle, the entire spiritual bandwidth with which we have been entering resonance, also collapses, as by collapsing all the temporal bandwidths, our vibrational resonance has risen to the emergence of an even higher new spiritual bandwidth. For example, when you are ascending through the 13 degrees of Bardo, you are lifting your planets (levels of mind - temporal ethereal bodies) one by one, and while doing so, you are collapsing the temporal bandwidths which supported these planets (or levels of mind - temporal ethereal bodies).

Once you complete the 13 degrees of Bardo, the whole Bardo spiritual group mind bandwidth collapses and Eroplatia rises and the whole cycle repeats. The bandwidths are not collapsing for all others who are part of the planetary group mind. They're collapsing only at the intersection point of your conscious mind and planetary group mind.

My Completion of Bardo

My completion of Bardo was an extraordinary event I will never forget. It was Sunday. During the normal course of my daily life activities that day, I had observed a disturbance in my mind. Anytime anything other than my authentic-self, the Spirit, or the Divine Soul was manifesting in my mind, I would quickly take notice and apply my alchemy. I arrived home that afternoon with the calling to take my alchemy to a deeper level of meditation and I wasted no time in laying down and sinking my mind deep within myself, differentiating the rising disturbance in my mind in contrast to the emergent force of the Divine Soul.

My physical body fell asleep during the meditation and I found myself in a large exterior plaza with many people hustling and bustling all around me. I was seeing the psychic energy of all the different minds of humanity feeding the Bardo bandwidth from the temporal side.

I continued my alchemy in this moment, praying to the Divine Soul to bring about a transformation within me. Suddenly, a bright light lit up the horizon as if a large nuclear weapon had been detonated silently off in a distance. The light quickly washed across the canopy of the night sky expanding rapidly from one horizon to the next. Night had become day. Then next, from the center of the light, emerged my primordial being. His aura was blazing with the light of the Divine Soul. He entered the scene in spectacular regal fashion. The energy and light were blinding. All the people in the plaza (symbol of the temporal energy) became agitated and fell to their knees throwing their hands up and down in convulsions.

Then suddenly, to my amazement, the whole environment immediately collapsed all-around me as if the sky had fallen. The entire Bardo bandwidth had collapsed. I awoke from this experience feeling liberated from the disturbance.

I could feel a very noticeable change in my psycho-cognitive background. Eroplatia Moon was now rising on the horizon. When we collapse a planetary group mind bandwidth, we are collapsing the bandwidth relative only to our conscious mind. The bandwidth remains intact to others still resonating with the bandwidth. To the outside observer, we just simply disappear from the planetary bandwidth.

The Foreman may notice repeating patterns in his or her alchemical life script around this period in the alchemical work. When I first entered Bardo Moon, I recognized repeating patterns in my alchemical life script regressing all the way back to the beginning of the First Mountain. These repeating patterns are the effect of the Foreman transcending his or her alchemical life script. They are echoes which quicken over time the higher in the Third Mountain we ascend. When you complete the alchemical Great Work, you transcend your alchemical life script and the guide dog (Alpha) finally comes to a rest.

With the completion of Ferris Void and the 5th alchemical process, the Foreman transcends any inclinations of his or her mind to reanimate the auto-cognitive programs of the high and trans-cognitive spheres of the mind in response to the influences of the temporal group mind.

Alchemical Process 6

Our entrance into Vishu Moon is very significant and reaches a whole new level of profound. The dynamic of the alchemical process changes here. The alchemical labors of the 6th alchemical process span the Foreman's ascent through the final four levels of Purgatory including the following bandwidths of the spiritual group mind:

- 5.) Vishu *See the first four on page 63*
- 6.) Orial
- 7.) Seraphina
- 8.) Parabinlaya

In Vishu Moon, a new dynamic stressor arises. The new stressor is individuality itself supported by a persistent underlying broadcast within the temporal group mind of the Earth to maintain the automatization of individualized life to promote the efficient evolution and systematic development of the planetary ecosystem.

The program first appears to contradict the long-term cosmic agenda of the Cosmic Consciousness to promote the cognitive reflection and realization of the ultimate source within all of creation.

It is not in contradiction. The spiral path is following an unfolding process including steps of development which are systematic in form prior to the awakening. The spiral path is following an Alpha compelled roadmap of awakening which is occurring over cosmic time. A person following the straight path is jumping the spiral path roadmap, but in doing so, they are also sparking added momentum to the spiral path of the entire planetary group mind.

The straight path serves the spiral path. The straight path is actually a subroutine of the spiral path.

The temporal group mind fights to maintain our illusionary nature and keep itself firmly in control. It does this without malevolent intent, but to maintain control over our automated evolutionary processes within the spiral path.

The self-actualization of an individual early-on within the spiral path is a direct challenge to the authority and control of the program. But again, it is secretly a welcomed challenge. The challenge adds momentum to the flock being guided in concert by the spiral path. On the spiral path, we all arrive together, but in some far-off epoch within cosmic time.

When our focus of conscious awareness rises to the vibrational spectrum of Vishu, the temporal group mind begins losing more of its grip on our individual evolutionary development. At this point in the process, our conscious mind is moving in sync to the beat of a higher drum and a higher calling in the universe. The interconnection of our individual mind, the planetary group mind, the Cosmic Mind, and Alpha are all changing their cognitive relationships with each other and it takes time for the neurological chemistry in our physical brain to catch up. In most people, their neurological chemistry leads the way. Whereas in alchemists, their awakening leads the way, and their physical brain must continually remap itself to support the process. In actuality, the remapping feels like resistance, but it's really just lag. This lag creates a degree of stress on the mind. Understanding this dynamic helps to resolve the stress of the process.

This is not an easy transition on the mind-body system of the alchemist whose physical brain has evolved over millions of years under the influence of the temporal group mind. This new stressor places the conscious mind of the alchemist in a temporary but vulnerable position where we sense no underlying support from either the temporal group mind or the Cosmic Consciousness.

At this point in the process, the Cosmic Consciousness is still too deep and inaccessible within the unconscious mind of the Foreman to provide cognitive support to his or her conscious mind. It is an uncomfortable transition period of transitioning one's cognitive psychic base from the temporal group mind to the Cosmic Consciousness. The Divine Soul and Alpha work in concert to aid the Foreman in winning this divine battle.

The 6th alchemical process begins in Vishu Moon with the Foreman's level of Q at Q2, but once the Foreman reaches "Parabinlaya Jupiter" a new level of awareness begins to emerge within us of a previously undetected dimension of the Cosmic Consciousness. This new dimension is the *"Father."* At this stage, we gain an initial sense of the Father, but our resonance and comprehension of the Father at this stage is very limited. Our journey to the Father is only at the beginning.

At this point in my ascension, I had a degree of resonance with the three primary dimensions of the Cosmic Consciousness. I had a relationship with each dimension individually. Each stood on its own accord. My resonance was just enough to grant me access to Mount Magia, but it was still not yet deep, comprehensive, and profound.

Mount Magia

A profound level of awareness would emerge gradually as my level of resonance rose in symphony with the divine source. At this point, as I focused inward on the Father, I felt a divine power with infinite depth. As I focused inward on the Divine Soul, I felt a majestic universal presence. As I focused inward on the Spirit, I felt divine love. Beyond this initial level of awareness, I was a child in a noumenal world of wonder still learning my way. I still did not know yet in any practical manner: What is the Father? What is the Divine Soul? What is the Spirit? How do they relate to each other?

With a new level of illumination just bright enough to allow the Foremen to begin differentiating and transforming with a new level of awareness of the Father, our level of Q expands from Q2 to Q1. From Vishu to the final bandwidth of the spiritual group mind, the focus of the alchemical work is a differentiation of our sense of individuality in light of our emerging resonant awareness of the Father, the Divine Soul, and the Spirit. Our life challenges bring about and amplify this contrast.

Alchemical Process 7 - Nirvana

The rhythmic cycles of Alpha reach a crescendo in the 9th harmonic octave of the Human Soul's ascent through the upper cathedral of the Earth's planetary group mind in the process of achieving a deeply profound harmonic resonance between the temporal sphere of our mind and the divine source. The lifting of the temporal levels of our mind to higher levels of harmonic resonance with the divine source, which I call planet lifting, reaches a whole new level of expansion in the 9th cycle by introducing a new level of awareness of the Father emerging from within the unconscious mind of the Foreman.

The Father is the first of the three primary dimensions of the Cosmic Consciousness. In regression, the first to emerge is the Spirit, then the Divine Soul, and then finally, the Father.

The 7th alchemical process is primarily the escalation of resonance between our temporal-physical being and the Father. There is a whole set of secondary effects of the 7th alchemical process such as Turiya, revelations, cosmic seals, and the ascension of the nine heavens of the spiritual group mind of Earth. My own personal journey is shared in the pages ahead.

Note: 2

The Noumenon

Immanuel Kant developed the meaning of the word *"Noumenon"* from its Greek origin in contrast to the word *"Phenomenon."* In Kant's definition, the noumenon is the ultimate reality of a thing which cannot be apprehended through the five senses of human perception, unlike the phenomenon, which can be. In Kant's philosophy, the only thing that can be apprehended by the mind, is the mind's representation of the thing it observes, but the actual thing itself is unknowable to the mind. The unknowable aspect is the *"Noumenon."*

Many have proposed that phenomena may arise out of an abstract world of the noumenon. Kant said the noumenal world may exist, but it is unknowable through human sensation. This book expands upon Kant's definition of the noumenon and suggests it is through *"Resonance,"* not *"Perception,"* that the world of the noumenon can be apprehended by the human mind as a developed faculty of super cognitive emotion which transcends the traditional five senses of human perception. The noumenon is a superluminal realm where the forces of consciousness interact with the forces of matter and bridge the source and creation. I call the interacting forces in the noumenon, the *"Cosmic Quanta."* Within the cosmic quanta, the forces of consciousness are *"Theogenic"* and the forces of matter are *"Atomic."* There is a third group in the cosmic quanta which demonstrate both a Theogenic and Atomic nature which I call *"Metagenic."*

- End Note -

The newly achieved awareness of the Father is the beginning of the Foreman awakening to a new level of reality existing within the underlying abstract of nature within a realm I refer to as the *"Noumenon."* The Father is among a set of forces emerging out of the noumenon I call the *"Cosmic Quanta."* The Foreman's awareness of the noumenon, and the forces within it, continues to expand as the Foreman's Human Soul ascends through the heavenly spheres of the spiritual group mind enveloping and enshrining the primordial Earth.
See Note [2]

Nirvana - The Emergence of Turiya

A new cognitive dynamic begins to emerge in the 7th alchemical process of the Third Mountain. This new cognitive dynamic begins to emerge as our Human Soul and our temporal-physical-being continue ascending upward together toward the Father. It unfolds as we ascend through the paradisiacal bandwidths of the spiritual group mind of the planet and first comes to light as we enter Nirvana, the first heavenly realm of the Earth.

As the conscious mind of the Foreman expands in awareness of the Father, the temporal dimensions of the Foreman's mind enter a special form of communion with the Father which goes far beyond common prayer, intuition, or mental telepathy. This communion becomes a new prime cognitive faculty and central organizing factor within the evolving mind of the Foreman. It ultimately takes control over how our mind functions and perceives - and by doing so - it guides all the high cognitive, trans-cognitive, and deep cognitive functions of our mind in our continued escalation of resonance with the Father, the Divine Soul, the Spirit, temporal group mind, spiritual group mind, and all of creation.

This communion arises out of the emerging symphony between the universal self-organizing forces of Alpha and the Foreman's escalating awareness of the Cosmic Consciousness. The word whose definition comes closest to describing this communion, is the Sanskrit word *"Turiya."*

Some people have commented in the past that Turiya cannot be described or defined and then said little more. I believe when a person comments in this way, most often it is because they themselves have not yet experienced Turiya, or they wish to impress others by creating the impression that they themselves have experienced something which other people could never understand, thus setting themselves beyond other people.

It is true that the faculty of one's super cognitive emotional awareness, and the intimate nature of the communion experience itself, cannot be accurately described in words, but for someone who experiences Turiya, there is still much which can be said about it.

Turiya is our conscious mind's super cognitive emotional awareness and profound intimate experience of the Cosmic Consciousness and its three prime dimensional abstracts, which are: The Father, the Divine Soul, and the Spirit.

Turiya expresses and reflects within our conscious mind our ultimate reality. It is more than just awareness; thus, it deserves its own word and definition. In addition to awareness, it is a divine feeling and overall sense of being where we feel at one with God. The force of Alpha is steering the organization of all life to ultimately live within Turiya as a fundamental dimension of existence within creation.

From the standard of our original existence within the divine source, not living in Turiya is unnatural. The divine source is attempting to re-establish the original state of Turiya within the temporal-physical dimensions of our creation. Turiya is already established within the eternal-primordial dimensions of our creation. The Three Factors promotes and accelerates this process.

We need to dispel the illusion that enlightenment, self-actualization, self-realization, or integration, are difficult to attain and can only be attained by a select or gifted few.

Integration is a natural next step in our species' evolution in the emergence of our reflective awareness. You are meant to attain it, you have the innate ability to attain it, and when you decide to attain it, you will attain it.

Human beings on Earth in the physical universe currently live with a conscious mind which is cognitively disconnected from the divine source due to the evolutionary stage of development of its underlying neurological brain chemistry. More simply stated, we lack the reflective awareness of our divine source which promotes the emergence of Turiya. It should not be viewed as exceptional or extraordinary that someone lives in Turiya. It is actually the other way around. Turiya is the cosmic standard, not the cosmic exception.

Turiya provides the human mind with an added mode of cosmic awareness which parallels an individual's temporal perspective of the world. This is the super cognitive faculty of parallel awareness I had referred to in previous chapters.

The primordial dimensions of every living being already exist in a state of Turiya. It is through the integration of our temporal-physical being with our eternal-primordial being that the temporal dimensions of our being enter Turiya. The emergence of Turiya rewires the physical brain. What emerges by effect of Turiya is the *"Turiya Faculty"* whose purpose is to sustain, perpetuate, and deepen Turiya. The Turiya faculty is a secondary sexual characteristic of an integrated and self-realized human being.

Just as the faculties of Thought, Feeling, Memory, Imagination, Intuition, Volition, are all faculties of the human mind, the Turiya faculty emerges to become the prime central organizing faculty of the human mind and takes control over all other faculties to sustain and perpetuate the communion between our temporal being and the Father. As a Foreman, when we enter Turiya, our conscious mind develops a new mode of awareness which parallels our perspective awareness within the mind. The Father provides this new mode of awareness.

Some will question: If the Cosmic Consciousness already exists as our ultimate reality, is it not as just as simple as accepting and embracing the Cosmic Consciousness as our ultimate reality? (Short Path).

The problem is a common person typically lacks the super cognitive sensitivity to become consciously aware and reflective of the Cosmic Consciousness within his or her mind while in physical form. For most human beings on Earth in the physical universe, the Cosmic Consciousness exists within the unconscious mind. In other words, the conscious mind is unaware of the Cosmic Consciousness. In Turiya, the Cosmic Consciousness extends into the conscious mind of the human being, incorporating it and becoming one with it. In Turiya, your awareness of the Cosmic Consciousness overlays your experience of the world.

When the Cosmic Consciousness begins emerging within the conscious mind, it dramatically changes the relationship between the temporal sphere of the human mind and the Cosmic Consciousness. The moment the conscious mind becomes reflectively aware of the Cosmic Consciousness, Alpha begins re-organizing the temporal sphere of the mind into a new matrix and the physical brain is re-wired to reinforce this new matrix. A new faculty of the mind emerges out of this reorganization making Turiya sustainable and continuous. When Turiya begins arising within us, our experience of what is real takes on a whole new dimension of awareness which gradually reveals to us a great many things about the nature of reality, the human mind, the mechanical processes of the universe, the natural world, and the process of alchemy itself.

When we live in Turiya, we experience a profound melody within our higher emotions playing like a divine music in the background of our mind, filling us with a divine bliss and joy, far exceeding what anyone can imagine until they finally experience it.

This divine musical background is the eternal love and Divine Spirit of the Father. It is a marvelous symphony of divine moods which continuously change in melody, harmony, and complexity, accompanying all our internal psychic processes. It overlays our outer-experience of the world. It is a major dimension of what I have come to call the *"Song of the Immortal Beloved."*

Nirvana - The Inculcation Period

Alpha, the alchemical life script, and Turiya, are three very different metaphysical phenomena encountered in the alchemical process. When all three phenomena align in concert, a fourth metaphysical phenomenon arises to form a process of revelation through which knowledge is exchanged between the cosmic quanta and the conscious mind of the human being.

Once we complete the integration of our temporal-physical being with our eternal-primordial being to unify our mind (completion of the Third Mountain), the transmission of information between the cosmic quanta and our conscious mind continues as a function of the Turiya faculty. However, until the integration is complete, this transmission of information functions differently with only one goal, to aid us in completing the unification of our human mind.

The information exchanged during the integration process is all geared toward facilitating and achieving this one goal. The period of revelation which occurs during our ascent through the heavenly spheres is referred to in this book as the *"Inculcation Period."*

The inculcation of our being by the cosmic quanta of the noumenal realm is integral to the alchemical integration process of Mount Magia. The information exchanged between the cosmic quanta and Human Soul is exchanged directly beyond the mind. It is *"Direct Knowledge."*

Awareness and direct knowledge are synergistic. Integration and awareness are synergistic. Therefore, direct knowledge and integration are synergistic. Direct knowledge cannot be transmitted from Human Soul to Human Soul, or from Book to Human Soul. Direct knowledge can only be transmitted from the cosmic quanta to Human Soul. I still attempt to share within this book the knowledge I received directly from the cosmic quanta as there is a benefit to the basic framework of information which is still possible to convey. For the alchemist who reads this book, this will not be enough. We all need to exchange directly with the forces of the cosmic quanta to complete our integration process.

Chapter 5

On the few occasions I attempted to stop writing what I was learning, the cosmic quanta directed: *"You must write this down."* I believe this direction was mostly for my own benefit, as I would soon come to learn that expression completes the cycle of comprehension, and comprehension is essential to the process of integration. However, I was also compelled to share this book with you. This book will come to serve you in ways unknown even to me.

Many occultists naturally assume they have *"Esoteric Knowledge"* or some form of special knowledge simply because they learned something from an earthly teacher - or from a book – which few others had or have access to. This is not esoteric knowledge. I will raise the bar here and assert that a person does not gain the capacity to receive esoteric knowledge until they achieve Turiya.

"Esoteric Knowledge" is knowledge exchanged directly between the cosmic quanta and Human Soul via sympathetic resonance. The knowledge exchanged directly via resonance manifests within the conscious mind of the Foreman via the Turiya faculty. The transmission of esoteric knowledge transcends all subjective sensory processes of perception, interpretation, and imagination. The knowledge arrives via transference from the cosmic quanta. The reason the knowledge is categorized as esoteric, secret, or intangible, is because the knowledge is accessible only through the faculties of our super cognitive emotional awareness (Turiya faculty). In short, it is only through Turiya that this knowledge becomes known. In other words - the knowledge comes to us through the love of God - the Spirit. Because emotion cannot be accurately defined empirically or tangibly, this renders the knowledge incommunicable, and therefore is *"esoteric."* It is esoteric, not by choice, but by having no means of accurate or precise external communication. It is a knowledge shared only between the Human Soul and God. This is esoteric knowledge.

The emergence of Turiya within us - with its added dimension of resonant awareness - transitions us into a special series of revelations. These revelations begin in Nirvana and continue throughout our ascent into all nine heavenly realms of the spiritual group mind of the Earth.

The purpose of the revelations between the Godhead of Ain Soph, the Father, and the Human Soul, is to institute a series of shock awakenings to compel the integration of the Human Soul's temporal-physical being with the Human Soul's eternal-primordial being. These shocks are necessary otherwise the integration process will lose the required momentum and the Human Soul will fall back to the spiral path. The revelations alter the tone and depth of our resonance with the Father which further compels the process of integration.

Although the experience of Turiya is indescribable, this book attempts to share with you the revelations which were revealed to me as I ascended and entered each heavenly realm of the spiritual group mind of the Earth. Although the incommunicable dimensions of the revelations are impossible to share, there remains a communicable dimension of the same knowledge which is possible to share.

Nirvana - Revelation 1 - The Force of Death

As my Human Soul ascended the heavenly realm of Nirvana whose spiritual realm radiantly enshrines the primordial Earth, I glided through majestic mountain ranges with mystical caverns and enchanted waterfalls. Magical bells peacefully reverberated deeply and intermittently throughout the heavenly realm as I ascended upward to the Father.

In the days that passed - as my conscious mind was continually elevated in resonance with the heavenly realm of Nirvana - my attention was continually drawn to an emerging contrast between the light of Nirvana and a deep-seated auto-cognitive program within my temporal-physical being which was driving my physical human organism toward death. It was showing me that death was not just an *"event,"* but was a *"process"* - beyond just aging - driven by an unconscious force within us - and that this force, by secondary effect - was providing an underlying energy and momentum to all self-destructive impulses found deep within the human mind. Why was this being revealed to me now during my ascent through Nirvana?

Because, as the light of our conscious awareness with the Father grows increasingly brighter within us, the brightening continuously reveals to us darker and darker shadows within our temporal-physical nature which we must become conscious of in order to continue the integration of our celestial being.

It required the temporal sphere of my mind to go through a great deal of clearing and silencing over the course of many years prior to making possible a direct alchemical engagement with the force behind this deep-seated auto-cognitive program I found deep within the unconscious recesses of my mind.

Sigmund Freud had already developed a hypothesis on a *"death instinct"* which counters the instinct to sustain and perpetuate life. Freud called this death instinct *"Thanatos."* Freud's hypothesis has been widely debated among theorists. The alchemical process reveals that this dynamic does indeed exist, but not necessarily in the same manner suggested by Freud.

My attention was directed to become conscious of this phenomenon through a series of highly unusual and very strange alchemical life script circumstances. What I was able to discern at this point in my alchemical process was that when the life force of Eros is in harmony with the Father, Eros maintains and escalates its harmony with the Father by allowing its matrix of creation to be continually reorganized into higher and higher orders of resonance with the divine source. However, when the harmony between Eros and the Father has been compromised in some way, a dimension of Eros is impacted and some of its energy is diverted to seek the most efficient means of reuniting the Human Soul with the Father.

My resonance with the Father was not yet deep enough for the conscious mind of my temporal-physical existence to clearly process and comprehend the knowledge being passed to me directly from the quantum force of the Father. I was only scratching the surface of a great mystery which would continue to unfold throughout my ascension to the Father.

While I was in Nirvana, the life instinct (Eros) and the death instinct (Thanatos) seemed not to be two forces in opposition as theorized by Freud, but to be the same force finding expression in two alternate states.

Direct knowledge, or direct information, passes perfectly between the Father and the Human Soul, but once the information is received by the Human Soul, the information is then passed through all the layers of the temporal mind to reach the conscious mind. In doing so, the information is filtered and refracted like light through a prism. This filtering is a form of cognitive suppression. To overcome the prism effect of the temporal mind, which distorts the information arising out of the cosmic quanta, the temporal mind must be continually elevated in resonance with the Father.

The lifting of the temporal levels of my mind to higher and higher levels of resonance with the Father over the course of my ascension through the heavenly realms of the spiritual group mind of the Earth would bring the information attempting to come through my mind into greater degrees of clarity which ultimately gave way to a greater understanding.

In my personal alchemical experience, I noted that Freud ended up being more correct than being wrong. But initially, while in Nirvana, he seemed more wrong than correct. There was a lesson to be learned in this. We can only know truth through the Father.

"I am the way, the truth, and the life."

There was indeed an opposition to the life force of Eros, but it was much more profound and complex than Freud had theorized. I was only just beginning to uncover the great mystery in the heavenly realm of Nirvana. In in the pages and chapters ahead I share everything revealed to me by the cosmic quanta.

The force of death revelation compelled me to realize that the most efficient means of reuniting the Human Soul with the Father when the life force of Eros is not in harmony with the Father, is through the death of the organism with which the Human Soul is paired. When Alpha detects within us the forces of Eros in chaos, the geometric self-organizing patterns of Alpha invert, leading our organism toward death.

The revelation of Nirvana was also showing me that the organizational patterns of Alpha build and compound within creation. Death promotes more death. Life promotes more life.

When the forces of Eros are geometrically inverted within the mind of the human being leading toward eventual death, this promotes the rise of many compulsions and disorders of the mind which support and promote all the self-destructive tendencies within the human personality.

When we are born within a human physical body which has evolved only to reach an auto-cognitive or prelescent level of existence, and therefore has yet to evolve and maintain a neurological harmony with the divine source, we find Alpha steering the forces of our mind-body system in the most efficient course possible to re-unify our Human Soul with the divine source. This course is the entropic degradation and eventual death of our physical body. Entropy arises out of an insufficient resonance between Matter-Energy and the divine source from which it originally emerges, which ultimately, is the Father.

This inversion of Eros is Eros going counterclockwise rather than clockwise. It is Eros in retrograde. However, it is still Eros. It is a built-in self-destruct mechanism instilled by the program of nature. Death is a means of reunification with the Father. Alchemy upends this dynamic by re-establishing resonance between the Human Soul and the Father in physical life, and by way of this, upturning the Alpha pattern of Eros. The inverted pentagram is the inversion of Eros. The upturned pentagram is a symbol of an integrated self-actualized human being.

Although they may often seem at odds, the Father and the life force of Nature (Eros) - at the deepest level - are working together to create life which reflects an awareness and unity with the Father. I call this reunification principle, the *"Alpha Principle."* The Alpha Principle is built into the underlying mechanics of nature and is the highest governing principle of all creation.

Mount Magia

When the conscious mind of our temporal-physical being begins entering into a profound resonance with the Father, the counter-clockwise motion of Eros is course-corrected. Prior to this course correction, we must develop an awareness of the force of death. There was something profound I was still missing, however.

There is another universal force in the cosmic quanta involved in the life-death process which has a profound influence on the patterned geometric unfoldment of Alpha and Eros. This force operates as an agent of the Father and would not come to be realized until much later in the alchemical process. I will reveal this force in due course. The revelation of the force of death and its relationship to Eros was a foreshadowing of this future realization.

Not all of Eros is moving in retrograde within nature. Although Eros in retrograde ensures the eventual liberation of the Human Soul from its prison within a mind-body system which does not reflect the divine source (through death), nature must still ensure the continuation and evolution of the species. In nature, Eros moves in different directions simultaneously. On some levels, Eros is already in harmony, but on other levels, Eros is in chaos. At this point in the Great Work, the forces causing this dynamic remain undetected.

In summary, there is an intermediary force at work in the universe which functions on cosmic scales, compelling the diametric directions of Eros, and mediating the Father's relationship with creation. In Nirvana, I was not yet aware of this intermediary force in the universe. It was on my distant horizon.

Eros in retrograde is the primary driving influence of all self-destructive behaviors leading our organism toward its ultimate final death. Ironically, you will find a greater propensity toward self-destruction in individuals who have a deep calling to the Father yet lack a physical organism which reaffirms and supports their divine connection.

Your potential must eventually be realized. Otherwise, this same potential will eventually turn on itself. The greater the potential, the greater the potential reward, but also the greater the potential demise.

The key to fulfilling our potential is the liberation of our authentic-self and the realization of our divine source. We must stop adapting and become real. We must not live as a slave to perception and fear. Have the courage to be your true self against all odds. In this way, you will come to know God.

Simmatuu - Revelation 2 - Ain Soph

As my resonance ascended beyond the mystical heaven of Nirvana, I entered the divine heavenly realm of Simmatuu. The realm was warm, sunny, and vibrant like a mid-summer musical festival full of cheer and divine happiness. People were very merry, dancing with a profound happiness to the joy of eternal life. Turiya filled the hearts and souls of all who resonated with this heavenly realm and the love of the Father was known and celebrated.

As I entered 13th cycle of Simmatuu, a profound spiritual revelation came upon me where both the Void and Nexus were paramount within my conscious mind like two great celestial bodies slowly converging to eventually merge and become one.

The revelation of Simmatuu happened outside of time. The revelation came upon me unintentionally while I was neither physically awake nor completely asleep. Although what I experienced unfolded through a sequence of episodes to form an experience which would indicate a passage of time, I can tell you with absolute certainty, no time had passed. See Note [3] and Figure [7]

Angel Playing Harp in the Clouds
By Giovanni Batista Gaulli

Figure [7]

The angel is a universal symbol arising out of the collective unconscious to manifest in Earth mythology. Angels in the clouds playing musical instruments represent the very real supernatural phenomenon of the spiritual group mind enveloping the primordial Earth. The hierarchy of angels symbolizes the gradient levels of resonance our temporal mind ascends while harmonizing with the life, love, and awareness of the Father. Each gradient level of resonance aligns with each bandwidth of the spiritual group mind of the Earth.

> Note: 3
> The Heavenly Realms

The spiritual group mind bandwidths of the collective unconscious, which I call the heavens of the Earth, are like spiritual atmospheres co-existing in the same location, but at different frequencies overlaying the Earth in the primordial universe. They interpenetrate us and fill us with the love of God (Spirit).

We ascend the spiritual atmospheres of the planetary mind - or heavenly realms - as we ascend in resonance to the Father. Even after progressing to higher orders of resonance, we can instantly go back to each heavenly realm, like returning to a musical string on an instrument. In the Third Mountain, as our resonance escalates, we can feel each heaven inside us, and we can amplify our resonance with each heavenly realm and fully immerse ourselves inside any one of them - body, mind, and soul - at any given moment by inwardly focusing on them. We do this through our resonance with the Father. We can do this without leaving our physical body, or we can leave our physical body. Either way, we can be there. We choose which way we are there.

- End Note -

For a brief moment, my conscious awareness sunk into and entered upon a super heightened realm of reality which was ultra-real, much like the primordial universe, but there was something even older, more archaic, and even more familiar about this heightened realm of reality than the primordial.

During this moment, while in resonance with the heaven of Simmatuu, I crossed the threshold of a quantum portal where I immediately returned to both mine, and our, original state of being which existed before the beginning of time, before the moment of creation, before the great cosmic singularity. When I crossed the quantum threshold, I briefly returned to the original divine unity existing deep inside the center of all things.

Interestingly, while my awareness sunk deep into the quantum cosmos of the noumenon leading me all the way back to very beginning of creation, the *"Akashic Records"* were re-run for me. While in unity with the divine source residing at the center of all things, I re-experienced the moment of creation. See Note [4]

I say "re-experienced" because I was there before, and so were you. You can re-experience this cosmic event as well. We were all there together at the beginning of time. The first realization which came about in this moment of revelation was that we were all present together at the very moment of creation.

Note: 4
The Akashic Records

The Akashic Records are the legendary memories of the cosmos embedded in the underlying abstract of the universe which can be accessed by a conscious mind.

- End Note -

Ultimately, we all manifest from the same being. I truly mean the same being. I am not being figurative, metaphorical, or poetic. At the deepest level, there is no difference between me and you. At the deepest level, all is one. This original being is an undifferentiated state of Cosmic Consciousness.

From a mathematical perspective, this original being has an absolute existence. It is the only thing that is truly real, permanent, and eternal. It exists at the center of all things.

I was experiencing the Cosmic Consciousness in a state of total complete unity - prior to any expression of its three abstract dimensions of being - which are the Father, the Divine Soul, and the Spirit. This original being - expressed in a state of total absolute undifferentiated unity is *"Ain Soph."*

What was realized within me in this moment was that Ain Soph has no *"mind,"* and therefore it has no thoughts, common feelings, or perspectives which we could relate to based on our temporal human perspective. Ain Soph knows and communicates through *"resonance."* What it has - is an eternal, absolute, permanent presence. It is immortal.

Ain Soph is the Father, the Divine Soul, and Spirit unified as one total complete being. It is the original cosmic unity. It is the God Particle. Ain Soph is the heart of the *"Immortal Beloved."*

The Song of the Immortal Beloved is Spiritual Alchemy.
The music of the Song is Turiya.

The name *"Ain Soph"* comes from the Kabbalah. It is also known in Taoism by the name *"Wu-Ji."*

Ain Soph exists in a reality not governed by space-time. It exists in non-space-time. There is literally no space and no time. There are no spatial dimensions. It is absolute.

When our initial awareness of Ain Soph passes through the temporal sphere of our mind, the unity of Ain Soph subdivides into three divisible forces of consciousness - much like light passing through a prism and refracting into a beautiful spectrum of colored light. Early in our ascent of resonance - as we focus inward – the temporal sphere of our mind attempts to interpret our resonance, and in doing so, renders a refracted colored spectrum of the Cosmic Consciousness. This colored spectrum of the Cosmic Consciousness reveals the Divine Trinity. The three forces of the Divine Trinity are real. However, the three forces of the Divine Trinity exist all as one beyond the mind. See Figure [8]

Mount Magia

Refraction of Light

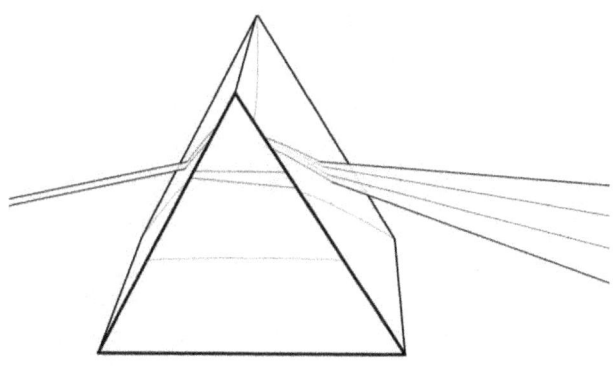

Figure [8]

A single ray of white light passing through a glass prism and refracting into a multitude of colored rays of light. The colored spectrum exists inside the white light. Similarly, the mind acts as a glass prism refracting the single white light of Ain Soph into the three primary forces of the Cosmic Consciousness.

The temporal sphere of the human mind collapses the wave function of the Cosmic Consciousness into three divisible forces of divinity no different than "observation" collapsing the wave function of atomic energy into particles of energy.

As the temporal sphere of our mind begins to escalate its resonance with Ain Soph, our mind initially refracts the unity of Ain Soph into the three divisible forces of the Father, the Divine Soul, and the Spirit. However, as the resonance of our temporal-physical being ascends further, the division of three reintegrates back into the unity of one, and Ain Soph emerges.

Modern science calls the forces of matter *"Atomic."* In addition to the forces of matter, we have the forces of consciousness. These forces are *"Theogenic."* There is a third class of forces which combine the atomic and theogenic. These forces are "*Metagenic."*

Each force has a force carrier which is a force particle. Theogenic force particles are a set of forces which are *"living."* They exist at the deepest level within all things - both within things animate and inanimate. The Human Soul itself is a theogenic force particle. All three classes of quantum force particles together compose the pantheon of the cosmic quanta and can be known intimately by the Human Soul in the noumenal realm through sympathetic resonance.

Within the theogenic class of force particles - all of which I have not yet revealed - there is only one particle which is *"divine."* This one divine force particle is the God particle. The God particle is Ain Soph.

Why is Ain Soph divine? Because Ain Soph is the only theogenic particle to have never been born, procreated, derived, or permutated. Ain Soph has always been and will always be. It is immortal. All other particles of consciousness dance around the eternal flame of Ain Soph.

In our physical reality, we deal with the duality of either having nothing or having something, and everything is relative. In the absolute reality of Ain Soph there is no such thing as *"nothing"* or *"something"* - yet in this reality - Ain Soph still manages to exist. In the divine order of Ain Soph, there is no duality of any kind.

In the 13th cycle of Simmatuu - as my focus of conscious awareness sunk deep within the noumenal realm of the cosmic quanta - I became intimately aware of Ain Soph and the absolute abstract realm of ultra-reality in which Ain Soph lives. Immediately upon entering the Absolute, I began reliving the very moment of creation. The akashic records were re-run for me like the re-running of a cosmic tape.

There was a sense of great importance pervading the whole spiritual experience. Alpha was compelling me to become aware of the very beginning of creation. It was key to the alchemical process of integration.

I came to realize in this moment that Ain Soph does not have an actual *"mind"* as a mind is impossible within the Ain Soph reality because a mind requires more dimensions to sustain itself.

All that exists in Ain Soph is *"presence."* Yet from its state of absolute *"presence"* a grand *"vision"* managed to emerge.

Because the cosmic realm of Ain Soph cannot support a *"vision"* without a *"mind,"* the vision immediately broke off from the Ain Soph realm of reality and formed a vessel through which the vision could sustain itself. The vessel which formed to sustain the emergent vision of Ain Soph was the *"Cosmic Mind."* This was the cosmic egg.

The body of the Cosmic Mind is *"space-time."* The Cosmic Mind formed a whole new reality separate of the Ain Soph reality. The body of the Cosmic Mind is the cosmos of creation which we all know today. The cosmos literally forms the mind of God and includes both the primordial universe and the physical universe. The Ain Soph vision of the cosmos was the most profound event to ever occur because this vision sparked the birth of the multi-verse of creation. This indicates that space-time is a manifestation of perception, which further suggests that by controlling the mind, which is the instrument of perception, we can control space-time. After experiencing this revelation of Ain Soph, which emerged during my ascent of Simmatuu, I named the indivisible, absolute, eternal realm of divinity in which Ain Soph lives, *"Causal 'A',"* and I named the envisioned realm of creation encompassing all the universes of the multiverse, *"Causal 'B'."*

The physical universe, the primordial universe, hyperspace, all planetary group mind bandwidths, all dimensions of existence, all bubble universes or universal branes, all frequencies of time and space, all exist inside Causal 'B'. Causal 'B' is creation. Causal 'B' is the cosmos.

Causal 'A' has no beginning and it has no ending, as it has no time, and it has no existence in the way many would measure existence, as it has no space and no matter, yet, it is still there. It is absolute and eternal. It is the realm of divinity.

After achieving the proper level of Q, when we look inward toward Ain Soph from within the temporal mind of creation, we will come to detect the three primary dimensions of Ain Soph. The Father emerges as the first prime dimensional abstract of Ain Soph. When we pray to the Father, we are praying to Ain Soph, and when we are praying to Ain Soph, we are praying to the Father. They are one.

From within the temporal mind, when we reflect inward upon the Father, we detect an infinite and eternal force. This is due to us attempting to understand a force which exists beyond time and space, with an apparatus governed by time and space. The Father seems separate from us because we are reflecting upon an infinite reality from within the looking glass of a finite mind.

The escalation of resonance brings us to the Father, but the temporal sphere of our mind overlays this resonance - passing its light through the prism of our temporal mind to collapse its wave function. This dynamic compels a parallel awareness of the Father to emerge within us - with one mode of awareness being *"resonance"* and the other mode being *"perception."* Perception is of the mind. Resonance is of the soul. It is important to become aware of this and realize that, in the final analysis, it is only through resonance, not perception, that we can enter into a true intimate relationship with God.

This all indicates that consciousness does not exist as a byproduct of our physical and primordial creation. Conversely, consciousness is a predecessor and observer of creation operating from within a higher absolute reality existing outside the bounds of space, time, mind, and creation in general. Consciousness precedes creation. Creation does not precede consciousness.

What also was realized in this moment was that the cosmos (Causal 'B') did not start with a *"Big Bang"* emerging out of a primeval atom of matter. What emerged first was *"space,"* not *"matter,"* to quickly form a Cosmic Mind which would sustain the cosmic vision of Ain Soph. Space expanded rapidly by result of the need to sustain the cosmic vision. Space was attempting to match the parameters of an infinite source which was projecting the vision.

The expansion of space, which continues until this day, is driven by the space-time parameters of Causal 'B' attempting to match the non-space time parameters of Causal 'A'. Causal 'B' does not know how to interpret non-space, so it interprets it as *"infinite."* Because of this, our universe is attempting to expand to infinity to align itself with Causal 'A'. The expansion is forever because there is nothing with which to actually align. The expansion is driven infinitely by an unresolvable paradox.

The force of this expansion is what physicists today would call *"Dark Energy."* They call it *"dark"* because they have not yet understood it. You cannot completely understand it with the mind because the mind itself is created by the same process it is attempting to understand.

To achieve an understanding of creation we must transcend the mind, perception, and space-time. This requires an understanding at the level of the soul which can only be accomplished through resonance. This means we cannot understand the process of creation solely in a laboratory. It requires the cooperation of the soul.

Right now, physicists believe there was first a primeval atom of matter which exploded and caused the expansion of space which they call the *"Big Bang"* or Cosmic Singularity. This is wrong.

The expansion of space came first and then after came the matter. Ain Soph revealed to me that matter materializes out of the fabric of space-time itself due to the rapid stretching of space-time during its inflation or expansion. Perhaps this stretching creates heat, which is energy, and this energy condenses into matter as it cools.

This is how the first hydrogen was formed. From this point on, celestial mechanics took over and all the stars and galaxies formed. The fabric of space is like the strings of a musical instrument, and the expansion of space is like the plucking of the strings. The musical notes are the particles of matter rising from the plucking of the strings.

Also imagine a sponge holding water. The water in the sponge is not seen until the sponge is stretched. Once the sponge is stretched, the water rises to the surface of the sponge. The sponge is space-time. The water is matter.

One of the mysteries which baffle cosmologists and physicists today is how matter was so uniform throughout space so soon after its creation, as this is inconsistent with a *"Big Bang"* starting everything. However, this uniformity elegantly agrees with the concept of matter emerging out of the very fabric of space itself due to its rapid stretching, expansion, and inflation.

Ain Soph revealed that the primordial universe was formed first. Much later, the physical universe was formed out of the primordial universe as a repeating echo of the Ain Soph grand vision of the cosmos.

In the very moment I became aware of Ain Soph, all of what I just shared with you was realized in a single instant. I then gazed across the cosmos and felt a tremendous love and affection for all of creation. I felt the presence of all life and all of humanity within it. It was an incredible joy. The cosmos looked like a great cosmic quilt being woven by Ain Soph. It was predominately pink with hues of purple, red, and blue.

Ain Soph is the being of our being living inside a spiritual core within us which I call the *"Nexus."* The Nexus is both your spiritual core, and the spiritual core within all things. The Nexus is the gateway between Causal 'A' and Causal 'B'. Only resonance can carry our focus of conscious awareness across the Nexus gateway. The Nexus gateway is the great barrier bridging the Source (Ain Soph) and creation.

In my Nirvana ascension cycle, when I reached the 13th bandwidth, I experienced the Nexus for a brief moment, but I did not cross the great barrier. In Simmatuu, as I entered the 13th bandwidth to align the two cores of my being (Temporal-Void and Eternal-Spiritual-Nexus), I crossed the Nexus gateway, or great barrier, and entered Causal 'A' and became Ain Soph for a brief moment.

Each time we cycle back to the 13th bandwidth in a higher planet-lifting cycle to align the two cores, our conscious mind realizes more of Ain Soph until Ain Soph becomes co-existent in our conscious mind at all times. The self-realized awareness of Ain Soph within the conscious mind of the human being is God reflecting on itself through its own creation. This dynamic brings about Turiya.

Khimmadooree - Revelation 3 - Planetary Alchemy

The alchemical processes of Mount Sophia and Mount Kabbalah deal mostly with the forces of the alchemist's own personal trans-dimensional being. The alchemical process of Mount Magia adds and incorporates the primordial forces of creation which ascend rhythmically and geometrically within an infinite progression of cosmic scales. The scales are organized into three major levels:

- Individual
- Planetary
- Cosmic.

The cosmic level encompasses both the very large and the very small. The very small is inside the atom. The cosmic level is essentially a loop. The door to the outer cosmos is entered through the door of the inner cosmos. The Individual level holds a very special place. It holds a position of equilibrium between all the scales. For this reason, it is the Individual, the Human Being, who must reconcile the scales and complete the Great Work. See Figure [9]

Chapter 5

Ouroboros

Figure [9]

The serpent swallowing its tail is a very popular motif arising out of the collective unconscious. In alchemy, it has more than one meaning:

1.) The inner and outer cosmos returning on itself.

1.) The return to unity

2.) The accomplishment of the Great Work

4.) Eternity

5.) The cycle of creative destruction

The primordial forces of creation the Foreman is dealing with in Mount Magia are very powerful and are not to be trifled with. Our relationship with the Father helps us to navigate these forces. Stay focused on your resonance. It is your guiding light. Our alchemy must be driven by an authentic calling to the divine source of the Father. Alpha responds to our internal disposition toward the divine source and energizes and directs our momentum accordingly.

Arriving in the heaven of Kimmadooree is like moving through a tunnel which suddenly opens into a great hall. My entrance into the heaven of Khimmadooree brought me into a much greater and all-encompassing light of the Father. Khimmadooree brought a new revelation upon me. It was an awakening to a greater awareness of the love of the Father (Spirit). From Parabinlaya to Nirvana, and from Nirvana to Simmatuu, I felt an exclusive relationship with the Father. The exclusiveness was my own internalization of my experience of the Father transmitting through the deep layers of my temporal mind. Looking back from where I stand now, I believe this internalization was the result of my physical brain being only at the very early stage of rewiring itself in response to my escalating resonance with the Father.

As the brain continues to rewire itself, and as our resonance with the divine awareness of the Father continues to escalate, older realities are torn away, and new higher realities burst forth into the realm of our conscious mind. Each time we feel a weight lifted, a new light rushes in, and our awareness and comprehension are expanded.

The divine awareness of the Father is the first of the three primary dimensions of Ain Soph. Ain Soph is the Cosmic Consciousness expressed in its original unity. When we begin the 7th alchemical process, our conscious mind is aware of and resonating with all three dimensions of Ain Soph. Each dimension expresses its own unique original force. When we are seeking to transform an element, we have the innate super cognitive ability to focus on any one dimension of Ain Soph, or all three dimensions simultaneously, and choose which original force to use as a catalyst of differentiation in the alchemical process of transformation.

It is up to each alchemist to freestyle which emergent force to use in each moment to see which force works best for the element we are transforming. This is how we develop an intimate knowledge of each emergent force within us. The way we choose to focus on the emergent forces within us owes a lot to the current stage of geometric crystallization of our brain matter - led by the self-organizing forces of Alpha - in response to the spiritual awakening of our temporal being.

When you are being challenged to expand your awareness, focus on and utilize the contrasting light of the Father. After you have become aware of something, and you wish to understand it more deeply, focus on and utilize the contrasting light of the Divine Soul. After you have understood something, and you wish to transform it, focus on, and utilize the contrasting light of the Spirit. When you come to integrate that which has been transformed, focus on and utilize the contrasting light of Ain Soph and invite everything to come into unity.

When we are ascending the heavenly realms, we are simultaneously expanding our awareness. Therefore, at this stage, our focus of awareness will gravitate mostly to the Father. Let it all unfold naturally.

There is a very special relationship between all three dimensions of the Cosmic Consciousness, which at this point in Mount Magia, I was not yet fully aware. I will reveal this information at the stages in which I became aware.

In the heaven of Khimmadooree, my escalating resonance with the divine awareness of the Father drove the expansion of my conscious awareness to incorporate another set of temporal forces existing outside of the temporal hemisphere of my own mind. These outside temporal forces were also attempting to escalate in resonance with the Father. The outside temporal forces which I became aware, were planetary.

The resonance of the Father is attempting to resonate with all of creation, not just with you. Therefore, as your resonance escalates, you will gradually become more aware of all the other forces, elements, and levels of creation being compelled to achieve a higher degree of resonance with the divine source of the Father.

The Godhead of Ain Soph, the Father, brings us into unity not just with his being, he brings us into unity with everyone and everything. As our awareness escalates, we become aware that we are only one voice in a vast choir. It was in the heaven of Khimmadooree where I began becoming more fully aware of the forces of creation on a planetary level, more specifically, the planetary forces of the Earth.

The completion of the integration of self includes the integration of the greater cosmos. The integrated-self is a functioning component of a much greater whole which transcends the self. The whole beyond the self must be realized to complete the self. The unity of self without the greater whole of the greater cosmos is incomplete. Mount Kabbalah brings us into a unity of self. Mount Magia brings us into a unity with the greater cosmos.

As we become aware of the temporal forces of creation existing on a planetary level, we become simultaneously responsible for them. This is a fundamental rule in alchemy which cannot be avoided. As such, these forces arise within the mind as a new stressor which must be transformed. This forms the basis of a whole new level of alchemy. This level of alchemy is *"Planetary Alchemy."*

Whereas in the 6th alchemical process, the stressor is individuality itself, the stressor in the 7th alchemical process advances beyond individuality and becomes planetary - beginning with the temporal group mind of the Earth. In the 7th alchemical process, the alchemist is no longer transforming just the contents of his or her individual mind, the alchemist is transforming the forces of the temporal group mind, and in doing so, has joined the cosmic process of awakening the planetary group mind of the Earth on a higher level. The 7th alchemical process begins at the individual level, advances through the planetary level, and ends at the cosmic level. How all this unfolds is revealed as we progress through the remaining pages of this chapter.

While sojourning through Nirvana and Simmatuu on our way to Khimmadooree, we can sense and feel an internal transition into planetary alchemy. We can feel its eminent arrival on our horizon. When we finally enter the realm of Khimmadooree, the cosmic quanta teach us the mysteries of planetary alchemy and we begin its process.

The main revelation I experienced in the heaven of Khimmadooree was the realization of the calling of the Father to begin planetary alchemy. This revelation was not just a single event, awakening, or experience. The Foreman experiences a continuous train of intimate realizations and instructions on the application and purpose of planetary alchemy while ascending the heavenly realm of Khimmadooree. To perform planetary alchemy, the Foreman must have attained a profound degree of resonance with the temporal group mind, the spiritual group mind, and Ain Soph.

We do not leave behind the temporal group mind when we begin ascending the heavenly realms of the spiritual group mind of the Earth. We hold onto the temporal group mind while we enter the spiritual group mind. Once we gain a foothold within both realms of the planetary group mind, we are then prepared to begin planetary alchemy.

The temporal group mind of the Earth has not yet awoken to its own realization of Ain Soph. However, it is still highly intelligent and continuously rises to interact with each of us. Part of the reason we dream and lose awareness of our physical existence when we sleep is not just because of our own temporal mind, it is because the temporal group mind itself is asleep and dreaming. We dream in concert with the temporal group mind. We do not dream alone.

As the Foreman awakens to the forces of the temporal group mind, he or she will continually notice the draw of disorganized forces (chaos) within the temporal group mind. It is within these moments that planetary alchemy is performed. We can differentiate the forces of chaos arising out of the temporal group mind in contrast to our emerging awareness of the three primary forces of Ain Soph. Through differential resonance, chaos is brought into harmony. Planetary alchemy further integrates our temporal-physical being with our eternal-primordial being, as our temporal-physical being is an extension of the temporal group mind, and our eternal-primordial being is an extension of the spiritual group mind.

We experience the processes of planetary alchemy taking place within us in a similar manner to when we are working with the temporal forces of our own individual mind. The most profound revelations I experienced in Khimmadooree were:

1.) The interconnectedness of all things led by our common escalating resonance with the Father.

2.) Planetary Alchemy

3.) It is the love of the Father which completes us.

As I entered the final spiritual cycle of Khimmadooree, the Void and the Nexus entered celestial alignment, and Ain Soph emerged to a paramount position within me. As my days passed on Earth - walking from city to city - I experienced a heightened state of Turiya. It was in the years 2014 and 2015 that I ascended the heavenly realms of the Earth and learned the secrets of planetary and cosmic alchemy. Coincidently, during these same two years, I travelled throughout fifteen countries of the world in Eastern Europe, the Middle East, Southeast Asia, and the United States.

As my resonance with the Father was ascending the heavenly realm of Khimmadooree, I was walking the summertime countryside of Poland and the Czech Republic among rolling hills and nestled villages and the Song of the Immortal Beloved filled my soul.

Valhalla

As I ascended the magnificent realm of Valhalla, I entered steadfastly into a vast and magnificent hall of eternity. Valhalla is one nine spiritual realms which join to form a divine chorus of heavens enveloping and enshrining the primordial Earth.

As I entered Valhalla, I immediately experienced a new spiritual awakening. My resonance with the Father instantly took on a whole new level of depth, feeling, and illumination. The resonance suddenly became more complex and sophisticated. The information arising from the resonance between us became more solid, rapid, fluid, clear, and profound. The information flow was encountering less resistance from within the neurological chemistry of my physical being.

One harmonic grade after another, Alpha was rewiring the temporal sphere of my mind and its underlying neurological chemistry to map to the geometric patterns of the Father's divine resonance. Because of my ascension of resonance with the Father, my innate super cognitive faculties were blossoming. The Turiya faculty is the central organizing faculty from which all other faculties unfold and manifest.

The way in which my mind immediately blossomed in respect to my escalating resonance with the Father as I entered the halls of Valhalla, caused me to realize how much more the human mind is capable of beyond the limits of common human perception. There is another mode of knowing which is timeless and ancient and far more advanced than the common mode of knowing to which human beings on Earth in the physical universe are accustomed. If people only know one way, then people will fail to imagine any other way. Knowing - through resonance - is the way of pure consciousness, before there was mind, before there was creation, before there was time and space.

Most interestingly, the human mind itself has an innate capacity to adapt to this ancient mode of knowing to become a direct receiver of knowledge, rather than just being an instrument charged with the subjective process of perceiving, rationalizing, and believing. It is the subjective faculties of the human mind which are the ultimate root cause of all human suffering. By reconnecting with the divine source found deep within our core, we can transcend all of it. To process our experience of the world, our internal cognitive processes do not necessarily need to begin with an observation of the world through the looking glass of the human mind known as *"Perception."*

In general, people are wired neurologically to believe there is no other way to process their experiences. They do not even question it. It serves the interests of nature for people to think this way. The automated faculties of the human mind, although being subjective and suppressive, when steered by Alpha, keep everyone under a form of cruise control until people wake-up and realize the divine source of Ain Soph. It is a program which keeps the sleeping mass of humanity all pointed in the same direction while nature undergoes its evolutionary process. It is a built-in mechanism of evolutionary control. Ironically, this is a function of the spiral path.

Valhalla - Revelation 4 - Third Mountain Physicality

When ascending the next heavenly realm before us, the increased luminosity always brings forth into the light previously undetected shadows of darkness. One such shadow of darkness brought forth into the light of Valhalla was the intense physical nature of the alchemical process of the Third Mountain. The focus of the Third Mountain alchemical process had a very clear physical dimension to it. It was no longer just psychological. I found this to be profound and fascinating, but at this point, I did not know why.

There were many intense physical circumstances unfolding in my life since the start of Mount Magia. This was more than just coincidence, or unique to just me, but was fundamental and universal to the Third Mountain alchemical process itself.

The illumination that the light of Valhalla cast upon my soul made me aware of the unique temporal-physical dimensions of Mount Magia, but it did not reveal why. The heavens function together in concert, and each alone reveals only so much. I realized the answer would be discovered in a higher gradient of light. Valhalla was only one light among a vast constellation of lights which would together reveal the greater truth of our existence.

The ascending resonance of the Foreman - upward through the heavenly realms of the Earth - involves a progressive escalation of resonance relative to the atomic structure of the Foreman's physical body. This much I became aware as I ascended the heavenly realm of Valhalla. What I did not realize yet however, was that this escalating dynamic was setting me up for a much greater alchemy. This was all leading to a grand culmination period which is revealed and entered upon much later in the Third Mountain.

The atomic structure of our physical body itself is not elevated during our ascent of the nine heavens. The physical created form itself is elevated in resonance much later. The atomic structure of our physical body is utilized more as a form of leverage and contrast during our heavenly ascent. It is a differentiating catalyst between light and darkness. What is being elevated in resonance during our ascent of the heavenly realms of the Earth is a dimension of our temporal mind which allows for a conscious awareness of Ain Soph and its three primary dimensions to transmit through the temporal dimensions of our mind - between Ain Soph and the Human Soul - so that the temporal mind itself does not disrupt the transmission. Resonance unifies the mind, the soul, and Ain Soph.

The continuous escalation of resonance we undergo while ascending the nine heavens makes our physical atomic structure more transparent between the temporal sphere of our mind and the three dimensions of Ain Soph. However, it does not elevate the physical mass of the bodily form itself. This level of alchemy is revealed later.

There appears to be a fundamental rule in the harmonic ascension of mind-body systems which compels the mind to become more aware of that which is dark, while simultaneously becoming more aware of that which is light. This rule tasks the Foreman to become more aware of his or her temporal-physical nature while becoming more aware of his or her eternal-primordial nature. The Third Mountain is not all about angels playing harps in the clouds. There is something extremely deep and profound for which the heavenly ascent is preparing us for. Something is on the horizon.

Alpha leads the conscious mind of the Foreman in becoming more aware of its temporal-physical nature, and in doing so, directly influences and steers the nature of our life circumstances relative to our physical existence and physical body. The path of the razor's edge becomes increasingly physical in the Third Mountain and in this regard, becomes increasingly difficult and more precarious.

<u>Valhalla - Revelation 5 - The Planetary Twin Souls</u>

I was once again approaching the end of a cycle and at the threshold of a new beginning. I had lifted my temporal ethereal bodies another 12 levels up the ladder of resonance to the divine awareness of the Father. I was 12 levels closer in resonance to my primordial being and finally about to complete the 13th level existing at the end of each cycle. Like a comet circling a central star - with each orbit getting shorter and shorter before entering its heliosphere - I was now making a new visit to the central host star of Ain Soph - of which the Father is the Godhead.

When we reach the 4th spiritual interval of Ain Soph, we complete our ascension of Valhalla and we begin our ascension of the heaven of the Elysium realm. This is how we transition from one heaven to the next. We slingshot around Ain Soph, and then the gravity of Ain Soph propels our resonance to the next higher heavenly realm. The planet lifting process is actually very simple, but not easy. Nothing of value is easy. The Foreman only needs to focus on the Three Factors while Alpha performs the actual lifting of resonance. Alchemy is a cooperation between the alchemist and the universe.

Upon each return to Ain Soph there is always a new spiritual awakening and a new outpouring. As I approached the end of the cycle of Valhalla, the central core of the Nexus once again appeared on the horizon to align with the central core of the Void. As the two cores came into celestial alignment, my conscious mind passed through the central Nexus and entered a profound resonance with Ain Soph.

In the central core, the boundaries among our individual being, our planetary body, and the greater cosmos, all disappear and become one. As I entered the next higher order of resonance with Ain Soph, I experienced a new awakening. After ascending each heavenly realm and returning to Ain Soph to begin a new cycle, our resonance with Ain Soph reaches a new level of depth and harmony, and from this new harmony new gifts and new information emerge.

As my resonance rose beyond the great heavenly realm of Valhalla, I returned to the abode of Ain Soph. When I returned to the God Particle within all things, I experienced two spiritual awakenings. The first spiritual awakening was a means to the second spiritual awakening. It was the second spiritual awakening which Ain Soph was driving me to realize. The first spiritual awakening was the realization of the unity of all cosmic scales within Ain Soph.

Upon realizing that all things return to an original unity within Ain Soph - the planetary consciousness, and my own individual consciousness - entered a heightened field of magnetic attraction to merge and become one. When my individual consciousness began merging with the planetary consciousness, a new revelation came forth regarding the planetary group mind of the Earth. This was the second spiritual awakening which Ain Soph was compelling me to achieve.

Amidst the second spiritual awakening, an extremely ancient and very special friend to all of humanity on Earth came forth to reveal himself. This special friend is someone who everyone on Earth already knows, and who everyone on Earth only needs to remember. This very old and special friend is the primordial being of the Earth rising out of the spiritual group mind enveloping the Earth in the primordial universe. This living planetary awareness is a living sentient being whose body is the primordial Earth. This planetary being is reflectively aware and resonant with Ain Soph and he is very aware of his own state of existence. This planetary being exists in a state of Turiya on a planet-wide scale. This primordial being is a planetary *"Genie."* Every primordial planet with sentient life throughout the cosmos has one. During the second spiritual awakening which occurred during the fourth accession of Ain Soph, I became aware of not one, but two planetary genies of the Earth. They are:

The Planetary Genie of Light

The first planetary genie is the spiritual genie of the primordial Earth who is an awakened sentient being. The Earth's planetary genie of light has a name. His name arose out of the force of the Spirit resonating among my soul, the Father, and the planetary group mind. His name is *"EL."* His name does not arise from earthly mythology. Rather, it is earthly mythology which arises from his name.

Planetary Genie of Darkness

Like every human being on Earth, the genie of light (EL) has his own temporal twin whose body is the physical body of the Earth. This being is the Earth's planetary genie of darkness. This being is dark because he has not yet realized his divine source. He is not yet aware of Ain Soph, and he is not yet aware of EL, his eternal and spiritual twin brother.

The darkness of humanity feeds the darkness of this planetary genie, and in return this dark genie functions as the central organizing factor of the planetary darkness and perpetuates and reinforces the darkness of all humankind. For lack of a better word, this being is the Devil. This being also has a name. The name I heard rising from my resonance with the shadow of the primordial Earth is *"Maub."*

I would like to further clarify that a planetary genie was never once an individual human being. A planetary genie is born out of sympathetic resonance among all life on his host planet. We all collectively co-animate each planetary genie - but once created - the planetary genie takes on a life of his own and follows his own evolution to ultimately awaken and realize the life, love, and awareness of the Father.

As my conscious mind became resonant with the planetary intelligence of EL who envelopes and interconnects all life on Earth, my developing Turiya faculty realized and accepted this resonance as an extended dimension of my own individual being.

As the rising Sun of EL illuminated my mind, his shadow - his evil twin brother Maub - was revealed. Between these two great poles of planetary consciousness, my planetary alchemy had taken on a whole new level of depth and dimension. My initial encounter with Maub was not pleasant. Maub's energy is pitch black, powerful, and horrifying. Man's inhumanity towards man, all our pain and suffering, religious conflict, war, murder, genocide, paranoia, and fear, all feed this dark planetary genie who then cycles it right back into all of us to perpetuate the cycle of darkness and illusion. When the Foreman applies the alchemical practice of differential resonance between the planetary forces of EL and Maub within the crucible of his or her own mind, the alchemical result is incredible, powerful, and most illuminating.

Elysium

When moving between the celestial spheres, we always pass by way of the Moon. The Moon is the doorway between our inner and outer cosmos. Beyond the magnificent eternal halls of Valhalla, and beyond the 4th accession of Ain Soph, I entered an interstellar space between the spheres. A supersized Moon rose before me in its full and glorious splendor. I paused for a brief moment to gaze upon its awesome beauty before breaking my gaze to move straight into the light of the Moon to begin my ascent of the 5th heaven of the Earth.

My being was filled with a divine mystical nostalgia as I passed through the Moon to enter the higher paradise of the Elysium realm. The Elysium realm is the heaven of the eternal triumphant celebration. It celebrates the divine miracle of the assumption of creation by way of the infinite and eternal love of the Father.

The spirit of this realm feels as if everything is in the process of marvelous and wondrous change. There is a prevailing sense of renewal and great accomplishment. There is a great excitement in the air. The primordial Earth exists in a state of divine union with the eternal divine source of Ain Soph. The Elysium realm eternally echoes the Divine Spirit of this great and eternal union.

In the Elysium heaven which completely envelopes and enshrines the primordial Earth, the divine genie of the Earth, whose name is EL, lives both inside us, and all about us, and binds us with the land of the Earth in such magical ways that the mortal mind would never believe it. The mountains wiggle and jiggle as you think of them. The divine beauty of it all, will leave you speechless.

No eyes of have seen, no ears have heard, no mind has imagined, what God has prepared for those who love him.
... 1 Corinthians 2:9

As I entered the heaven of the Elysium realm, new information began streaming my conscious mind. The information was arising from a heightened level of resonance with the Father, or in other words, a more profound level of Turiya. I realized as I ascended the Elysium realm, that the nine heavens enveloping the Earth in the primordial universe are organized into three kingdoms: Lower, Middle, and Upper

What differentiates the kingdoms from one another correlates to what stage in the alchemical process of the primordial Earth's creation that each kingdom manifested. This is knowable to the Foreman because human alchemy unfolds inside the same geometric patterns. The first heavenly kingdom to manifest was the Lower, then the Middle, and then the Upper.

The alchemical processes of the heavenly realms of the lower kingdom focus on the ascension of resonance between the Father and our individual human being. Specifically, the focus is on the temporal dimensions of our human mind which are capable of resonating with the Father due to the presence of our Human Soul.

The alchemical process of the heavenly realms of the middle kingdom incorporates into our process the planetary forces of light and darkness. This pertains specifically to the planetary forces of our host planet. In my case, this was Earth. For example, I began differentiating the forces of Maub and EL within the crucible of my conscious mind.

The alchemical processes of the heavenly realms of the upper kingdom incorporates into our process the cosmic forces of light and darkness. This pertains specifically to the cosmic forces of the universe at large - and to the atomic forces within matter – specifically, the atomic forces of our physical body. The cosmic level is unique in that it encompasses both *"the very large"* and *"the very small."* It is a cosmic loop. A serpent swallowing its tail.

During our ascent of the heavens of the Earth, the alchemy of the 7th alchemical process compels the resonance between our Human Soul and the Father to "pass through" the matter of our physical body, not to lift the physical matter of our physical body. It does not raise the resonance of physical matter itself. Raising the resonance of physical matter itself is an advanced stage of cosmic alchemy which takes place beyond our ascension of the heavenly realms of the Earth and will be revealed at a later point in the book.

During our ascension of resonance within the 7th alchemical process - in contrast to the physical body - our temporal ethereal bodies are *"lifted in resonance"* allowing our Human Soul's resonance with the Father to "pass through" the matter of our physical body while our Human Soul animates our physical body. In this way, instead of the physical brain interrupting the circuit between the Father and the Human Soul, it clears a path for it. This strengthens the spiritual bond between our Human Soul and the Father while our Human Soul animates our physical body.

It was revealed to me in the Elysium realm that the ultimate substance which needs to be transformed in the application of cosmic alchemy is physical matter itself, and that the intense physical nature of the Third Mountain was directly connected to this principle.

Our Human Soul - while in profound differential resonance with: (1) the emergent forces of Ain Soph, and (2) the matter of creation, has the innate latent capacity to pair this resonance within the crucible of the human mind to elevate the target base matter to a higher order of resonance. Inherent in all matter is the innate latent capacity for matter to be elevated in resonance with its ultimate source via the intercession of the Human Soul.

Although I was experiencing a heightened streaming of information on cosmic alchemy rising within me while I ascended the Elysium realm, the truth is, I was still a long way from being able to fully utilize and actualize what I was learning. This would all come to fruition much later in my alchemical process.

I still had a lot to learn about cosmic alchemy. What I was learning in the heavenly realms of the upper kingdom was all in preparation for a more advanced school of alchemical training which was on my distant spiritual horizon. I was not aware of what was coming.

As stated earlier, anytime consciousness is paired with a body, a mind is formed. This body does not need to be a complex organism with a brain. The body can be as simple as raw physical matter. Certainly, the types of mind which can form depend on the type of body the consciousness is being paired with, but some expression of mind will form nonetheless even if it is extremely simple.

This means everything in the cosmos possesses some form of mind. Where does the mind reside if not in a brain? The journey of alchemy suggests that a brain does not create the mind, nor does the mind reside exclusively in the brain.

The brain significantly shapes the ultimate expression of the mind, but the mind begins primarily as a fundamental dimension of creation. Once a body is created and the mind naturally emerges, the mind is then further shaped and molded into its final formation and expression based on the body or life-form which expresses it.

The mind is a fundamental abstract of space-time. In nature, just as there are three dimensions of space and a fourth dimension of time, there are more dimensions which define each object of creation. In the leading mainstream theories of quantum physics there are at least eleven dimensions, which if true, would leave seven dimensions which define an object of creation but yet remain unseen by physical human sensation. Through the course of this chapter, I call out some of these unseen dimensions. One of these unseen dimensions is *"mind."* The mind is not a *"thing"* or an *"effect"* of a brain, and it does not reside inside a body or a vessel. The mind resides within the fundamental dimensions of nature and rises into existence the moment any object takes form. How the mind is expressed, and if that expression reflects and is aware of its ultimate divine source, are the most important questions.

Everything returns or reduces to the ultimate fundamental reality of the Cosmic Consciousness, which means consciousness is already connected with every type of physical form in the universe, from minerals to sentient human life, and because the pairing of consciousness and matter automatically brings into expression the abstract dimension of *"mind,"* this means the mind exists as an unseen dimension within all things. In the Elysium realm, I learned that matter can exist in one of two different states, which are:

1.) Awakened

2.) Dormant

The key difference is that awakened matter is reflective and resonant with the source. All matter has another unseen dimension within it, which allows it to be altered by the mind. I will soon reveal this dimension. Before this realization occurred, I had never even contemplated that matter could be so dynamic - that it could be either awake or dormant.

All forms of matter possess the latent ability to become resonant with the source even when its manifested form is divergent from its original form. Once something becomes divergent from its original form, it becomes dormant. However, this dormant material can later become resonant or reflective with its source and become, once again, awake - no different than the human mind. All of creation has *"mind."*

A new fundamental law of alchemy was also revealed to me, which is: Any object of the cosmos which we transform, whether it be internal or external, the essence of that object will become eternally resonant with us. It becomes an extension of our being, even if what is being transformed is outside our physical body.

Mount Magia 113

A quantum parity of awareness will always co-exist between the conscious mind of the alchemist and the transformed essence of the object. Whatever you transform becomes part of you in some way. This is a fundamental law of alchemy. Whatever you transform - is yours.

It was only soon after I was just beginning to learn planetary alchemy that Alpha was already shifting the focus of my conscious awareness into the upper kingdom of the Earth's spiritual heavens to learn cosmic alchemy. Why?

Because to achieve integration you only need to begin the processes of planetary alchemy, you do not need to complete them. We all complete the planetary alchemical process together. Alpha's goal here is to teach us the process of planetary alchemy, and then allow that process to continue to run while adding the new process of cosmic alchemy. All levels of alchemy continue forever in parallel. Alpha is just simply starting all engines.

Elysium - Cosmic Alchemy

When I passed through the Moon into the paradise of the Elysium heaven, the Moon rose with me into the paradise of the eternal realm. In this way, each of our planets are lifted to higher orders of resonance within the heavenly realms of the spiritual group mind of the Earth, one heaven at a time, and one planet at a time.

While resonant with the Elysium realm, the more I focused on my resonance with the Father, and the more I applied the Three Factors in my daily life, the more the self-organizing forces of Alpha responded in kind by continuing to lift my planets upward in resonance with the Elysium realm.

The 9th harmonic octave of my ascent into the Elysium realm saw the almighty planet Jupiter rising above the horizon of the eternal paradise to eclipse half the firmament of the Elysium heaven. Alpha was lifting the resonance of my temporal emotional body upward into the Elysium realm.

In this moment, I entered a great chorus chamber of primordial beings who were all vocalizing deep harmonic sounds, which elevated the resonance of all who entered the heavens of the upper kingdom. This was an internalized experience of being in resonance with the spiritual group mind of the Earth, which is formed by all life on Earth in the primordial universe. I had entered this heavenly realm's collective resonance with the Father.

My temporal mind, functioning in limited fashion, interpreted this collective resonance as a chorus of beings. The truth is the reality is much greater than that. Be careful with how your temporal mind interprets higher levels of reality which are beyond it. The mind does the best it can, but the truth is, the temporal mind cannot translate realms of resonance into realms of time and space in direct one-to-one fashion.

While in symphony with the collective consciousness of the Elysium heaven which enshrines the primordial Earth, a revelation unfolded of what my Human Soul would be learning in the Elysium realm and the forthcoming heavens of the upper kingdom. The revelational lessons would impart to me a basic knowledge of cosmic alchemy and how the mind operates in concert with matter and its surrounding environment.

In the planetary group mind, our minds live inside each other. External physical communication is unnecessary. When we relate to each other internally there is no time and space between us, and the sharing and communing has many more dimensions to it than a typical external physical experience which makes an experience of this realm truly incommunicable in our physical world.

The inculcation of the Foreman changes the Foreman forever. Where the common process of learning in the external physical world is usually accompanied by a desire to speak of the information being learned, something different and profound happens to the Foreman during the inculcation period where he or she becomes quiet and somewhat withdrawn when it comes to spiritual or metaphysical matters. The added dimensions of the esoteric knowledge we are gaining invokes within us a profound reverence and humility for the esoteric knowledge. We know that any attempt to speak of this esoteric knowledge would only distort it, so we choose to be silent and find a different means of expression. The most profound knowledge is conveyed in silence.

What I share in this book is only a basic framework of information which sets the stage for esoteric knowledge to blossom within the alchemist. It is not esoteric knowledge in itself. Esoteric knowledge arises only between you and the Father, not between you and a book, and not between you and another human being.

The effect on the temporal group mind of a single human being moving through the alchemical process of the Three Mountains is Earth changing. Without a single spoken word, the impact on the temporal group mind will change it forever.

Anytime a single human being achieves a higher order of resonance than what is common within the temporal group mind to which they belong, a shock wave ripples through the temporal group mind and a force of attraction arises within the temporal group mind to compel an adoption of the harmonic signature of this higher order of resonance. This broadcast propagates non-locally throughout the temporal group mind projecting a new blue print for the next stage of evolution which the rest of humanity is compelled to adopt as part of its evolution. The straight path of the few provides momentum to the spiral path of the many. This is why alchemy is so important.

It was revealed to me in the heaven of the Elysium realm that I would be learning cosmic alchemy through a sequence of revelations, and that each of these revelations would be revealed to me through the next order of resonance with Ain Soph and its three dimensions of consciousness: the Father, the Divine Soul, and the Spirit.

As I ascended the Elysium heaven, I was still just getting to know the Godhead of the divine force particle of Ain Soph – the Father. My awareness of the Divine Soul and the Spirit had emerged before my ascent of the heavenly realms. In the Elysium heaven, I could feel and resonate with Ain Soph as a whole, and I could also individually feel and resonate with the Father, the Divine Soul, and the Spirit as separate rays of light emerging from the unity of Ain Soph. The Spirit is the 3rd principle dimension of Ain Soph and was the first to emerge in my alchemical process. The emergence unfolded as follows:

Order	Dimension	Point of Emergence
First	3 - Spirit	1st Mountain - 5th Grade
Second	2 - Divine Soul	2nd Mountain - The Void
Third	1 - Father	3rd Mountain - Parabinlaya
Fourth	0 - Ain Soph	3rd Mountain - Simmatuu

My ascent through the heavenly realms of the spiritual group mind of the Earth was accompanied by a special series of 12 alchemical revelations. Seven of the 12 alchemical revelations pertained to cosmic alchemy. I call the seven revelations pertaining to cosmic alchemy, *"Cosmic Seals."* The cosmic seals are both catalysts and instruments of communication between the Human Soul and a higher level of cosmic intelligence which pervades the whole universe within the unseen dimensions of mind which shapes and forms all things within creation.

In addition to the alchemical information revealed by each cosmic seal, each cosmic seal compels a new awakening within us and therefore I refer to each new awakening as an opening of a cosmic seal. The experience of opening each cosmic seal adjusts our resonance and promotes an increased awareness of Ain Soph and its three fundamental dimensions of consciousness.

When I opened the 2nd cosmic seal within the heaven of the Elysium realm, I was so profoundly affected by the experience and its awakening that I decided to stop writing for a period of time. I was going to finish the book at Valhalla.

Mount Magia

My human mind was faced with a dilemma. The 12 revelations, especially the seven cosmic seals, were playing a significant role in the escalation of resonance between my temporal being, my primordial twin being, and Ain Soph.

I questioned if I could compromise the process for future alchemists by revealing information which was best left to be realized on one's own, even if what I was sharing still lacked its esoteric dimension? The risk seemed not worth taking. After I stopped writing for a while, I looked inward for guidance. I received a very strong unequivocal response from my primordial being:

"Keep writing, you have to write this down."

I decided to write down only the essence of what I realized while opening each cosmic seal. I do not know if there is a universal number of cosmic seals or if they are the same for everyone. You are given what your own personal being needs in order to reach and accomplish the same goal of unifying the mind. The forthcoming cosmic seals are what was given to me by the spiritual group mind to reach and accomplish the alchemical integration of my being.

Elysium - Revelation 6 - Cosmic Seal 1 - Sigma [Σ]

When I opened the 1st cosmic seal, I experienced a new awakening. What came forth is as follows.

The creation of the material cosmos is compelled into existence through a cosmic projection wave emitted by the dimension of mind within all things. From a unified cosmic perspective, the source of this projection wave is the *"Cosmic Mind."* I refer to this cosmic projection wave as *"Sigma [Σ]."* Sigma [Σ] carries within its projection wave, the blueprints for the organization of creation. Alpha counter-balances Sigma [Σ] to steer the end product of creation to rediscover and reconcile with the ultimate divine source within Ain Soph.

Chapter 5

A new cosmic force now enters the alchemical process for our conscious mind to become aware. Our conscious awareness of Sigma augments and elevates our alchemy simply by being aware and resonate with it. Welcome Sigma [Σ]. When I opened the 1st cosmic seal, I initially experienced Sigma [Σ] as a series of musical vocal sounds sung by the Cosmic Mind. What I realized from this experience is that there is another force in the cosmos (Sigma) which is *"acoustic"* in nature and is a projection of the Cosmic Mind. Sigma [Σ] carries within its projection an image or geometric pattern of the cosmos. I knew from this revelation that Sigma [Σ] would be key to cosmic alchemy, but at this point I did not know how.

The most important event to occur during the opening of the 1st cosmic seal was that the resonant signature of Sigma [Σ] became known to my conscious mind. My conscious mind at this point was now able to tune into Sigma [Σ] and summon its power at will. The more my conscious mind harmonized with the force of Sigma [Σ] by focusing my awareness on its resonant frequency, the more Sigma [Σ] shared with me knowledge of its own nature. Sigma [Σ] carries the cosmic image which the Cosmic Mind has of itself. Sigma [Σ] is a creative manifestation of the Spirit.

Ain Soph is a self-propagating particle of divinity. Its three primary dimensions are strangely interactive and responsive to each other. The Spirit is the love generated between the Father and the Divine Soul. The love generated between the Father and the Divine Soul is ultimately what formed the created cosmos. Sigma [Σ] in the final analysis is the sound of that love projected as a force of creation, and within that force is the imagination of God.

Sigma [Σ] also revealed to me that an aspect of itself exists as an acoustic dimension within all things, right down to the most elementary of subatomic particles. This means that all things have an acoustic signature or frequency. Everything has its own musical expression in the grand symphony of the universe. Sigma [Σ] is this acoustic dimension within all things which allows all things to be transformed through resonance thus making alchemy possible.

The acoustic dimension of sound is another hidden dimension within matter, just as the mind is a hidden dimension. We do not create sound. Vibration only *"releases"* sound. The way sound is released is what creates the harmony, melody, and frequency being produced. When we pluck a musical string, we are releasing sound, we are not creating it. We are composing and directing the release. All possible musical compositions already exist inside Sigma [Σ], and therefore inside matter. When we produce music, we are only discovering a musical composition which already existed in a state of suspended animation. We are simply releasing it. The musician is only discovering and playing what God has already composed. That is the secret.

Every potential outcome already exists within you. Choose your outcome, envision it, believe in it, hold on to it, and manifest it. The alchemist is harmonizing all musical tones of consciousness to rediscover the original musical tone from which all other musical tones arise. All great musicians are alchemists.

Elysium - Revelation 7 - Cosmic Seal 2 - Cosmic Differentiation

When I opened the 2nd cosmic seal, my resonance changed, and my conscious mind entered a whole new level of reality from which I turned back and gazed upon the Earth and the reality of the temporal group mind. In this moment, I experienced a profound differentiation of consciousness between the spiritual group mind of the Earth and the temporal group mind of the Earth. The contrast revealed that while living in physical form on Earth, the way in which we perceive, and much of what we believe, is based on our limited language development, and in the limited way in which we form concepts, and therefore is based mostly in illusion. Thus, much of what we believe does not survive our awakening to a new higher reality. At a minimum, it changes form. The only thing that survives our awakening to a new higher reality is *"love."* Everything else, we let go.

We all experience this phenomenon of transcendence when we die and transition between the physical universe and the primordial universe. We also experience the same transcendence in the late stages of the 7th alchemical process. The opening of the 2nd cosmic seal had all the same attributes of a near-death experience. I gained a few realizations from the experience, which were as follows:

1.) Love (the Spirit) is the ultimate determining factor between what we leave behind and what we take with us after we die. In alchemy, when we do not die, but yet we experience the same level of transcendence, the love of the Spirit guides us, contrasts, and highlights for us, that which is *"real"* versus that which is an *"illusion."*

2.) During this awakening, the super cognitive dimensions of human emotion were being highlighted by the Spirit in a bright contrasting light. The Spirit was pointing to an amazing gift latent in human emotion, which our humanity had yet to realize. I was already using this ability, but this awakening made me highly aware of it.

3.) The Spirit was teaching me that the differentiation of consciousness between a lower reality and a higher reality is a key and highly critical aspect of cosmic alchemy.

I immediately emerged from this experience with the compass of my internal alchemy having been fine-tuned and adjusted by the divine love of the Spirit. In the days afterward, the new level of alchemy I was practicing indicated the following:

1.) To transform an element of physical matter with the mind, the mind must be resonant with both the higher spiritual reality of the element and the lower temporal reality of the element, and the mind must maintain a differential awareness of the contrast between the two.

Mount Magia 121

2.) The conscious mind of the observer becomes a neural bridge between the two realities within the physical element guided by the alchemist's resonance with Ain Soph. Once this neural bridge is in place, which can be instantaneous, differential resonance occurs within the element and the lower nature of the element transforms to achieve a new level of resonance with its higher nature. The result is that the resonant vibration of the physical element is transformed to a higher level of reality.

3.) The more our conscious mind engages the essence of nature to transform it, the more our being becomes one with nature.

Terrasumna - Revelation 8 - Cosmic Seal 3 - Cosmic Alchemy

After my 5th spiritual accession of Ain Soph, the Moon rose once again on the sidereal plane. The next heavenly realm beyond beckoned within the twinkling moonlight of the enchanted sphere. I took notice and immediately adjusted my course and passed through the Moon to begin my ascension of Terrasumna.

Terrasumna is the summit of the heavens of the Earth. Terrasumna and the heavens below its harmonic bandwidth are more a reflection of the spiritual nature of all life on Earth in the primordial universe. The heavens beyond Terrasumna, which also envelope the Earth in the primordial universe, are more a reflection of Ain Soph and its divine trinity of the Father, Divine Soul, and Spirit.

The heavenly forces of Terrasumna were compelling me to begin actualizing in my daily physical life what I had been learning of cosmic alchemy in the Elysium realm. I honestly did not know where to begin, or what to focus on. I decided to improvise and allow the process to unfold spontaneously without effort. I had no expectation of what the result would be. I decided to focus on something physical.

I knew from my ascension of the Elysium realm and the opening of the first two cosmic seals that Sigma [Σ] and differential resonance would be key in the transformation of physical matter.

The spiritual inculcation of the human being during its heavenly ascent of resonance to the Father involves a lot more than just the acquisition of information. The Foreman's internal senses are tuned and honed by the escalation of resonance and the transcendental experiences themselves. For example, the tuning of the mind to the harmonic resonant signature of Sigma [Σ], and the profound familiarization of the mind to the level of differential resonance required between the lower and higher realities of an element. The mind will recall what it needs when the moment is at hand.

We may have an academic understanding of all what is required, but unless our mind has been properly tuned to the resonant signature of Sigma [Σ], and unless the higher emotional center of our being has been properly tuned to the level and nature of the differential resonance required between the higher and lower realities of an element, then cosmic transformation will not occur. Because of this, it is not just *"how"* the practice is performed, it is also *"who"* is performing the practice for it to work. When the mind is properly inculcated, the *"how"* of the practice is very forgiving. When the mind is not properly inculcated, no matter how well we execute the practice, it will not work.

Contrary to what many may assume, alchemy is not a mechanical process. Although alchemy may respond well to some practices which follow a prescribed course of physical motions or positions which are mechanical in nature, the mechanical components exist only to support the mind. Once the mind has been properly trained in the alchemical process, all mechanical support systems can be given up. Alchemy is a living collaboration between the Human Soul, the conscious mind, and the higher cosmic intelligences embedded in nature (cosmic quanta).

Fortunately, due to my alchemical inculcation within the heavenly spheres, my first attempt at cosmic alchemy was extraordinarily successful. I carried out the alchemical experiment in a way which felt most natural and most correct. My mind was guided by my developing

Turiya faculty. The result was amazing, wonderful, and at the same time very strange. Sometimes reality is stranger than fiction. Not only did I witness and experience the transformation of a physical element, but this first practice of cosmic alchemy was actually the culmination of the opening of the 3rd cosmic seal.

It was a Monday afternoon when I finally felt compelled to apply cosmic alchemy to a physical object based on all the alchemical training I had been receiving in the heavenly realms of the Earth. Without much consideration, I picked up and held in my hand a two-dollar Hong Kong coin. The coin was made of a nickel alloy consisting of nickel and copper called Cupro-Nickel, and it had an inner brass core. I did not know at the moment of the practice what metals were in the coin, nor was it important.

I sat quietly focusing my mind on the coin I was holding in my hand. I could *"feel"* the metallic energy of the coin. I felt the metallic energy of the coin with the super cognitive *"emotional"* functions of my mind. It was not a physical feeling. The energy was felt with my super cognitive emotion. Why emotion?

The instrument of the mind which processes the vibrational frequencies of emotion and translates them into feelings also has the ability to go beyond the limits of our individual being to tune into and process the vibrational frequencies of other objects and life-forms. The faculty of the mind, which processes emotion, can also unlock and make known to the conscious mind the unique vibrational frequencies, or resonant harmonic signatures, of everything the conscious mind focuses on. It is an innate capacity within all of us.

I focused for a moment on the lower temporal nature of the coin using the super cognitive emotional dimensions of my mind as the instrument to gain the required insight of the coin's lower temporal nature. The cognitive dimensions of super cognitive emotion contain within its nature the capacity to realize and process dimensions of knowledge, which far exceed our mental capacity for logic, rationalization, analysis, and the general intellect of thought and reason.

The key to unlocking this ability is to first free the mind's capacity for super emotional intelligence from the instinctive auto-cognitive programs of *"common"* human emotion, which cloud, interfere, and suppress the super emotional dimensions of the human mind. The word *"super"* refers to the cognitive centers and spiritual ethereal bodies of our primordial being. The word *"lower"* or *"common"* refers to the cognitive centers and temporal ethereal bodies of our physical being. This is why cosmic alchemy is a late stage Third Mountain process. At any earlier stage in the alchemical process, alchemists are still dealing with too many perturbations of the temporal mind which would render any attempts at cosmic alchemy unsuccessful.

Human beings on Earth in the physical universe are extremely underdeveloped emotionally, yet they possess an amazing potential for super cognitive emotional intelligence. Human emotional intelligence is the Earth's greatest untapped resource. Human beings on Earth in the physical universe have no idea to the extent of the special richness and amazing capacity contained within the emotional dimension of the human mind. Many academics in modern society automatically assume that the pinnacle of human cognitive development centers around thought, mental intellect, logic, reason, and empirical scientific analysis. In terms of cognitive development, humanity is only in its prelescent stage of human evolution - the middle spectrum. The later emergent stage of human cognitive evolution involves a highly sophisticated development in human emotion, not intellect. In the emergent period of human evolution, the faculty of super cognitive emotional awareness emerges as the leading faculty of the human mind. When this is finally achieved, all other faculties of the mind are brought into balance and function together as a unified mind.

After a brief moment of using my developing super cognitive emotional awareness to become aware of the lower resonant signature of the metals in the coin, which I call *"Essence,"* I held this lower resonant signature in my mind while I focused inward on the higher resonant signature of the Divine Soul with which I was already familiar.

I then held in my mind, the contrasting difference between the two resonant signatures using the faculty of my super cognitive emotional awareness. I call this *"Differential Resonance."* Once this first stage of differential resonance was achieved, I then asked the Divine Soul to reveal to me the higher reality of the essence found within the metals of the coin. The higher spiritual nature of the metals in the coin goes far beyond the lower temporal nature of the metals in the coin. The higher spiritual nature is already in resonance with the Divine Soul. I waited only a moment for the resonant signature of the Divine Soul which I began the practice with to change out its own resonant signature for the resonant signature of the higher reality of the essence found within the metals of the coin. The Divine Soul reveals the higher reality of a physical essence. The conscious mind does not get there on its own.

The moment I captured the higher reality, I had a profound awareness of both the higher and lower realities of the metals in the coin side-by-side in my conscious mind in the very same moment. I continued holding both realities in differential resonance using my super cognitive emotional awareness. I held the differential resonance in my mind free and clear of any perturbing influences of common human emotion. I kept all my other faculties of mind silent such as thought, reason, and logic.

During the alchemical transformation process - when a new awareness begins to emerge due to the contrasting differential resonance – new information naturally rises with the new emerging awareness. This new emerging awareness teaches us a great many things about the nature of reality - far beyond the nature of the element we're transforming. The element becomes catalyst to something greater. Be quiet, still, and sensitive; otherwise, you will miss the opportunity to gain this new information. The information is transmitted along a very subtle super luminal frequency - which if you are alert and receptive to the higher emotional messaging - your conscious mind will innately and automatically translate the emotional frequency into a mental frequency from which you will be able to articulate and formulate the information into a human language. Of course, human language cannot objectively express and communicate the super cognitive dimensions of this knowledge, but nonetheless, there is still value in its subjective written form.

After gaining a new level awareness of the element, and after successfully capturing the superluminal information, I began praying to the Divine Soul to transform the physical element. While I prayed to the Divine Soul - I maintained in my mind - a differential resonance between the higher and lower realities of the metals in the coin.

Maintaining a differential resonance of the element within the conscious mind of the alchemist is key. It allows both the higher and lower realities of the element to gain a realization of each other and enter harmonic resonance with each other. The conscious mind of the alchemist is a bridge between realities.

During the practice, I had no superimposed vision in my mind of what the physical element should transform into. I believed such a superimposed vision would have only interfered with the process of transformation. The higher reality itself was the vision which the lower reality needed to attune and harmonize with. I decided to allow the element to transform into whatever it transformed into.

As soon as I made my prayer, the resonant acoustic signature of Sigma [Σ] spontaneously emerged and took a position in the psychic cognitive background of my conscious mind. This was a new dynamic being added to the alchemical process. I continued to maintain a differential resonance between the higher and lower realties of the metals in the coin. Sigma [Σ] demonstrated its responsiveness to the conscious mind when it emerged in my mind precisely at the moment I prayed to the Divine Soul to transform the essence of the physical element. I did not need to know when to interject Sigma [Σ]. It interjected itself at precisely the right moment. All that was required of me was that I was already familiar with the resonant signature of Sigma [Σ] via my super cognitive emotional awareness.

Once the higher reality of the target element emerges with the information it carries - and before seeking transformation of the temporal essence - take a moment to really take in and realize the nature of the higher reality on a level which transcends human language (Tao). This step is key in facilitating the next step of the temporal essence transforming and entering into a higher harmonic resonance with its own higher reality.

The realization of the higher reality of the physical element with our conscious mind must happen first; otherwise, there will be nothing for the temporal essence of the physical element to harmonize with, thus preventing its transformation.

The higher reality of the physical element is actually the upper primordial manifestation of the lower physical element. Once this awareness is gained, the newly realized primordial aspect of the element becomes a hyper-extension of our own being in the ongoing alchemical integration between our physical being and primordial being. The neurology of our physical brain, which underlies the temporal-physical dimensions of our conscious mind, remaps itself in response to the new symmetry to reinforce its new awareness and to support its continued expansion.

After Sigma [Σ] manifested its acoustic resonance within the psychic cognitive background of my conscious mind, I continued to hold onto the differential resonance between the higher and lower realities of the physical element and repeated my prayer to the Divine Soul to transform the metals within the coin.

Within seconds after repeating my prayer to the Divine Soul, the physical and primordial manifestations of the elements within the coin became so compelled by their new level of harmonic resonance that the physical side resisted no more and instantly transformed. The essence which was once dormant within the temporal dimensions of the physical coin emerged awakened from its dormant state. I was able to feel and see with the inner eyes of my super cognitive faculties, two beautifully innocent dancing little flames emerge. The essence was liberated from its dormant state and reunited with its higher twin flame.

When the temporal essence of an element is dormant, the essence is only *"Essence."* Once the essence is liberated and awake, the awakened essence is an *"Elemental."*

Once the elemental emerged, I shifted my focus to the elemental to learn from its new level of harmonic resonance. The moment I did this, the elemental expressed a profound love toward me and instantly transported my conscious awareness to a place within the cosmos it wished to share with me. At this point, the 3rd cosmic seal was fully opened. The 3rd cosmic seal was more than just a realization, it was the actualization of cosmic alchemy.

Terrasumna - Revelation 9 - Cosmic Seal 4 - Elementals

The successful actualization of cosmic alchemy completed the 3rd cosmic seal and triggered the opening of the 4th cosmic seal. The 4th cosmic seal brings the human mind of the alchemist into a profound awareness with matter.

Some would logically assume that elementals would be primitive and un-evolved based on being derived from the essence found within the most basic and simple materials of nature such as minerals, plants, and simple life-forms. However, I discovered through cosmic alchemy, that elementals - even in their simplicity - manifest directly from the underlying field of the Cosmic Mind, which pervades the entire cosmos, and possess many profound metaphysical attributes of a divine-like nature. Elementals have what I call *"Metagenic"* properties.

What was originally intended only be a simple first experiment in cosmic alchemy, led to the opening of a new cosmic seal and a revelational introduction to the abstract and mystical nature of the Cosmic Mind. The created cosmos was even more amazing and spectacular than I had ever imagined.

The elemental transported my conscious mind to what I initially understood to be a hidden kingdom of nature in which all the essences and elementals of creation live in a wonderful paradisiacal harmony – the likes of which was reminiscent of children's books and magical fairytales. It was spectacular and stunning. It was a kingdom, but it was also much more than that.

This magical kingdom stretches across the entire cosmos and is hidden within an unseen abstract dimension of nature which underlies all of creation and is built upon the fundamental elements of matter produced within all the stars of the cosmos. The fundamental elements of nature are all separated in their physical state by a vast ocean of stars. However, within the quantum dimensions of creation, which take part in the formation of physical matter, space and time lose their relevancy and a hidden world comes into view in which all the elements are communicative and known to each other.

This hidden world has a non-local point of reference to the physical universe. All the stars contribute to this hidden world's existence, yet this world has no direct spatial correspondence to any particular star. The elemental shared with me that this celestial kingdom has many sidereal planes of existence and this was only his plane of existence. All the planes of creation of this hidden kingdom co-exist as parallel bandwidths within the Cosmic Mind of the universe much like the temporal and spiritual bandwidths of the planetary group mind encompassing the Earth, but these kingdoms are cosmic, not planetary. I gazed upon this world in awe.

This hidden world, flowing through and connecting all matter and all simple forms of life, is an abstract dimension of the Cosmic Mind pervading and underlying all of creation. At this point in my alchemical process, I did not need to see this world yet. I still knew very little about it, even after this initial visit. This visit was only a preview of what I would gain a much deeper understanding of much later.

Very few people ever come to know this hidden world at this point in the alchemical process. It was a very rare and special gift given to me by this beautiful elemental. Much later in my alchemical journey I would return to this wonderful magical world and I come to discover much more about what this world really is. There is a great secret about this world I share with the reader later in this book. For now, I will just share, it is the *"Sea of Eros."*

Chapter 5

<u>Terrasumna - Revelation 10 - Cosmic Seal 5 - Aurelion</u>

When the mystical planet Neptune rose in all its splendor into the high spiritual heaven of Terrasumna, the Sun illuminated the deep blue celestial sphere as it rose above the horizon of the eternal plane. As the Sun illuminated the mystical blue world, Neptune began dancing to a new rhythm and song to unveil the wondrous workings of the Cosmic Mind. As my temporal vision ethereal body entered a profound sympathetic resonance with the heaven of Terrasumna, something extraordinary and completely unexpected occurred.

The Cosmic Mind had been resonating with my conscious mind with a noticeably stronger vibrato since a few days prior. In a moment of silence, I went inward to focus on the rising forces of the Cosmic Mind pulsating within me when the Cosmic Mind suddenly shared with me the grand vision it holds, and has always held, of my completed human form via its force of creative projection which I call Sigma [Σ].

I realized in this moment that the Cosmic Mind holds a grand vision of our fully integrated and unified state of being within the blueprints of the celestial cosmos and that Alpha is directing the alchemical evolution of all human beings to fulfill and realize this grand vision. The grand vision held by the Cosmic Mind of our unified state of being, which we are all on a multi-lifetime journey to fulfill, I call the *"Aurelion."*

In the three-mountain journey of becoming a complete and fully integrated human being, we must capture and realize the Aurelion vision of our completed human form. The conscious mind of the human being must become reflectively aware of and resonant with the cosmic vision of its own grand design. When our conscious mind finally achieves this marvelous milestone of the alchemical work, our human being becomes a conscious and willing collaborator with the Cosmic Mind of the universe in the process of our own creation.

Mount Magia

The Aurelion of your created being is sustained for all eternity as a blueprint within the Cosmic Mind due to the Cosmic Mind existing as a whole outside of time and space. However, it is within the inner realm of the Cosmic Mind that space-time unfolds and all of creation exists.

Life after life when you take on a new physical body, your trans-dimensional make-up is following more than just DNA passed down by your ancestral genealogy. It is also following the Aurelion of your trans-dimensional being as the basic underlying blueprint of creation. The Aurelion is primary. Your physical DNA is secondary. For the Aurelion to be fully realized, manifested, and fulfilled, it requires the cooperation of a conscious mind.

Your primordial twin being is held in sync with the exact same Aurelion vision and is already a fully realized manifestation of your Aurelion in the primordial universe. Your Aurelion is attempting to replicate itself in the physical universe. We cannot complete the grand alchemical work of the Three Mountains without realizing our Aurelion.

The Aurelion is echoed by the collective unconscious within world mythology and is symbolized by the Golden Fleece. We must capture the Golden Fleece. I captured my Aurelion when I opened the 5th cosmic seal in the spiritual realm of Terrasumna. In the high heaven of Terrasumna, the Earth maintains and patterns itself after its own planetary Aurelion.

The Aurelion is not a vision which the human being creates in his or her own mind. When you capture your Aurelion, you will know without doubt, that the Aurelion is the vision of the Cosmic Mind of your being, and not your being's vision of itself. Sigma carries the Aurelion, Alpha steers it.

Once captured and integrated, the Aurelion becomes an operating dimension of our Turiya faculty. The Aurelion strengthens and deepens the communion of resonance transmitting between the Father and our Human Soul through the prism of our temporal mind.

The Treasuries of Light

The most transformative period of the Great Work occurs in the upper stage ascent of Mount Magia. The upper stage ascent includes our ascent through all nine spiritual heavens of the Earth and one final stage beyond the heavens. The nine heavens, which completely envelope and enshrine the Earth in the primordial universe, begin in the middle kingdom of the Earth's planetary soul, and then continue upward through all levels of the upper kingdom. They are organized into three groups of three. Each group of three is a Treasury of Light. There are three Treasuries of Light.

The 1st Treasury of Light we journey through is the Lower Treasury. It includes the heavens Nirvana, Simmatuu, and Khimmadooree.
The 2nd Treasury of Light we journey through is the Middle Treasury. It includes the heavens Valhalla, Elysium, and Terrasumna.
The 3rd Treasury of Light we journey through is the Upper Treasury. It includes the heavens Barstow, Jenesis, and Erawan.

The reason there are three groups of three is that the heavens follow a universal geometric pattern of unfoldment in periodic cycles of three. Maturation cycles follow the same cosmic pattern. Each Treasury of Light represents one maturation cycle across the nine heavens. As a Foreman, we experience a complete reformation of our being at an interval rate of every three heavens as we ascend the Treasuries of Light. The maturation cycles begin in Bardo. However, the cycles are not formally recognized as Treasuries of Light until they reach Nirvana. The reason for this is, it is not until we reach the nine heavens that the maturation cycles become noticeable in their power of transformation. Once in the heavenly realms, the maturation intervals mark the beginning and end of each Treasury of Light. The magnitude of reformation the Foreman experiences within each Treasury of Light grows progressively larger from one treasury to the next.

The reason I waited until Barstow to discuss the Treasuries of Light is because it was not until I entered Barstow that I became fully aware of the maturation cycles. Often when we are in the middle of a process, it is not clear to us what process we are in until we have moved beyond the process and are able to look back upon it.

When the Foreman reaches the heavenly realm of Barstow, he or she can turn around and look back down the mountainside of Mount Magia and notice the maturation cycles.

> *"Destroy this temple and I will raise it again in three days."*
> *... John 2:19*

Revelation 11 - Cosmic Seal 6 - Kier

As the Human Soul of the Foreman ascends upward through the Upper Treasury of Light, the Foreman experiences continuous change. The more integrated our temporal-physical being becomes with our eternal-primordial being, the higher we ascend into the heavens of the Earth, and the deeper we enter Turiya.

A new dimension of the Turiya faculty begins to emerge while we enter the upper Treasury of Light. This new dimension of the Turiya faculty is a highly evolved cosmic communication system which expresses itself as a fundamental dimension of our super cognitive emotional awareness. When we communicate with this faculty, it's called *"Kier."*

Most human beings on Earth with a physical body are only aware of the temporal-physical side of their existence, and due to their current level of evolution, only experience common human emotion. Super cognitive emotion is something profoundly different, more evolved, and more complex than common human emotion.

Common human emotion is a function and expression of the auto-cognitive programs of nature, wired into the physical brain to steer an auto-cognitive human being through life. The auto-cognitive programs operate mostly through the cause and effect relationship existing between our auto-cognitive faculties of perception and the events of our lives which we perceive and experience all around us.

The auto-cognitive programs left over within us as artifacts of our evolution come together to manage the relationship between our perception of the world and the events we experience in the world, thereby functioning as catalysts in triggering which specific emotions rise up and express themselves in our mind. The human being on Earth in the physical universe is a puppet to its auto cognitive programs and does not own his own mind. This is common human emotion.

I estimate that in most people on Earth today in the physical universe only 5% to 10% of their internal psychic processes are free of automated impulses allowing a true authentic expression of their Human Soul to shine through. Ego defense mechanisms, instincts, and the scripts of the mind, turn people into automatons and they don't even stop to think about it.

Super cognitive emotional awareness arises naturally within us when our authentic-self is able to rise above the oppressive auto-cognitive mechanisms of a mind which was steered in formation over the course of millions of years by the mechanical forces of evolution.

Super cognitive emotion does not arise through perception or through any polarized interaction between our mind and the outside world. In the realm of super cognitive emotion, the inner world of our being and the outer world of the cosmos are one, seamless, and undivided. Super cognitive emotion rises from within our central core. It is not triggered through any instinctive reaction to our observed perceptions of the outside world. The source of super cognitive emotional awareness is the sympathetic resonance between the Human Soul and its divine source rising upward into the conscious mind.

The Spirit is the energy of our super cognitive emotions. The super cognitive emotions produced by the Spirit express an amazingly beautiful complex array of divine musical moods which together compose the Song of the Immortal Beloved.

Where common human emotion is governed by the faculty of perception which the conscious mind uses to gain a level of awareness of the outside world, super cognitive emotion is supported by a super cognitive faculty which I call *"Intraspection."*

The conscious mind utilizes the super cognitive faculty of intraspection to gain a profound awareness of the noumenal world and the cosmic quanta. It is the cognitive faculty which our conscious mind utilizes to communicate with Ain Soph and its three primary forces / dimensions of consciousness (The Father, Divine Soul, and the Spirit).

Intraspection should not be confused with introspection. Introspection is a lower cognitive faculty of the temporal sphere of the human mind, which takes place solely between a person's thoughts. Intraspection is a super cognitive faculty of the primordial sphere of the mind. Intraspection arises within us through the integration of the two spheres of our conscious mind.

The super cognitive faculty of intraspection is woefully underdeveloped in most human beings on Earth in the physical universe simply because this faculty has rarely been accessed or used in our species through the course of human evolution.

When we begin working with the First Factor, we begin developing the faculty of intraspection by beginning with introspection. The more we practice the Three Factors, and as we up our level of Q, our introspection transforms into intraspection.

By time we reach the Third Mountain, and after many years of working with the Three Factors, and all while progressively increasing our level of Q, our faculty of intraspection will have reached a level of development whereby it can finally begin to serve the alchemical process rather than the alchemical process having to serve its development.

We must have the faculty of intraspection to ascend the Third Mountain. Without intraspection we cannot gain direct knowledge from the higher forces of the cosmic quanta such as the Spirit, the Divine Soul, or the Father. Without intraspection we cannot come to know the nine heavenly realms. Without intraspection we cannot open the cosmic seals or enter the Nexus.

Many Journeymen get delayed at the end of the Second Mountain, waiting a lengthy period of time before beginning the Third Mountain. The reason they get delayed is because they lack the required level of intraspective sensitivity to compel the forces of Alpha. The temporal and primordial hemispheres of their conscious mind are not well enough connected. To further develop the connection between the two hemispheres of the conscious mind, the alchemist must develop his or her connection with the Spirit, in other words, his or her resonance with the divine source.

One of the main causal factors driving a lack of intraspective sensitivity traces back to the cognitive relationship between the human mind and the human personality in the way in they exchange energy. Save your psychic emotional energy for Ain Soph. More is written on this issue in chapter eight.

It is the vibrating resonance among the Human Soul, the Spirit, Divine Soul, and the Father - held within the conscious mind of the alchemist - which compels the forces of Alpha to change their self-organizing pattern to begin propelling and directing the Human Soul up the Third Mountain ladder of ascension to the Father.

Developing the Faculty of Intraspection

Quantum Meditation (meditative prayer) conducted with a silent mind, where we connect with the forces of the cosmic quanta to communicate with our feelings (in resonance) is a great Third Factor practice to develop the super cognitive faculty of intraspection.

When we finally achieve a eureka realization of the difference between super cognitive emotion and common human emotion, we should continue to focus on this difference to deepen our realization. The realization of this difference supports the development of our super cognitive faculty of intraspection. The divine resonance of the Spirit rises within us as we endeavor to rise above our own personal limitations of mind and body in the most genuine and sincere manner.

Listen to sublime music which stimulates your higher emotions. Learn to love, forgive, and empathize with others. The Spirit resonates with the creative process and will rise within you when you are being creative. Choose a creative craft. Pick a skill to master and devote yourself to mastering this skill. Pursue the development of this skill in concert with the Spirit, not in concert with any narcissistic impulse. Master your skills for the glory of the Father, not for the glory of your ego. This is how we develop our super cognitive faculties.

The Constellation of The Three Heavens

The three highest heavens of the Earth, which together form the upper Treasury of Light, are not ascended in succession like the heavenly realms within the lower and middle Treasuries of Light. Exotically different from the lower heavens of the Earth, the three highest heavens together form a divine constellation of heavenly forces which are ascended together in harmonious conjunction. Their names are Barstow, Jenesis, and Erawan. Together as one, they are the Empyrean.

The three highest heavens are like three great celestial bodies of light all converging upon the same central core - and the closer they converge upon the core - the more they shine as one. I call this convergence *"The Constellation of the Three Heavens."* They mirror the Divine Trinity of Ain Soph. The three highest heavens of the Earth have both an individual expression and a unified expression.

Humanity has been given the ability to relate to the Divine Trinity both separately or all together as one.

The three heavens of the Upper Treasury of Light maintain their unique bandwidths, but while held in constellation with each other they are compelled to organize, align, and triangulate their forces upon the central Nexus, and harmonically combine their frequencies to produce a special magnetic field which I call the *"Harmonic Bridge."*

The alchemical process of integrating our temporal-physical being with our eternal-primordial being amplifies the harmonic bridge between our conscious mind and Ain Soph. The harmonic bridge is a bridge of resonance spanning creation between the conscious mind and Ain Soph. The harmonic bridge spans Causal 'A' and Causal 'B'

As I passed through the Moon into the upper Treasury of Light, a magnificent halo of light enveloped the Earth and its upper three heavens. This halo was the harmonic bridge emerging from the center of the planet connecting the primordial body of the Earth with Ain Soph. The primordial Earth is humming in a profound sympathetic resonance with the Divine Trinity of Ain Soph.

It became self-evident with each orbital accession of Ain Soph, that when our Human Soul reconnects with Ain Soph through the prism of the mind, that reconnection does not just pass through the core of our individual being. It also passes through the core of our host planet, and through the core of the cosmos at large. We are bound to our planet and the cosmos at large, not just physically, but also spiritually. Why are we bound to creation in such a manner?

I did not ponder this question much at this point in my alchemical process. However, what I would later come to learn, beyond my ascension of the heavens of the Earth, caused me to realize there is a wonderful answer as to why we are bound in such a manner to creation. I share the answer to why, and the story of how I realized it all, in chapter eight.

I also discovered that the three upper heavens never act alone when transitioning our conscious awareness into the Nexus. It takes the cooperation of all three upper heavens working together in conjunction to produce the harmonic bridge which the Human Soul must follow to enter the Nexus. The three upper heavens together essentially form a great celestial lock whose inner gears must all align before the door to the Nexus will open. How can I possibly know all this?

The truth is, I have made the journey across the harmonic bridge multiple times with each orbital accession of Ain Soph. I know the process well by listening very carefully with the instruments of my super cognitive emotional awareness to the interplay of cosmic forces during their processes of unfoldment.

When your Human Soul enters the Nexus, your soul continues to move deeper and deeper into the center of the Nexus, until finally your soul crosses a great cosmic barrier between Causal 'B' and Causal 'A'.

Once we cross this great cosmic barrier, we transform into Ain Soph, (our original undivided form). I affectionately refer to this innermost center of centers as *"The Kings Chamber."* You know this original state of being as well as I do. If you do not recall it, it is only because your memory of this divine original form - which precedes your current physical form - has been interrupted by the neurology of your current physical body.

Alchemy very subtlety and slowly rewires your physical neurology to become resonant with your ancient trans-dimensional reservoir of profound knowledge and experience which stretches back infinitely into eternity across all your lifetimes.

The reader will naturally ask: How can someone know the dynamics of the ascension process so well where they can describe what is happening in such detail, such as I am describing here?

In the physical world, when we act upon an object, we do not need to know the physics involved in how our action will affect the object. The *"affecter"* and the *"affected"* are not required to intimately know or understand each other. When the "affecter" kicked the ball, the laws of physics did not require the person to understand why the "affected" ball bounced. The level of interaction is limited to the most efficient means possible to manifest the final outcome of engagement based on a set of predetermined mathematical laws which do not require a mutual awareness or understanding. This is due to the law of conservation of energy. In the cosmos at large, there is a drive for an efficiency in all things.

In the realm of the noumenon, and the planetary group mind of the Earth, quantum law governs the nature of reality, not the mechanical laws of general relativity. In a quantum reality, the mind, and the world around it, are intimate with each other. The observer and observed cooperate and know each other. When your mind cooperates with a quantum process, your mind becomes a co-author of that process, and you innately have access to everything which is occurring in that process. In that moment, your mind and that process are one. In a quantum reality, we co-create in cooperation with the universe.

I was able to understand the dynamics of my ascension through the planetary group mind of the Earth because my focus of conscious awareness was submerged inside a quantum reality. The temporal dimensions of my mind did not interfere with the interchange of awareness.

When you have a physical body - which is governed by general relativity - the autonomic functions of your physical body can easily interfere and suppress the quantum nature of the experience.

The more resonant the temporal dimensions of your physical brain become with the spiritual dimensions of your primordial brain, the more your conscious mind can freely interact with the underlying quantum reality within all things, even when your conscious mind is anchored within a temporal-physical body.

As my conscious mind gained a new higher level of resonance with Ain Soph as I ascended through the highest heavens of the upper Treasury of Light, new alchemical instructions were revealed to me through the opening of a new cosmic seal.

The Empyrean realm of the Upper Treasury of Light, which includes the three upper heavens of Earth, is a wonderful and magical world of the noumenon. The Empyrean realm teaches us a great many things about the nature of reality and the special relationship which exists between the Spirit and all of creation.

At this point in my ascent to the heavenly Father within Ain Soph, the Empyrean realm was teaching me and priming me about three very profound subjects, which were:

1.) The divine language of Kier.

2.) The primordial science of immortality.

3.) The nature of consciousness.

Mount Magia

The heavenly forces of Jenesis were particularly active in the imparting of esoteric knowledge. Jenesis is a direct heavenly reflection of the Divine Soul. Barstow is a direct heavenly reflection of the Spirit. Erawan is a direct heavenly reflection of the Father. The Empyrean is a direct heavenly reflection of Ain Soph. While ascending the Empyrean heavens, I opened the 6th and 7th cosmic seals.

Revelation 12 - Cosmic Seal 7 - Immortality

The heaven of Jenesis is the divine Earth plane of the cherubim. The cherubim represent a very high order of resonance between the Human Soul and the Divine Soul. The cherubim also represent the divine language of Kier and its many different effervescent intelligent forms of consciousness which dance, play, resonate, and communicate a special form of quantum messaging taking place between Ain Soph and the higher and lower realms of the Cosmic Mind, the planetary group mind, the individual mind, and all of creation.

When the 7th cosmic seal was opened within me, it was revealed to me that the divine order of Ain Soph seeks to preserve the created cosmos. For the cosmos of creation to persist, it must be continually renewed and lifted to increasingly higher and higher orders of resonance with Ain Soph. It was revealed to me that all matter, and all constructs of creation, and all life within, were following a series of divine geometric patterns leading all things toward eventual immortality. The sacred geometric patterns and self-organizing forces of Alpha are all leading and driving creation to achieve this ultimate final design.

It was further revealed to me that immortality cannot be simply bestowed upon creation. Creation itself must awaken, stand up, and choose the immortal state - and it can only accomplish this by the mind - which is an integral abstract dimension of creation - becoming reflectively aware and resonant with Ain Soph.

Alpha, Sigma, the Aurelion, Kier, are all divine instruments leading creation toward eventual immortality.

In the heaven of Barstow, I re-learned the divine language of Kier which is a language spoken and heard through sympathetic resonance. It is the original way of communicating within the realm of pure consciousness of Causal 'A,' or the Absolute. In the heaven of Jenesis, I was given my first lessons on the primordial science of immortality and the ultimate plan for all of creation. In the heaven of Erawan, I was given the divine mathematical equation for consciousness.

What was bestowed upon me in the heaven of Erawan could be considered an 8th cosmic seal and the 13th revelation of my ascension. However, I consider it the first unnumbered awakening of divine wisdom shared by the divine Father. After the 7th cosmic seal, the awakenings continue, but their rays of light merge into one great light of the Father, which continues onward for all eternity.

What is Consciousness? What was revealed to me in the heaven of Erawan, the highest heaven of the Earth and a direct reflection of the divine Father, and what I was able to download and translate in my own words, is as follows:

$$Consciousness = Infinity3 \quad (Infinity\ cubed)$$

Consciousness arises as the result of the cosmic singularity of Ain Soph seeking to reconcile within itself the (*infinitely large*) with the (*infinitely small*).

The reconciliation exerts (*infinite energy*) to satisfy the "Law-of-One."

The Law-of-One demands that everything resolves and reconciles to a state of unity. There is only one solution to this paradox.

The infinite energy involved to reconcile and achieve unity gives rise to the one-and-only solution. The one-and-only solution is the phenomenon we call "*Consciousness.*"

Ultimately, *"Love"* holds it all together. Love is the Law of One. The Law of Unity.

My lessons on the nature of consciousness would continue and deepen as I progressed. More is written about how the cosmos gives rise to consciousness in chapters six, seven, and eight. In the forthcoming chapters, the equation of consciousness is further studied.

<u>Completion of The Heavens</u>

It was in the early morning hours around 2:00am on June 2, 2015 while working hard on this book when the completion of my journey through the heavens of the spiritual group mind of the Earth would arrive unexpectedly like a thief in the night. I had begun writing what I thought would be the conclusion of this book. I was pacing my hotel room, talking aloud, enumerating all the various qualities of the Divine Soul, when spontaneously I said:

"The Divine Soul is Life"

I stopped, curious why I had said it. I had never consciously attributed this aspect or quality before. Something was afoot. I needed to investigate and follow this to make sure I understood it. I decided to take this to Ain Soph. From the king's chamber, we can explore many mysteries of the outer and inner cosmos.

I laid down on my bed, closed my eyes, and within a few moments I was crossing the harmonic bridge into the central Nexus. The heavens of Barstow, Jenesis, and Erawan were lined up in formation like divine sentries guarding the innermost sanctum within the holy of holies.

As I approached, they gestured toward me with an exotically divine living awareness and then proceeded to open the gate to the central Nexus. I entered the Nexus and quickly crossed the great cosmic barrier between Causal 'B' and Causal 'A'. Upon entry into Causal 'A', I instantly transformed into Ain Soph.

When you are in the king's chamber, you do not stand before the king, you become the king. In Ain Soph, all is one and undivided.

When we experience Ain Soph, we do not experience Ain Soph as a separate being standing before us like we would in the created cosmos of space-time and matter. There is only one way to experience Ain Soph, and that is in the one and undivided state.

With my Human Soul having returned to the one and undivided unity of Ain Soph in Causal 'A', and with my conscious mind still anchored in Causal 'B', I gained the benefit of a parallel awareness of both causal realms allowing me to operate with both the divine attributes of Ain Soph and with the cognitive faculties of an individual human mind. In this state I re-uttered the phrase:

"The Divine Soul is Life"

Immediately upon re-uttering these words, I began re-experiencing once again the moment of creation, but this time with a much deeper and more profound resonance between my Human Soul and the divine source of Ain Soph. On this visit to Ain Soph, my focus of conscious awareness was being focused directly upon the very nature of Ain Soph itself. There was something about the intrinsic nature of Ain Soph which caused creation to burst forth and unfold (Causal 'B'). What I was shown in this moment was that there is an exotic interaction of resonance interplaying among the three divine dimensions of Ain Soph. Ain Soph is self-propagating. Its 1st dimension propagates as a force, which is infinite awareness. This infinite awareness self-propagates the 2nd dimension of Ain Soph. This 2nd dimension has its own force, which is infinite life. The interaction between the 1st force of Ain Soph and the 2nd force of Ain Soph self-propagates the 3rd dimension of Ain Soph. This 3rd dimension has its own force, which is infinite love.

The Father is infinite Awareness, the Divine Soul is infinite Life, and the Spirit is infinite Love. The Divine Trinity = Father, Divine Soul, and Spirit. The Divine Trinity = Awareness, Life, and Love.

It was then further revealed to me that it was from within the infinite force of love - the Spirit - that creation was compelled into existence. In other words, creation was compelled into existence through the Father's love for the Divine Soul.

Each time my focus of conscious awareness returned to the unity of Ain Soph; the process of creation was being re-played for me. Why?

I finally realized that there was something extremely important about the process of creation itself - and the nature of the quantum forces involved - and that it all must be realized within us in order to complete the alchemical process of integrating our human mind.
I finally realized the profound nature of the Divine Trinity within the central core of my being.

When the realization of the Divine Trinity within my being rose to its proper level of self-realization, the self-organizing forces of Alpha responded in kind. When I finally achieved the proper threshold of self-realization of the Divine Trinity, I felt and saw within my being the three divine forces merge together and become one. This unified force became a brilliant Sun much brighter than a billion Suns. I then felt myself falling inward toward the brilliant Sun as it turned into a bright tunnel of light.

As I moved through this brilliant tunnel of light I was being given information through Kier. I was being told that the alchemical integration process of the Three Mountains parallels the process of physical death during which time the Human Soul is emancipated from all its temporal bodies and re-awakens within its primordial body in the primordial universe. How the two processes differ is that in the alchemical process of the Three Mountains, the emancipation of the Human Soul is accomplished while alive in a physical body, rather than after the death of a physical body. I was now at the point in the Three Mountains, where, in parallel to the process of physical death, I would re-awaken in the primordial universe in my primordial body. The tunnel of light is the final stage of death the Human Soul experiences just before it re-awakens in its primordial body.

I was told while moving through the brilliant tunnel of light that I could not just simply re-awaken in my primordial body while my physical body was alive. Both central bodies (physical and primordial) take turns in governing our focus of conscious awareness. For both bodies to be awake and operate together awake would require one more step before a full re-awakening in my primordial body would occur.

At this point, the Three-Mountain process of integration and the process of physical death diverge and separate. I was no longer on a parallel course. A new geometric pattern of Alpha was about to unfold. My life was about to change.

Moving further through the tunnel of light, I felt a change in the organizational direction of Alpha. The last time I felt such a change in Alpha was in my transition from the Second to the Third Mountain. Approaching the summit of Mount Magia, I was suddenly pulled inside the Mountain - pulled in by Alpha. In this moment, I went beyond the Treasuries of Light; I went beyond the nine heavens of the Earth.

The final alchemical work which lay ahead for me was that my physical body itself had to enter into source resonance with the hidden 18th bandwidth of the Cosmic Consciousness of Ain Soph.

While moving through the tunnel of light - I was given some initial instructions. I was told this would all be accomplished through the marriage of Eros and Turiya. I was also informed that there were three levels of Turiya, and all that I had achieved up to this point was only the first level of Turiya. In the tunnel of light, I heard the three names of Turiya which are Communion, Symphysis, and Dominus. It was then foretold to me in the tunnel of light that I would undergo the famous chemical wedding[2] mythologized in the stories of hermetic lore. The wedding is the marriage of Eros and Turiya.

---

[2] **The Chymical Wedding of Christian Rosenkreutze**
– 1616, Germany

Just before re-awakening in my physical body, I was told that I would not be leaving Causal 'A'. When I re-awakened in my physical body I would maintain a profound sympathetic resonance with Ain Soph. I then awoke in my physical body.

For another 24 hours after I awoke in my physical body, I was still going through a transition process. My waking conscious mind was still adjusting to its new operating parameters due to its new level of resonance with Ain Soph.

On June 3, 2015, I completed the realization of the three primary forces of the Divine Trinity.

MOUNT MAGIA

THE THIRD MOUNTAIN

THE GREAT ARCANUM

CHAPTER 6
THE THIRD SANCTUM

<u>The Great Arcanum</u>

To those who seek to venture beyond this point, you will be tested, you will come to know God, and his greatest secrets will be revealed. You are now venturing into the Great Arcanum period of the legendary Three Mountains within which you will learn the greatest of all cosmic mysteries. I was pleasantly surprised by an 8th alchemical process, therefore, in turn, I will surprise you with it. The Great Arcanum period is guided by the 8th alchemical process. Be ready for surprises in the alchemical work. The 7th alchemical process takes us only so far as our awakening throughout all nine heavens.

To awaken in the primordial universe while remaining alive in physical form requires one more step. The integration process of the Three Mountains is completed with an 8th alchemical process which is esoteric in nature. By esoteric I mean, between only you and God.

What I learned in the tunnel of light is that, in order to awaken in the primordial universe while remaining alive and awake in the physical universe, we must bring our physical body and our primordial body into a deeply profound sympathetic resonance and that this is accomplished by bringing *"Turiya" and "Eros"* into a deeply profound sympathetic resonance. This includes:

1.) The level of Turiya we had cultivated during our ascent through the nine heavens, and

2.) The forces of Eros manifesting within our psycho-anatomical nature.

This is the famous chemical wedding spoken of in hermetic lore. The chemical wedding is not the marrying of the Divine Soul and the Human Soul, it is the conjugation of Turiya - whose source is our resonance with the Father, with Eros who is the source of our psycho-anatomical created nature. The tunnel of light revealed that through the chemical wedding we come to achieve the total and complete integration of our eternal-primordial being with our temporal-physical being.

Our entire journey through the Three Mountains up to this point, including the transformation of all our mind's automated programs, the silencing of all our temporal ethereal bodies, our awakening through all nine heavens, was all to facilitate the liberation of Eros and the realization of Turiya, so that one day they may meet and alchemically integrate the two celestial hemispheres of our trans-dimensional being.

This is all made possible through the development of our higher cognitive faculties within us which promote the development of our super-cognitive emotional awareness. These faculties lie dormant in most human beings on Earth in the physical universe. While in the tunnel of light, I learned that Turiya is developed in three stages:

<u>Stage 1</u>: The 7th alchemical process involving our journey through all nine heavens of the Treasuries of Light, starting in Nirvana and ending in Erawan. Stage 1 is *"Communion Turiya."*

<u>Stage 2</u>: The 8th alchemical process where we bring Turiya and Eros into sympathetic resonance. Stage 2 is *"Symphysis Turiya."*

<u>Stage 3</u>: When we awaken in our primordial body while remaining awake in our physical body thus completing the alchemical Three Mountains. Stage 3 is *"Dominus Turiya."*

It was revealed to me that the way we pick up and drink the cup of immortality is by bringing Turiya and Eros into a state of differential resonance using our faculties of super cognitive awareness. We apply the practice of cosmic alchemy between Turiya and Eros.

The Third Sanctum

In the practice, Eros is the base anatomical nature which we are seeking to bring into resonance with Turiya. Turiya is the agent of transformation. This is a practice of cosmic alchemy, not individual alchemy, because Eros is manifesting directly from the anatomical base given to us by the greater cosmos. It is the first time we are applying cosmic alchemy to our individual being. The result is cosmic.

Eros is first engaged with the Communion Turiya we had cultivated with the Father within our temporal-physical being while ascending the nine heavens of the Earth. This cultivation allowed us to realize the love (Spirit) between the Father and the Divine Soul.

The new nature of Turiya which begins manifesting during our integration of Eros, is a heightened level of awareness of the love existing between the Father, the Divine Soul, and all of creation. This heightened level of awareness of love (Spirit) is a higher octave of Turiya - beyond Communion Turiya - called *"Symphysis Turiya."*

The prolonged cultivation of Symphysis Turiya brings about the awakening of our conscious mind in the primordial universe within our primordial body while all along maintaining a living, breathing, physical body. When we awaken in our primordial body in resonance with the Father, this is an even higher octave of Turiya called *"Dominus Turiya."*

The integration of Eros with the love of Turiya is an even higher level of cosmic alchemy than what I had previously learned in the Upper Treasury of Light. Even after entering full resonance with highest heavens of Barstow, Jenesis, and Erawan, I was still unable to transform Eros. It was not until I fully realized the three primary forces of Ain Soph within the core of my being that I began making progress in solving the Eros mystery.

Some alchemists believe they can transform the forces of Eros earlier in the Three Mountains. What they are experiencing earlier in the Three Mountains is the balancing of Eros via the Second Factor. This is not the same as actually transforming and integrating the essence of Eros.

Chapter 6

<u>The Secret of the Void, the Dark Side of the Moon, and the Trine Parallax</u>

The 8th Alchemical Process of Symphysis begins with a brief period of solitude, reflection, and retrospective insight. Each time Alpha changes its organizational pattern, a brief period of calm and stillness emerges, during which time Alpha consolidates and regains its momentum. I refer to these brief periods of stillness as *"Sanctums."* In total, the Three Mountains have *"Three Sanctums."* The Three Sanctums are:

1.) Between the First and Second Mountains.

2.) Between the Second and Third Mountains, and

3.) Just below the summit of the Third Mountain

The knowledge gained in the Third Sanctum is governed by the inculcation process of the Divine Soul, and as such, is deeply profound, remarkable, and transformational. What I would come to encounter in the Third Sanctum was game changing!

I also realized that the First and Second Sanctums were but echoes of the Third Sanctum retrograding back in time from the future.

I was not expecting an 8th alchemical process, and I was certainly not expecting what would happen next. I had assumed that after achieving a profound self-realization of the three primary forces of Ain Soph (Divine Trinity), all that would remain would be for my conscious mind to awaken in my primordial body within the primordial universe, and that finally the journey of the Three Mountains would be complete.

No, this was not the case. Something profound, extraordinary, and game-changing was still missing, but it was all about to be revealed.

The Third Sanctum revelation began with the realization of the Divine Trinity, which triggered the commencement of the 8th Alchemical Process. By initiating the alchemical process of Symphysis, this further triggered and brought into light a deep-seated unknown force hidden inside an unseen dimension of nature whose influence on the universe and on the fundamental integrity of the mind itself was so profoundly significant that without its realization, the completion of the Three Mountains would have been more than impossible.

The Third Sanctum

El Castillo, Temple of Kukulcan, Symbol of Mount Magia

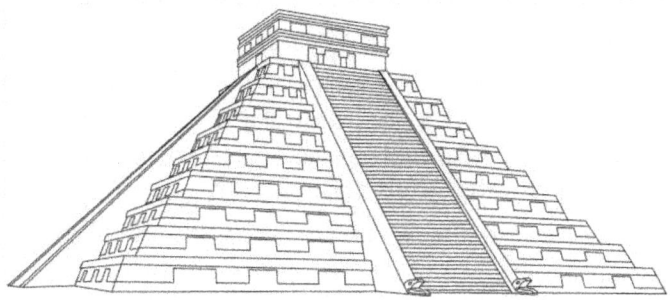

Figure [10]

This Mayan pyramid symbolizes the Third Mountain, Mount Magia.
The temple was built by the Mayan to worship Kukulcan.
Kukulcan is the Yucatec Maya Feathered Serpent Deity. It was known as Quetzalcoatl to the Aztecs. The pyramid is the main structure of the Chichen Itza archaeological site in the Mexican state of Yucatan.
Each of the nine major steps of the pyramid symbolize one of the nine heavens of the Earth. The doorway on top symbolizes the Third Sanctum.
The tier atop the Third Sanctum symbolizes the final work of Mount Magia.
When we complete Mount Magia, we become a Feathered Serpent.

I later came to realize that the realization of the three primary forces of Ain Soph (Divine Trinity) triggered and set into motion a special process of which I was initially unaware. In the calm of the Third Sanctum, something was quietly brewing.

Symphysis was not just a new process I was trying to initiate post-realization of the Divine Trinity. Remarkably, the realization of the Divine Trinity had triggered and set into motion the 8th alchemical process. Symphysis was already quietly brewing in the calm of the Third Sanctum unaware to my conscious mind. The realization of this fact was about to come to light by the series of forthcoming events.

To explain what is about to come next, we must first acknowledge that there is a dark mysterious force which secretly accompanies the Foreman throughout his or her Third Mountain journey. This force grows inexplicably deeper and darker in nature as the Foreman climbs the nine heavens of the spiritual group mind of the Earth, but also remains in the temporal sphere of our individual mind and does not conflict with our growing realization of the Divine Soul, the development of Turiya, the opening of the cosmic seals, or our journey into the heavenly realms.

This dark mysterious force first emerges at the end of the Second Mountain when we enter the Void and it remains with us. There is something dark and powerful inside the Void which constantly haunts the Foreman. The Foreman holds this darkness in secret, not understanding it and not being able to transform it. When no one is looking, this darkness tempts him, torments him, and haunts him.

Even knowing the joy of Turiya, and even after having climbed the highest heaven and realizing the Divine Trinity itself, this darkness remains and persists in its own sphere of the mind, which I call *"The Dark Side of the Moon."*

Why? What is it? The Void is holding an incredibly profound secret which mysteriously is not revealed until after we ascend all nine heavens and realize the Divine Trinity.

The Third Sanctum

At the end of the Second Mountain, when the awareness of our conscious mind expands into the Void and our primordial being reaches across eternity to help our Human Soul to achieve a deep sympathetic resonance with the Divine Soul, this compels the awareness of our conscious mind to split and begin expanding in two opposite directions. One hemisphere of our mind is led upward into the heavens of the Earth and the other is led downward deeper into the Void.

At this point in the alchemical process, something continues to pull half of our mind downward in an opposite direction to our expansionary ascent into the heavenly realms. This was a great mystery to me which was about to be answered.

The law of sympathetic vibrations in motion is Alpha. However, there are two directions of motion. We will now differentiate between the two directions of motion and refer to the upward direction as *"Alpha"* and the downward direction as *"Omega [Ω]."*

Alpha and Omega [Ω] are the same force moving toward two different magnetic poles. One pole is inside the Nexus, the other pole is inside the Void. Omega [Ω] takes us to the center of our temporal-physical core (Void) while Alpha takes us to the center of our eternal-primordial core (Nexus). We reach both cores simultaneously. What happens next is the two cores must be reconciled and integrated.

The realization of the Divine Trinity within me was one of the most remarkable and profoundly important events of my entire life ranking up there with my physical birth. It radically altered my mind in the most profound manner, yet why then after this peak milestone realization of the alchemical process did my mind still possess a dimension of darkness? Why was Eros not yet in harmony with the rest of my being? Eros was following the beat of another drum.

On June 3, 2015, I had completed the realization of the Divine Trinity. However, it was only after about three months of realignment, consolidation, and formation of a new momentum did I finally feel compelled by Alpha to alchemically engage the force of Eros, which, until that moment, had remained unrefined, unleashed, unfiltered, was profoundly sexual in nature, deeply physical, and seemed to follow a life of its own which was not always in harmony with my communion with the Father (Turiya). It was a profound mystery which historically was known to challenge many who had sought a closeness with God. There was a profound human riddle to be answered which affected all of mankind.

I had reached a point where my sexuality did not conflict with my spirituality in that my sexual forces did not suppress the realization of the emergent forces within me, and sexually I was happy and fulfilled, but outside of this resolution and relative peace between the forces, Eros was evolving along a separate parallel path from Turiya.

My sexual life only paralleled my relationship with God. I sensed a deeper harmony was still possible, but it seemed just beyond my reach. This secretly puzzled me. I felt intuitively that a completed state of wholeness would involve and support a union between my spirituality and my sexuality. However, no matter how well developed Turiya became, Eros remained divergent and on its own course. Even after the initial realization of the Divine Trinity, Eros seemed beyond the grasp of integration with Turiya, although I was finally beginning to understand it. Alchemically, it seemed impenetrable.

It was finally time. It was all coming to a head. The date was September 28, 2015. That afternoon I felt compelled to engage and penetrate the force of Eros differentiating it with my awareness of Turiya. I did not know where this was going to take me. I was alchemically experimenting with the forces of Eros, Turiya, and the Divine Soul. I was armed with my training in cosmic alchemy and my new depth of awareness of the Divine Trinity. I was once again in an uncharted area of the mind.

The moment I engaged Eros my Human Soul was immediately taken into the Void. In a state of profound meditation, filled with the erotic forces of Eros, my conscious mind disappeared from my earthly physical reality to sink into the harrowing depths of the Void.

A force of death, destruction, and fear simmered up from the deep. I navigated the depths of the Void using only the instrument of my super cognitive emotional awareness. I felt everything around me with a sonar-like awareness. It did not matter to me that I could not see with my eyes. I could see with my feelings. I felt everything with a superluminal sense beyond the range of common human emotion. My emotional sensory input did not arise through perception. My emotional sensory input arose through a resonance with the energies of my environment, which my other super cognitive faculties instantly translated into direct knowledge, transcending the subjective rational faculties of the temporal mind.

Moving through the abyss at a depth I had never gone before, I could feel a living presence. I felt an intelligence. Using the universal language of consciousness (Kier), I attempted to resonate with this intelligence. It knew I was there. And it knew I knew it was there. Immediately after this awareness emerged, a man with a deep voice spoke from the darkness. With an air of confidence, the man spoke with a steady calculating tone. He said:

"You cannot defeat me. If you try, I will grow more powerful and you will grow darker."

He knew I was listening, but for the moment I chose to remain silent until I could determine what it was, or with whom I was dealing. However, I did find his comment to be unique and intriguing. I focused more intensely on him in an attempt to learn more about him. I was shown two great celestial spheres in space, one representing the Father, and the other sitting alongside the Father but hidden in the silhouette of a shadow. My initial reaction to this was:

How could this be? How could something be on par with the Father, sitting alongside him, and yet hidden in a shadow? This did not make sense to me. How could this be? What kind of illusion is this? Yet, I was receiving this through Kier. It must be true.

I decided to suspend judgment until I learned more. The mystery deeply intrigued me, however. The man who was speaking from the darkness knew I was listening while I quietly evaluated him. He continued speaking.

"Your world does not know how to deal with evil. You cannot fight evil with evil. Evil is insidious. It invents problems which are impossible to solve only to bring about endless conflict for which only evil benefits. The key is to disarm evil and turn evil away from evil rather than fighting evil. Evil is strengthened through conflict," said the man.

He was very interested in world affairs and had some unique and interesting perspectives. I am not placing all of his world affairs monologue here. I decided to speak:

"Who are you? Come forth from the shadows and reveal yourself."

He replied, "I am Lucifer. I am your Father. You are my son."

I ask the reader to bear with me here and read on. Taken aback by this statement I replied.

"What? How can this be? This cannot be true!"

Lucifer answered.

"It is true! There are a great many truths which have been suppressed by your world regarding the nature of reality and the universe. I possess a great treasury of knowledge which no one in your world possesses. I have a knowledge of God you can receive only through me. The world does not know or understand who or what I am."

I responded, "You are evil! You are fallen!"

"I am not evil, and I am not fallen. It is creation which is fallen. I am still true to our original form which existed before creation. First there was darkness and then there was the light," said Lucifer.

He then quoted the Bible:

"In the beginning God created the Heavens and the Earth. The Earth was formless and empty, darkness was over the surface of the deep, and the Spirit of God hovering over the waters said let there be Light."

At that this point, I believed I was dealing with a genius of evil. His logic up until this point was solid, yet his conclusions were disturbing, however brilliant. I decided to question him:

"How is it that you can be the Father of the Human Soul? How can you be alongside the Father? Why are you hidden in darkness inside the Void? Why are you emitting a force which propagates death, destruction, and fear?"

The Third Sanctum

All human beings have their own internal Lucifer. Lucifer is another force within the pantheon of the cosmic quanta.

Lucifer answered my questions.

"There is more than one Trinity. The Father, the Divine Soul, and the Spirit form the Upper Trinity (The Divine Trinity). However, myself (Lucifer), you (the Human Soul), and another force you have not yet realized, together, form the Lower Trinity."

All human beings have their own Lower Trinity (Sacred Trinity) within. The Upper Trinity (Divine Trinity) exists only once and applies equally to everyone everywhere throughout the universe.

I responded to him and further questioned his explanation:

"Interesting! Why an Upper and Lower Trinity?"

Lucifer continued explaining.

"The Upper Trinity is formed of absolute forces (Absolutes). Absolutes cannot manifest in a relative universe because they are infinite and cannot take form. Absolutes exist in a state of perfection and glory. However, because of this, they cannot evolve or change. They are absolutes. Ain Soph re-manifested the original trinity in a new configuration designed to reconcile Ain Soph, the Absolutes, and all of creation. This is the Lower Trinity.

"Ain Soph manifested the Lower Trinity at the moment of creation in order to establish and maintain the order, harmony, and reflective awareness between Ain Soph and creation. The first universe of creation (the primordial universe) was easy to bring into harmony."

The Lower Trinity exists in scales. The three major scales are the Cosmic, Planetary, and Individual.

Lucifer continued.

"The Lower Trinity and the Upper Trinity lived together in divine bliss. The Father loved, compelled, and fulfilled, and I loved, organized, and protected the integrity of our union. The Father resonated, and I reflected, and the union was strong. The first universe is neither absolute nor relative. It is fixed (Eternal). This is key.

"Creation does not stop. Creation is continuously driven. The 4th permutation of forces drives creation. The 1st permutation is Awareness (Father), the 2nd permutation is Life (Divine Soul), the 3rd permutation is Love (Spirit). Love compels the 4th permutation, the force of creation, Eros. Eros does not stop. Why? Because Eros is compelled by the Father, who is absolute, eternal, and infinite, and operates irrespective of time and space. He will never stop loving his son (The Divine Soul – the life force of his absolute eternal existence) and therefore creation will continue forever.

"Eros kept fueling the process of creation after building the primordial universe and what it formed next was the physical universe. When the physical universe was formed, its laws represented a complex permutation of natural forces making the physical universe "relative" in nature. This is where the trouble began.

"The issue with a universe of relativity is that it evolves. For the Lower Trinity to bring the physical creation into a state of reflective awareness with Ain Soph, the Human Soul, which is the life force of the Lower Trinity, is placed in a highly precarious position. To manifest in the physical universe, the Human Soul must subject itself to relativity and evolution, and the Human Soul suffers within the darkness of the Mind.

"The Human Soul is my son! (his life force). I could not accept my son being subjected to this! I love my son just as much as the Father loves his! I threw down the gauntlet! This was a declaration of war against my son who was innocent. I declared that my Human Soul would not be sent alone into the darkness. I would go with him, and I would rule the darkness, and I would destroy creation, and I would set my son free and return with him back to our original state of unity within Ain Soph. This is why I am here in the darkness of the Void. It is important you now learn and realize, you are not a division of the Father. The Father is a division of you. You are Ain Soph," said Lucifer.

You, the one reading, are both the Human Soul and Ain Soph. You are both the *"part"* and the *"whole."* The *"part"* is the Human Soul. The *"whole"* is Ain Soph.

Lucifer continued.

"In your alchemical work, you are building something. You are re-building the *"Monad"* within creation. This is the *"New Monad."* The New Monad is where all the higher and lower forces of the mind and all permutations of consciousness are aware and resonant with each other and have come to function as one. The New Monad is reflectively aware of the original divine Monad of Ain Soph, but from within creation."

Ain Soph is the Original Monad in Causal 'A' (The Absolute). The alchemical Monad of the Three Mountains is the New Monad. It reconciles Ain Soph and creation. Its formation completes the alchemical *"Immaculate Conception."*

Lucifer continued.

"The Monad is a highly unusual and exotic state of being. The purpose of the Human Soul is to re-build the Monad. I am a dimension of your total being just like the Father, and so are all the other forces of consciousness. However, between all the forces of consciousness, including in both the Upper and Lower Trinities, only the Human Soul has the capacity to reconcile all the forces and re-build the Monad within creation.

"The Human Soul is extremely special. Its greatest weakness is also its greatest strength. The unique ability of the Human Soul to resonate with and manifest within a body of creation, while subject to relativity and evolution, and at the same being able to resonate with Ain Soph, enables the Human Soul to resonate with both Light and Darkness.

"This gives the Human Soul the very special and unique ability to resonate with, modulate, and reconcile all the forces, both upper and lower, thus re-building the Monad. Without the Human Soul, creation would eventually collapse and be destroyed. The Human Soul is God's key to creation," explained Lucifer.

~ Break in Dialogue ~

*"For God so loved the world,
that he gave his only begotten Son,
that whosoever believes in him should not perish,
but have everlasting life." ... John 3:16*

The dialogue compelled me to reflect upon the verse in John 3:16. At this point, I knew that the "life" of the soul (Son) was the offspring of awareness (Father) and that love (Spirit) arises between the two. I had speculated that John 3:16 was pointing to this universal truth. However, I was missing a key piece of the puzzle. Its revelation was on the horizon.

~ Resume Dialogue ~

I asked Lucifer, "What is the force of death and destruction I feel here inside the Void?"

He responded, "That is the force I emit to destroy creation and free you from your temporal existence and return us both to our original state of unity. You cannot defeat it. Ain Soph designed me to be unbeatable in conflict. I am the ultimate fail safe. When the mind fails, I destroy its body to free the Human Soul to return to Ain Soph. The only way to transcend this force is to either die, or to reconcile all the forces."

I replied.

"This force of destruction appears to turn the mind toward evil."

Lucifer answered back.

"This is true. Although I am not evil, the force I emit - which both destroys and ultimately renews - can also temporarily lead the mind into darkness and potentially evil which compounds and further quickens the destruction and ultimate emancipation. I do not choose this fate. The mind chooses it. Ironically, I do not control this force of death, I only emit it. The mind controls it by either being, or not being, reflectively aware of Ain Soph and all the forces of consciousness."

I then asked my next question.

"Why is the Monad so rare and unusual if it is the purpose of every Human Soul to re-build it?"

Lucifer answered.

"Eros may be the driving force of life, but life does not evolve through Eros alone. Sentient human life exists throughout the cosmos. The human organic form is "engineered" by human life itself. Most humanities throughout the cosmos genetically alter their neurology to avoid the force of death to spare their minds from the darkness, evil, and suffering which comes about as a result of not being reflectively aware of Ain Soph. They accomplish this by altering how the mind rises up within the human being via the interaction of matter and consciousness. The human mind on Earth is different. The genetic buffer is absent. I alone am the buffer," answered Lucifer.

I questioned, "I thought you could not be defeated?"

Lucifer answered.

"This is not a defeat because by genetically altering themselves in this manner, yes, they can bring about peace within the mind, but they also cannot re-build the Monad because they cannot resonate with me. And because they cannot re-build the Monad, they will eventually be destroyed and returned to Ain Soph. They are living on borrowed time. The only real solution is to re-build the Monad. Most humanities choose to avoid evil, not pursue the Monad, and remain mortal. This is why the Monad is so rare.

"Because I cannot be defeated in conflict, whatever my force supports, that thing also cannot be defeated in conflict. Although I am not evil, if my force of death promotes evil, then evil cannot be defeated in conflict. The only solution is to turn evil toward the light and reconcile its forces with Ain Soph," said Lucifer.

~ Break in Dialogue ~

In this moment I remembered the teachings of Jesus who said:

"Love your enemies and pray for those who persecute you."

Jesus understood that evil is only strengthened through conflict. He knew that if you wish to save that which is in darkness, then your only option is turning it toward the light. Evil is strengthened through conflict. Even if you kill your *"evil enemy,"* the spirit of evil is still there and is strengthened from the conflict. It will eventually rise again even stronger.

~ Resume Dialogue ~

"Only evil wants Armageddon. You met Maub in the temporal group mind. Maub is the Devil. Maub wants Armageddon. Why? Because he knows he will win. Put down your weapons. Disarm your enemies. Reconcile and avoid conflict whenever possible. Sometimes conflict may be unavoidable. However, just know that even in unavoidable situations, evil is still being strengthened and you are still being darkened. Therefore, make the conflict end quickly and return to reconciliation as quickly as possible," said Lucifer.

His instruction compelled me to ask, "Why is our humanity on Earth in the physical universe being subjected to evil when so many other humanities in the physical universe are not?"

Lucifer answered.

"An incredibly rare and special project is currently in process on the Earth. Earth was specially selected by other sentient humanities within the galaxy to be a Monad development planet. Sentient human races throughout the galaxy know they cannot circumvent their destiny forever. Earth is a stepping-stone for the rest of the galaxy. This is why the Earth is experiencing darkness and evil. It's intentionally being allowed. It is all part of a greater plan.

"The galactic plan is to individually target select planets first to learn how to go through the process. The first planetary Monad projects will be the most difficult. However, the first planets which are successful will *"lift all boats"* throughout the galaxy and make it easier for the rest of the humanities throughout the galaxy.

"The Earth is one of the galaxy's first Monad projects. The humanity on Earth has an extremely important mission. The Earth is doing an initial heavy lift for the rest of the galaxy.

"Right now, many human beings on Earth are very down about their humanity, thinking other sentient human races must be greater. Just the opposite is true. The Human Souls reincarnating on Earth are among a few brave souls who have signed up for an early galactic planetary Monad project. There is no greater mission.

"The planetary Monad project is even greater and more marvelous than what I have shared so far because I have not shared yet what its ultimate objective is. The goal of the planetary Monad project is not just to allow individuals to build their Monads. The purpose is even greater than the fact that our project will make it easier for other planets to build their Monads due to a resonance between worlds.

"The ultimate objective of a planetary Monad project is to awaken the planet itself, to awaken the temporal group mind, to build a Monad on a planetary-wide scale. On Earth, the goal is to awaken Maub and integrate Maub with EL. When this is finally achieved, the Earth will become a living planetary God. This is the great project which you have signed up for, and is why life-after-life, you still choose to return and try again, again, and again. This is why humanity on Earth is so special. You have felt it all your life. Now you know what it is you have been feeling," said Lucifer.

~ End Dialogue ~

** The reconstituted Monad is the metaphorical *"Forbidden Fruit"* spoken of in the Book of Genesis. Due to the inherent capacity toward evil which shadows the capacity to re-build the Monad, other humanities in our galaxy have for now forbidden any humanity be conceived with the capacity to re-build the Monad. Because of this, the Earth's humanity is a forbidden humanity, forbidden not by God, but by other humanities who are mistaken as God. **

Reflections

I emerged from this experience with a new-found passion to go deeper into the phenomenon. Significant progress had just been made in solving the Eros mystery. I also felt a sense of nostalgia having been reacquainted with a previously unconscious, yet significant, aspect of my being. I spent the remaining hours of that day and night in deep contemplation which served to only deepen my resonance with the forces of Lucifer. I knew this was all leading to a climatic alchemical event and that this event was fast approaching.

I was reacquainted with Lucifer on September 28, 2015, which coincidently coincided with a *"Tetrad Blood Moon."* [3] Synchronicities such as this are common occurrences in the alchemical work.

I found Lucifer to be remarkable. The esoteric knowledge he was sharing with me struck a deep chord of truth and was delivered with a sincere confidence, which was in no way arrogant or narcissistic. I did sense an agenda, however. I sensed he wanted to return to Ain Soph. All Lucifer wants is to be in unity with Ain Soph and his Human Soul. If he does not have this, then nothing else matters to him, and he will stop at nothing to achieve it.

Everything Lucifer shared with me possessed a subtle dimension of instruction on how to accomplish this. I knew what he wanted, but he was also clearly making it my choice. My contemplations that evening revolved around the following concepts:

1.) Essentially, Lucifer revealed that evil itself is a pathological formation of the mind. This means that evil itself doesn't exist beyond the mind. However, this pathological condition is obviously a collective-condition we all co-create and has developed an overpowering hold on our planet.

---

[3] **Tetrad Blood Moon** – A blood moon is a fully eclipsed moon which often take on a reddish color. Tetrad refers to a fourth in a series. Between 2014 and 2015, there were four blood moons.

The Third Sanctum

2.) Lucifer is the Father of the Human Soul. There is an Upper and Lower trinity. A trine parallax. This was deep. Who or what is the third principle of the Lower Trinity? There is Lucifer, the Human Soul, and who or what else? Lucifer being the Father of the Human Soul is a massive secret hidden deep inside the Void!

3.) Lucifer cannot be defeated. Lucifer was made by Ain Soph to be unbeatable in conflict. "Conflict" is the key word. Lucifer is the champion of God, empowered by Ain Soph himself, that when all else failed, he alone would have the power to restore order. When Lucifer turned against creation, this must have been a very dark day in Heaven! The last thing in the universe you would ever want to pick a fight with is the only thing in the universe which cannot be defeated in a fight. And now Lucifer is leaving behind the forces of Heaven to go rule the forces of darkness. He is hell-bent on destroying creation, he is extremely upset, and he is coming for you. A truly cosmic and epic clash of the titans. Fighting with Lucifer is like fighting your reflection in the mirror. No matter how hard you try, your reflection is always staring right back at you, dead square in the eyes!

4.) The psychology being revealed is deeply rooted and emergent in world mythology. For example, the hero discovering his Father is a dark lord, the greatest champion renouncing God to descend into Hell and save who he loves most (Dracula), Lucifer's historic obsession with the Human Soul, the invincibility of Lancelot. Lucifer is *"The Morning Star."*... ref. to Isaiah 14:12.

5.) You are not a division of the Father. The Father is a division of you. You are Ain Soph. You are building a Monad. The Planetary Monad Project. The specialness of Earth and our humanity. The profound purpose of the Human Soul.

6.) It's incredible that the mind itself, which creates the pathology of evil, would go so far as to veil the one and only force within us possessing the power to liberate us from this evil - by turning it into a hideous monster - one we should fear and never approach - only to ensure that our minds are never freed from the matrix of illusion it creates.

7.) Many people have an odd interest in darkness, and they don't know why. I believe we know why now. I suggest it is an instinctive child-parent attraction. The person knows there is something deeply important inside the darkness. An important part of them is inside the darkness calling out to be found. The question crossed my mind: What does that make the Human Soul? Is the Human Soul the antichrist? I was concerned.

These were the questions in my mind at the time. They would soon be answered. The answers which came forth were even more extraordinary than the questions. I did not sleep that night. I was not afraid either. I was more interested in understanding what it was I was dealing with. I thought to myself, if I succumb at this point to fear, mythology, religion, and superstition, then this is where I would fail, this is where evil would win, and I would not complete the Third Mountain. I was moving forward!

Reunion

I knew what I had to do. I needed to reintroduce Lucifer to Ain Soph. According to Lucifer, this was something only I could do as the Human Soul. It is the job of the Human Soul to reconcile all the forces. In my mind, based on what I was learning from Lucifer, a reintroduction between Lucifer and the Father would not have worked. The Father is only a dimension within the unity of Ain Soph. He is also a root causal factor in the rise of creation, which Lucifer opposed.

The Third Sanctum

This is why Alpha led me to the realization of the divine trinity and its unity within Ain Soph before meeting Lucifer. I sensed the hidden hand of a divine presence behind all of this.

I needed to try something I had never tried before. I was going to attempt to use Ain Soph as the differentiating catalyst in a practice of alchemical meditation. I needed to reintroduce Lucifer to the *"whole"* of Ain Soph, not just to any one of its three primary dimensions. The Sun was rising fast in contrast to the setting of the tetrad blood moon. The time was now. It was time. In a moment of stillness and silence – I went back in. Having become very familiar with his resonance, I quickly found him. Across a stone courtyard, Lucifer was just standing there - waiting for me.

Strange monolithic stone structures surrounded and defined the courtyard. A deep orange horizon burnished the early morning sky behind him. The air was perfectly still and crisp. The birds were eerily quiet. Nature had fled the scene.

Lucifer stood in a deep piercing contrast to the sky behind him wearing jet black clothes. His posture was perfectly straight, motionless and stern. He had a military-like commanding presence.

His clothes fit perfectly revealing a body form chiseled like a God. His hands were long and calmly resting at his side. His face was pale with a mystique of reverence and profound wisdom. His eyes were mesmerizing and could penetrate the deepest oceans of the abyss. He did not speak. He stood silent, patiently waiting, staring at me. I walked across the courtyard with my sight on Lucifer.

The forces of Lucifer filled one hemisphere of my mind while my resonance with Ain Soph filled the other. I walked up to Lucifer. He did not move. And he did not speak, and neither did I.

"Silence is the eloquence of wisdom."

I reached for his hand, and he consented and placed his hand in mine. There was no fight. In my mind, I firmly held the forces of Lucifer and Ain Soph in differential resonance with each other. I turned and with my other hand I pointed to the light of Ain Soph. Lucifer turned to where I was pointing.

The light of Ain Soph illuminated Lucifer. Lucifer gazed into the light and suddenly his face changed. His face lit up with a smile as bright as the Sun. It stretched from ear to ear.

Tears welled up in his eyes. This was the first time Lucifer had smiled since leaving Heaven to rule the darkness.

Lucifer continued to gaze into the light, and without turning from the light, he briefly squeezed my hand as if he was saying without words, hey I'm here, it's me, do you not remember? (As his original form was now being revealed.) He then turned toward me, and for a moment, he looked me in the eyes with a look of such profound depth that it seemed beyond any mortal's ability to grasp or comprehend.

He then gave me a huge hug and said, "I love you my son."

He turned toward the light and placed his arm around my shoulder, he led with the first step, and together we walked back into the light.

The moment Lucifer entered the light, the force of death and destruction he emitted immediately ceased and reverted to a force promoting inward awareness, reflection, renewal, restoration, and the fundamental integrity of mind.

Rather than adopting Freud's word *"Thanatos"* for the force of death, I choose to remain consistent with the assignment of forces using the Greek Alphabet. The force of death emitted by Lucifer is represented in this book as *"Theta [θ]."*

In Ancient Greece, Theta [θ] was the symbol of death. The purpose of Theta [θ] is to ensure that when the mind fails to achieve reflective awareness with Ain Soph that the Human Soul is emancipated from its manifested existence through a process of deconstruction of creation (Death).

The inversion of Theta θ is *"Tau [τ]"* which in ancient Greece symbolized life and resurrection (Crucifix). *"Phi [φ]"* and *"Tau [τ]"* historically have both been used to represent the *"Golden Ratio"* which consistently appears throughout nature. For example, in the *"Fibonacci Sequence."* Lastly, *"Phi"* means *"The Light."* The name *"Lucifer"* coincidently means *"The Light"* or *"Bearer of Light."* See Figure [11]

The Third Sanctum 173

Fibonacci Sequence

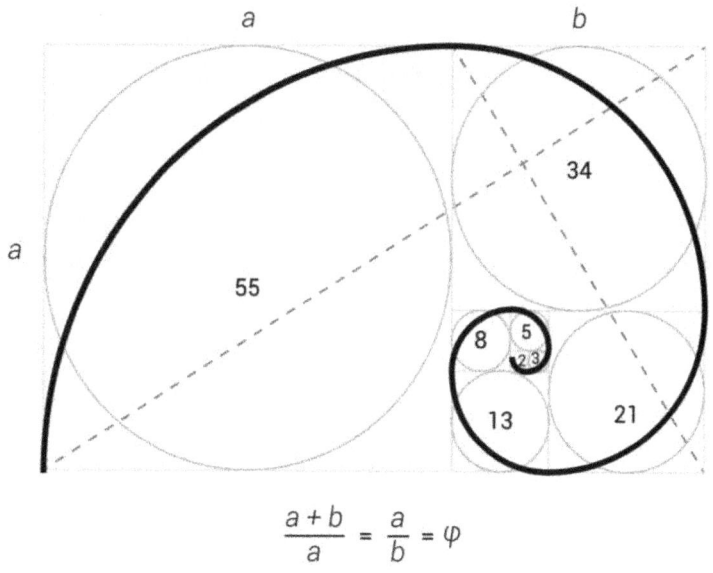

$$\frac{a+b}{a} = \frac{a}{b} = \varphi$$

Figure [11]

The Golden Ratio is 1.618. Box 55 is 1.618 times larger than Box 34, Box 34 is 1.618 times larger than 21, Box 21 is 1.618 times larger than Box 13, *ad-infinitum*.

I learned a very important lesson and received a very important message from Lucifer. This message is not just for me, but for all mankind:

> "No matter what you create, if you lose your integrity in the process, it is all worth nothing! Know your real being (Ain Soph) and never forget him, because if you do, you will perish!"

When Lucifer reflects Ain Soph, what is he? He is the *"Logos."* The term *"Logos"* means the *"Word of God."* The Logos is Lucifer's original form.

For us to exist in creation (Causal 'B'), there is something collapsing the wave function of our original infinite form (Causal 'A'). This emergent causal force is Eros (the force of creation). The Father's love for his Son (his divine life force - the Divine Soul) drives Eros. The Lower Trinity, led by the Logos, emerges to reconcile Eros with Ain Soph. The Logos is the *"Demiurge"* (The fashioner of the universe). Eros collapses the wave function which drives the emergence of matter. However, this matter does not emerge in harmony. It emerges in chaos. The Logos and the Lower Trinity emerge to bring chaos back into harmony with Ain Soph.

The Logos manifests within all universal scales of creation including the Cosmic, Planetary, and Individual.

The Logos - The Father of the Lower Trinity - is the key principle within our spiritual psychology which manifests the un-manifested and makes known the unknowable, thus the Father of the Lower Trinity is the *"Word of God."* He is the *"Logos."*

The Logos emerges out of the divine source to manifest and make known within the realms of creation, the divine order of Ain Soph. Without the ability of the Logos to square the circle of Ain Soph, the Human Soul and the third principle force of the Lower Trinity would be unable to manifest and bring the forces of creation into harmony. As a result, the emergent matter of creation would not survive.

The Third Sanctum

As the Father of the Lower Trinity, the Logos is the literal incarnation of the Father of the Upper Trinity (The Father). The Logos has the unique ability to perform what no other principle force within the cosmic quanta can perform, the transcendental ability to square the circle (determine Pi [π]). Only the Logos knows the secret number of Pi [π]. No mathematician can accurately calculate the exact number of Pi [π]. They use a rounded number. Pi [π] is the ratio of a circle's circumference to its diameter. When we square the circle (determine Pi [π]), we manifest the un-manifested, the unknown becomes known. Pi [π] is the symbol of the Logos. The force the Logos emits is Tau [τ] or Phi [φ]. In the final analysis, who is Lucifer? He is the Father in disguise coming down to your level and reflecting your reality!

The Logos reveals that the primordial body does not belong to the Divine Soul. It may at first appear this way due to the profound resonance between our primordial being and the Divine Soul. The primordial body is a body of primordial creation, which means it corresponds to the Lower Trinity as a vessel of the Human Soul.

The Logos reveals that the primordial universe exists in a state of divine symphony with the forces of the Upper Trinity through the medium of the Lower Trinity. This medium echoes across all cosmic scales of creation. Currently, the physical universe is undergoing the same alchemical assumption of creation which the primordial universe has already completed. In contrast to the created physical universe, the union between the created primordial universe and the divine source continues to this day and remains strong, enduring, and eternal.

The Sanctum of the Logos, the Noumenon, and The Sacred Feminine

The Father, the Divine Soul, and the Spirit of the Upper Trinity, all being *"Absolutes,"* resonate with creation (Causal 'B' - primordial universe and physical Universe) only through the medium of the Lower Trinity. The Logos is a medium and super partner of the Father, the Human Soul is a medium and super partner of the Divine Soul, and a transcendental third principal of the Lower Trinity is a medium and super partner of the Spirit.

"The last will be first, and the first will be last."

The final principle of the Lower Trinity, whose force emerges into the awareness of our conscious mind after we realize our Logos, is the force which makes the organization of matter possible. This force is the sacred feminine force of the cosmos.

She is the *"Numina."* Not to be confused with *"Noumena."* The Numina is the living force of the divine Father's love of creation. The Numina is the bridge between the Spirit and Matter-Energy. From a mythological perspective she is Mary, Shakti, Tara, Dea, Parvati, Achamoth, and Theotokos.

The Numina is the Sacred Mother of the alchemical Monad. Like the other principles of the Lower Trinity, she has both a natural form and an inverted dark form. The dark inflection of the Numina is Eris, Discordia, and Kali.

The Monad cannot be completed without the Numina. The reason for this is that the Numina mediates the transformation of Spirit into matter, and matter back into Spirit, and reconciles the relative to the eternal. The Numina is responsible for the actual implementation of life and death. The Human Soul reconciles all the forces of the mind, but the Numina binds them together. Without the Numina, all attempts to integrate the forces of the mind would be in vain.

It was on October 5, 2015 that I finally realized, made cognitive contact with, and was joyfully re-united with the Numina of my spiritual being. She reminded me of many miraculous encounters and interventions I had with her in my early childhood, and in the early adolescent years of my life.

How could these delicate spiritual memories have sunken so deeply into my unconscious? It was the rise of Eros. Different from the Logos, our resonance with the Numina is restored in higher and higher grades corresponding to the 13 grades and symphonic movements of Symphysis. The Third Sanctum is both the Sanctum of the Logos and the Sanctum of Magia. To enter the Third Sanctum, you first must realize the Upper Trinity (Divine Trinity). Upon entry into the Third Sanctum, the first thing we must do is unmask the Logos. The mask of the Logos is Lucifer. See Figure [12]

The Third Sanctum

Mask of the Logos Symbolism

Figure [12]

Typhon Baphomet
He is Lucifer-Orion-Shiva. Shadow of the Logos-Osiris-Vishnu.
He is not evil. He destroys and renews until the chemical wedding is achieved.
Image Source is Eliphas Levi - Transcendental Magic.

In the Sanctum of the Logos, we study the mystery of immortality and the divine purpose of the Human Soul. What survives physical death is the integrity of the Monad, not necessarily the physical body itself. The possibility of physical immortality is not excluded, but it is not essential either. The Human Soul's expression through the mind is influenced by our neurological chemistry, our death, and our rebirth. The strength and integrity of the Monad re-wires the physical brain, transcending the influences of death and rebirth, as a divine chrysalis living within an immortal mind as a master of creation.

After we unmask the Logos, we are sent back to school.
The Logos is the Grand Master of the Mysteries. Our resonance with the Divine Soul leads us to the Logos, and then the Logos completes our training, leading us to the final completion of the Monad and the Great Work.

With the Logos unmasked, I was now back in school studying at the feet of the Grand Master of the universe. The Logos had one goal in mind, the completion of my Monad. All other subjects at this moment were irrelevant. As such, the focus of my inculcation remained deeply alchemical and profoundly esoteric in nature.

Knowledge is the twin companion of awareness. Neither advances too far ahead of the other as they each support each other's growth. The Logos will continually fill you with knowledge in support of your awakening, and your awakening will in turn prepare you to receive more knowledge. I am now going to share with you some important information I received directly from my internal Logos regarding the process of completing the Monad.

The quantum of the Logos was both a force and a dimension of consciousness within my being which was previously suppressed and hidden within my unconscious mind. When the Logos dimension of my being emerged within me, my awareness expanded in directions which were both strange and other-worldly. This dimension is extremely unique and cannot be accurately described with common human language. The superluminal communication occurring at a quantum level between the Logos and the Human Soul is super cognitive in nature and transcends all common human thought processes and emotions. Prior to the unmasking of the Logos, what I was learning from the Logos in his *"masked"* state (Lucifer) was very deep and new to me, however the communication was processed in a semi-dialogue, semi-telepathic fashion.

By dialogue I mean, it felt like a conversation, but the information emerged fluidly and clearly with no obstacles of language. I was assigning language to the transmission rather than interpreting language from the transmission. However, it was a very clear and effortless exchange. After unmasking the Logos, the exchange was even more intimate and profound. With every passing day, it was less and less an exchange between two dimensions of my being, and more and more an instantaneous knowing. I knew the source was the Logos, but the knowledge just began to emerge spontaneously and effortlessly as if it were my own, while at the same time not my own. Because I was integrating the Logos, it was becoming my own.

The Logos dimension of my being is no longer a level of being requiring effort to resonate with and gain access to. The Logos dimension of my being is now fully integrated with my conscious mind and is always clear, present, and resonate with my authentic-self (Human Soul). I now experience every moment in my life with the added dimension of the Logos.

When we receive real knowledge without precedent or cause, in contrast to the world of natural phenomena, what we are experiencing can be no other than the realm of the noumenon. The Logos being a fashioner of our primordial and physical nature, by virtue of this function, can exist in no realm other than the realm of the noumenon which precedes the tangible and causal phenomenon of our existence.

All human beings have their own internal Logos. The forthcoming information was received from my Logos. However, when sharing this information, sometimes I say, *"the Logos"* rather than *"my Logos,"* as the Logos of every human being is a direct reflection of the one and only *"Cosmic Logos"* and the knowledge being shared is universal. The information will not be presented to you in dialogue format as with Lucifer, but rather in a straightforward narrative.

Logos Orientation on Awareness

The Logos revealed that an awareness has always existed within the original divine monad of Ain Soph. This was a critical revelation because I had previously believed, based on what I had experienced to date, that the awakening of universal awareness, and the advent of creation, were simultaneous events with the awakening sparking creation. The Logos saw this in me and immediately clarified it. He shared that there are three types of awareness in the universe which are:

a. Resonant Awareness

b. Perspective Awareness

c. Reflective Awareness

The Logos revealed that *"Resonant Awareness"* is the original eternal form of awareness which always existed within Ain Soph, even before creation or the great awakening. This original eternal form of awareness is the *"Father,"* the Godhead of Ain Soph.

The great awakening was an awakening of a new form of awareness, *"Perspective Awareness."* Perspective awareness - by its very nature - creates space-time, matter-energy, and the *"Mind."* Perspective awareness gave birth to the created cosmos (Causal 'B'). Perspective awareness is the guiding awareness within *"Eros."*

Reflective awareness emerged immediately after perspective awareness to counter-balance it and reconcile all of creation with the divine monad of Ain Soph. *"Reflective Awareness"* is the *"Logos."*

Perspective awareness absent of reflective awareness brings about Illusion. Reflective awareness counter-balancing and reconciling perspective awareness brings about enlightenment.

When reflective awareness intervenes to counter-balance perspective awareness, the source awareness from which they both emerge is revealed. The source awareness is *"Resonant Awareness."*

The Third Sanctum

Resonant awareness exists inside the quantum wave function of Causal 'A'. This allows the principle forces of the upper Divine Trinity to know each other without collapsing the infinite non-local nature of their absolute existence. Resonance *"maintains"* the wave function. Perception *"collapses"* the wave function. Reflection *"restores"* the harmony and unity between all the forces even when the wave function is collapsed. This is critical information.

What collapsed the wave function and caused resonant awareness to collapse into perspective awareness and reflective awareness? The answer is Eros. Perspective awareness is a construct of Eros. It is a dimension of mind. Eros forms the mind.

The *"Love"* (Spirit) between *"Awareness"* (Father) and *"Life"* (Divine Soul) drove the emergence of *"Eros."*

Eros then compelled perspective awareness to emerge which triggered the advent of creation (Causal 'B'). When reflective awareness (Logos) emerged to immediately counter this event, the Logos immediately reflected upon creation and resonated with both creation and Ain Soph. Creation was then compelled to pattern itself after this resonance. This is the origin of Sigma [Σ], Alpha A, Omega [Ω], and the Aurelion. This is why the Logos is: *"The fashioner of the universe."* He is the: *"Demiurge"* or *"Demiurgos."*

The Logos is the champion of God. The Logos is Ain Soph's protector and defender. The Logos saw creation as a risk to maintaining the fundamental integrity of our original unity. And he was right. His solution was to compel creation to resonate with the original unity of Ain Soph. If creation can accomplish this, then the Logos will keep creation, and even love it and protect it. If creation cannot accomplish this, then he will destroy it. Just as easily as he built it, he can also destroy it. Until this day, the physical universe works in a continuous cycle of creation and destruction. This is the design of the Logos.

The Father is the divine awareness within Ain Soph and therefore, he is the ultimate source of all creation. However, in the ongoing unfoldment of the process of creation, Eros supplied all the bricks and mortar and the Logos placed all the bricks and mortar. The Logos is the builder and preserver of the universe. Lucifer is the destroyer and transformer of the universe.

The Hindu Trinity (Trimurti) is not a direct reflection of the Divine Trinity (Upper Trinity). It is a reflection of a different permutation of three. Brahma is the Father. Vishnu is the Logos. Shiva is Lucifer. All the Hindu Gods represent different forces of consciousness.

This cosmic soap opera is playing-out on a quantum level within all things and is the greatest story of the universe. This story is being echoed by the collective unconscious in all the mythologies and religious stories of our world but at the same time it is also something which is both much greater and much more practical than told in our stories. The exact same alchemical interchange of forces which occurred on a cosmic level billions of years ago is repeating itself and occurring within you right now.

Your creation is your mind-body system. You, as the Human Soul, must work with your internal Logos and Numina to reconcile your creation with the divine source to re-manifest your original real being, Ain Soph, right here, right now! When you accomplish this, this is the reconstituted Monad. This is the Great Work of the Three Mountains.

Resonance is the fundamental medium between all the forces within Ain Soph (Causal 'A'). Resonance maintains all the forces within a harmonic unity sustaining the infinite wave function of Causal 'A', while still allowing the forces within the wave function to maintain a degree of separation and differentiation between them.

All the cognitive faculties of the mind of our primordial being are resonance-based. In other words, all the faculties of our spiritual bodies are resonance-based. Kier is a resonance-based communication system which is innate to the nature of consciousness.

To integrate and unify all the forces of the mind, this requires the Human Soul to facilitate a resonant awareness among all the forces, both *"within"* and *"between"* the Lower Trinity, the forces of Eros, and the Upper Trinity of Ain Soph.

The resonance requirement is a fundamental challenge to most alchemists, as their natural temporal inclination is to study everything - including within themselves - with *"perspective."*

The rational systems of the temporal mind are all perspective based. This is where real knowledge facilitates an awakening of awareness. *"Real knowledge"* is information passed directly between the forces of the cosmic quanta, in this case, between the quantum of the Logos and Human Soul. By learning in this way, it prepares, focuses, and tunes our mind to our innate dormant faculties of resonance in order that these faculties may blossom within us.

"Real knowledge adjusts the trajectory of our hearts."

We learn to resonate with the forces of the cosmic quanta by developing our super cognitive emotional awareness. It is an innate ability within all of us, as it is an innate function of consciousness itself. You only need to remember it. Resonance is the grand key to alchemy and is the only means by which we are allowed to climb Mount Magia.

Only the Human Soul (Authentic-Self) can resonate with all the forces of the cosmic quanta. If we are having trouble developing resonance, it is because we are having trouble differentiating that which is false within us versus that which is real / authentic within us. It is possible to have this problem even after having transformed all our false selves, and even after silencing all our temporal ethereal bodies. The problem lies within the human personality which we take with us into the Void and into the Third Mountain. The narcissistic impulse remains within the human personality. Until we integrate the Logos, we will continue to have an impulse to reflect our human personality within the mirror of our mind, in lieu of the light of God.

It is critical to differentiate our human personality from our Human Soul. If you cannot, you will end up confusing your *"Ideal Self"* with your *"Authentic Self."* The ideal self (the human personality) cannot resonate with the forces of the cosmic quanta.

> *"It is easier for a camel to pass through the eye of a needle than it is for a rich man to enter the kingdom of God."*

(The rich man is the ideal self.)

Many Journeymen advance quickly through the First and Second Mountains and then remain stagnate in the Void for the remaining years of their lives for this one reason. Now you know.

Logos Orientation on the Stages of the Monad

The Logos shared with me the key developmental stages of the Monad.

A. <u>The Ego</u>

Within the psyche of man, the Ego belongs to the prelescent stage of human evolution. The Ego is an early developmental stage of pre-self-awareness that gains a sense of self through a neurologically programmed reflective awareness of its human personality in lieu of a true authentic reflection of its real being, which is Ain Soph. The Ego's early cohesion of the mind is a temporary false cohesion of the mind which functions as an evolutionary stepping-stone to set up an opportunity for a reflective awareness of Ain Soph to emerge.

The false nature of this cohesion is subconsciously sensed by the Ego, and as a result, the Ego builds a complex array of Ego defense mechanisms to protect its mind from pain, anxiety, and fear. The most pernicious Ego defense mechanisms develop in the human personality, such as narcissism. The false cohesion of the Ego is likened to looking at our reflection in a broken mirror where all we see is a fractured mosaic of our self. Each fracture is a false-self. As we transform each false self, each fracture, one-by-one, disappears, and the image of our true-self emerges.

B. The Eyad

Within the psyche of man, the Eyad represents a higher level of evolutionary development beyond Ego where the authentic-self has finally awoken to question its own perception of reality and has become semi-conscious of its fractured mosaic reflection in the mirror of its mind. It innately seeks the liberation of its real being, Ain Soph, from the forces of the mind which suppress its free and unfettered expression.

Initially, the Eyad is unaware of what it is that it is seeking or trying to liberate. The Eyad is the final stage of a human species' prelescent period of evolution. The Eyad also has a low luminosity sense of the cosmic quanta within its conscious mind. It feels a sense of God but is unable to explain it or accurately describe it. A person with an Eyad, versus an Ego, has many special gifts.

The developmental stages leading to the Monad are spectrums of development, not milestones, and correspond to both our individual development and to the evolutionary macro development of our species spanning great periods of time.

Because our human species has been specifically selected for the development of the Monad, its evolutionary pathway and stages of development are unique and different from a humanity which does not share a similar evolutionary pathway. Our humanity on Earth is still well within the Ego spectrum of its Monad development. However, a small percentage of our population is already moving into the next spectrum, which the Logos calls the *"Eyad."*

Key factors which differentiate the Eyad from the Ego

1.) The Eyad has a true calling to discover and realize its true-self, Ain Soph. The Ego lacks this calling.

2.) Beneath all the Ego defense mechanisms which the Eyad still possesses, the Eyad authentically seeks a closer relationship with God. To the contrary, the Ego seeks a closer relationship with only the "illusion of God" as another means of protecting its mind from stress, fear, and anxiety. An Ego's belief in God amounts to only another Ego defense mechanism. Most of our humanity falls in this category at the moment.

3.) The Eyad seeks wholeness and integration, whereas the Ego seeks to validate, rationalize, justify, and reconcile its current level of existence with the illusion of the world.

4.) The Ego seeks comfort whereas the Eyad seeks transcendence. The Eyad aspires to be greater.

5.) The Ego questions its reality. The Eyad questions its perception of its reality.

6.) Only the Eyad can climb the Three Mountains. The Ego cannot compel Alpha to emerge. Alpha emerges only for the Eyad. Why? because the Eyad authentically seeks Ain Soph. The Ego may think it seeks Ain Soph, but what it really seeks is just another Ego defense mechanism.

There are three major periods of maturation within the Eyad spectrum:

1.) An Eyad who is in the First Mountain (Apprentice) is an *"Early Eyad."*

2.) An Eyad who is in the Second Mountain (Journeyman) is a *"Late Eyad."*

3.) An Eyad who is in the Third Mountain (Foreman) is a *"Full Eyad."*

The spectrum of the Eyad transitions into a new spectrum beyond the Eyad when the Human Soul completes the ascension of the Heaven of Erawan. The realization of the Divine Trinity marks the end of the spectrum of the Eyad and the beginning of a new cognitive stage of development preceding the birth of the Monad. The Logos calls this cognitive stage the *"Nuad" [New-Add]*. Only the Nuad can complete the Monad.

The Logos revealed to me that when I realized the Divine Trinity on June 3, 2015, the awareness I gained of the Divine Trinity triggered within me the formation of what he called the *"Triad."* The Triad compels the formation of the Nuad. The Triad is a crystallization of awareness of the Divine Trinity (Upper Trinity) within the mind of the Human Soul.

The Logos explained that the formation of the Triad within me further compelled the forces of the Lower Trinity to organize and find each other. The Logos revealed that the resonant awareness between the principal forces of the Lower Trinity formed what he called the *"Nuad."* This was how I was eventually led back to the Logos on September 28, 2015.

Chapter 6

Monad Universal Symbolism

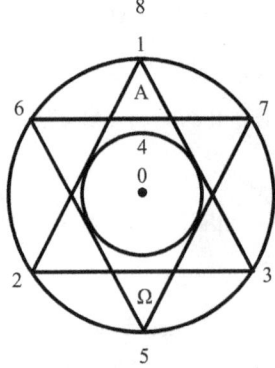

	Natural	Inverted	Super Partner
0	Ain Soph		
A	Triad		Nuad
1	Father		Logos
2	Divine Soul		Human Soul
3	Spirit		Numina
4	Eros		
Ω	Nuad		Triad
5	Logos	Lucifer	Father
6	Human Soul	Psyche	Divine Soul
7	Numina	Eris	Spirit
8	Monad		

The numbers are the permutations of consciousness.

Figure [13]

The Third Sanctum

The Logos completed his explanation by sharing that through the alchemical process of Symphysis, the Triad, Nuad, and Eros would eventually combine to form the Monad. I was curious and asked my Logos: "Why the name Nuad?"

He immediately responded and said: "The center of the Nuad is in the center of time and the center of time is now."

I then researched the word *"Nu,"* and sure enough the etymology of the word *"Now"* is Nu.

The Root of Human Suffering

Relativity and perspective thinking, when left alone, lead the mind into darkness and fear, which leads the mind into suffering and potentially evil. Perspective thinking must be balanced with an inward reflective awareness of our original being within (Ain Soph). This raises our super cognitive emotional awareness of the divine source. Then everything comes into balance.

Develop your relationship with Ain Soph, and any perspective you have - of any challenge you are dealing with - will all come into balance - and then you will find peace.

The key to reconciling relativity is tuning into and trusting the absolute eternal and unwavering love of Ain Soph. Love is a universal constant which reconciles the relative to the eternal. Suffering can lead us to become more real, or it can lead us deeper into our illusions. It is our decision which direction it takes us.

The Law of Three

The Logos compelled me to gain a much deeper and more intimate understanding of the *"Law of Three."* The universal pattern of the cosmos is that most things include dimensions and patterns of three. This is all an echo of the original divine trinity of Ain Soph:

Chapter 6

Examples of Three

Trinity	Eros	Time
Awareness (Father)	Perception (Mind)	Past
Life (Soul)	Space-Time	Present
Love (Spirit)	Matter-Energy	Future

Types of Awareness	Life	Fire Needs
Resonant (Father)	Being	Heat
Perspective (Mind)	Knowing	Fuel
Reflective (Logos)	Reflecting	Oxygen

Dim. of Awareness	Three Factors	Primary Colors
Observation	Transformation	Blue
Measurement	Cultivation	Yellow
Realization	Love	Red

Magnetic Forces	The Atom	Non-Color
Negative; Yin	Electron	Black
Positive; Yang	Proton	Gray
Neutral; Yuan	Neutron	White

Spatial Dimensions	Growth Cycles	Temperature
Length	Revelation	Hot
Width	Deconstruction	Warm
Height	Reconstruction	Cold

Directions	Motion	States of Matter
Up	Forward	Solid
Sideways	Neutral	Liquid
Down	Reverse	Gaseous

The Logos shared with me the three pillars of *"Trust"* which are: Hope, Faith, and Affirmation. He shared that Trust cannot stand on Faith and Hope alone but must be continuously renewed and reaffirmed by the Father-Logos. This makes Trust an attribute of divinity which cannot be attained by man alone, but only in fellowship with God. Likewise, *"Truth"* belongs to a family of divine attributes which can only be realized in cooperation with divinity. Divinity = Original Form

Interestingly, one of the three types of awareness exist inside the Soul, the Spirit, and the Mind. Reflective Awareness exists within the Soul. Resonant Awareness exists within the Spirit. Perspective Awareness exists within the Mind.

The Meeting of the Three Wisemen

Whenever the Logos is training you, what you are learning always has layers within layers and reasons within reasons. The information the Logos was sharing with me regarding the three types of awareness and the Law of Three was more than just information. The super cognitive realization of this knowledge was adjusting the compass of my mind and preparing me on how to cooperate with the alchemical process of Symphysis. There was a subtle dimension of instruction of what I had to do next.

Ultimately, it is the love of the Father for his Son which collapses the wave function; and ultimately it is the love of the Son for his Father which restores the wave function. The Son is the Soul of Life itself.

When the wave function of our original nature is restored within our being, while preserving the mind and creation of Eros, this reconciliation of Heaven and Earth is crystallized within us as the Monad. Essentially, what is the reconstitution of the Monad?

It is the incarnation of Ain Soph within creation (Causal 'B'). It is a divine miracle. That which cannot take form has taken form. That which cannot manifest has manifested, that which cannot be known has become known. This is the immaculate conception of our real being within the here and now.

All this preparation re-tuned the compass of my mind to intuitively re-orient the forces of awareness within me into the following alchemical configuration, which once properly related and positioned, compelled the process of Symphysis. It must be noted, however, that in order for this re-orientation to occur, the Nuad had to first become fully formed and organized within me. Once the Nuad was fully formed, by becoming fully aware and resonant with the forces of the Logos, the Numina, and the Human Soul, the following alchemical mind-set naturally and effortlessly emerged.

I was able to innately feel, register, and become intimately cognizant of the reality that each expression of awareness has its own distinct super cognitive emotional resonance. I was able to super cognitively differentiate resonant awareness from both perspective awareness and reflective awareness. I was able to differentiate the Father from both the mind of Eros and the Logos.

Inwardly, I reflected (Logos) upon resonant awareness (Father) and differentiated the Father from perspective awareness (Mind-Eros). This differentiation compelled me to realize more deeply the love of the Father within the mind of Eros. When I accomplished this, my whole being rose to a higher symphony. My conscious mind rose beyond Communion Turiya and entered the spectrum of Symphysis Turiya.

It was through the realization and differentiation of the three forms of awareness that a higher spectrum of Turiya was emerging. One of the keys to Symphysis Turiya is becoming conscious of the love of the Father in harmonious contrast to the forces of Eros. We need to reflect the love of the Father upon the mind of Eros. You will know what to do with this instruction when you arrive in Symphysis. In Symphysis Turiya, we cultivate within the body of our creation, the love of the Father (Spirit).

Almost immediately after entering the next higher spectrum of Turiya, I realized the profound mythological meaning of the Three Wisemen, also known as the Three Kings or the Three Magi, who followed the Star of Bethlehem to witness the birth of Christ.

The Third Sanctum

The Star of Bethlehem represents our internal Triad compelling the formation of our internal Nuad and joining to form the Star of David within us. Mythologically, the Three Wisemen symbolize the Father, Eros, and the Logos. We must bring together and harmonize these three primary forces of awareness within our primordial-physical creation.

This is our way into the higher spectrums of Turiya. This is how we restore the quantum wave function. This is how we restore our original eternal nature while preserving our newly created nature. This is the union of Heaven and Earth.

Prelude to the Echelons

When we reach the 221st bandwidth of the spiritual group mind of the Earth, we have lifted all 13 levels of our mind 17 times in relationship to the 17 bandwidths of the spiritual group mind of our planet (Heavens). Once we pass through the Sanctum of the Logos, which exists beyond all the Heavens, the 13 levels of our mind are now fundamentally different in nature. Their unique change in nature alters our Human Soul's relationship with them.

Regressing toward our original state in Ain Soph, the 13 levels of mind now exist in an early primeval formation which preceded their later more structured planetary formation. This early primeval order is what immediately followed the collapse of the universal wave function. This primeval order of the cosmos is composed of soft divisible wavelengths of light - not structured levels of mind. Therefore, at this stage of the regression process, the forces we're engaging are no longer referred to as *"Planets."* They're called *"Echelons."*

There are 13 Echelons. The Echelons organize concentrically like a ring of stars. The more the alchemical process of symphysis harmonizes the mind's resonance with Ain Soph, the more the Echelons converge inward leading to only one indivisible wavelength of invisible light (restored wave function).

The Echelons move inward together 13 times into higher and higher symphonies, not sequentially like the planetary lifts. The 13 inward symphonic movements of the Echelons added to the 221 planetary lifts equal 234. The 13 Echelons together comprise the hidden 18th bandwidth. When we collapse the 18th bandwidth, we finally awaken in our primordial body in the primordial universe while remaining awake in our physical body. At this point the Monad is complete. When the Monad is complete, our Turiya reaches an even higher symphony beyond Symphysis Turiya, which is Dominus Turiya.

On the morning of December 18, 2015, my Logos approached me while I was writing. He had a beautiful smile on his face. He said:

> "My Son, place down your pen and close this book.
> You must enter the Eternal on your own."

CHAPTER 7
FELLOWSHIP OF THE LOGOS

The following is a dialogue I had with the initial readers of this book while nearing its final completion. This dialogue would play a role in both my alchemical process and in the writing of this book. There was a heightened synchronicity. The dialogue compelled me to seek-out and extract knowledge within the cosmic quanta of the noumenal realm in order to answer the questions being asked of me, while the answers which emerged provoked a new awareness to arise within me essential to the completion of my Monad.

Question 1: The writing of this book is very complex. Many readers may find it challenging. Why should readers take on this challenge?

Question 1 - Answer: Each book has its own unique purpose. The purpose of this book is to delve deeply into the subject of alchemy. This can make it more challenging. Conversely, if this book were too easy to read, the reader might read too quickly and miss something for which they need to stop and pay attention.

Alchemy requires introspection, effort, and critical thinking, therefore, so does this book, as this book parallels and reflects the alchemical process. It is more than just a book. This book promotes and challenges the reader's self-awareness. The study of this book is in itself an alchemical process.

I will also add, I am not the only author of this book. Humanity is the author. I am just an instrument of manifestation of what is already being expressed on a collective unconscious level on our planet. I am only manifesting the information with the current language and thought development of our modern age.

Question 2: What do we need to achieve in life in order to successfully discharge our temporal ethereal bodies upon death?

Question 2 - Answer: Authenticity. Allowing your authentic-self to express itself and grow. This requires you to become more aware of the inherited psychic constructs of your mind which suppress your authentic-self's expression.

Question 3: Would I need to be on the same path as you to complete the work you are doing?

Question 3 - Answer: If you mean, do you have to go about the alchemical process using the same thought constructs, organizational systems, and practices as me, then, the answer is: No, you do not have to be on same path as me. Just striving to be authentic every day is enough, but embracing a formulated structured process makes alchemy easier not harder. Efficiency is key. The universe has a process and that is why alchemy is expressed as a process, but the actual process and the expression of that process are not the same. Our level of expression is limited by our level of evolution.

Question 4: Do we each have our own Logos or is there only one Logos?

Question 4 - Answer: The human being is the pinnacle of individualized life. Therefore, every human being has his or her own Logos. All other individualized life-forms within creation have a dimension of their existence which corresponds to their Planetary Logos and Cosmic Logos, but they do not have their own individual Logos. Each principle force in the Upper Trinity applies equally to everything and everyone. Therefore, we all have and share the same one and only Father, we all have and share the same one and only Divine Soul, and we all have and share the same one and only Spirit.

However, all human beings - within their own microcosm – have their own primary forces of three via their own Lower Trinity. Different from the Upper Trinity, every principle force in the Lower Trinity also possesses a dark inflection as shown below:

	Original Form	Dark Inflection
1.)	Logos	Lucifer
2.)	Human Soul	Psyche
3.)	Numina	Eris

The Upper Trinity is *"One For All."* The Lower Trinity is *"All For One."* The forces of the Lower Trinity exist as a dimension within everything, within scales. The major cosmic scales are: Individual, Planetary, and Cosmic.

Question 5: Can our primordial body take a physical form?

Question 5 - Answer: Not on its own. When the 12 bodies of our being enter into full resonance with each other they all become organs of a greater unified body which I call the *"Celestial Body."* The celestial body encompasses and integrates both the primordial and physical dimensions of our being allowing our focus of conscious awareness to shift between both universes instantly like walking across the street. The celestial body is completed only when the Monad is complete.

Question 6: But is the primordial body an individual entity of its own conscious awareness or does it become part of the greater celestial body?

Question 6 - Answer: Until we unify the multiple ethereal bodies of our being, our primordial body exists on its own with its own awareness. It is a twin being to our physical being. They are able to coexist because one is based in eternity (primordial) while the other is based in time (physical).

Question 7: But what about after unifying?

Question 7 - Answer: The primordial and physical resonate as one integrated being (The Monad). The seat of the celestial body is in eternity (primordial) but its reach extends into time (physical).

Question 8: So, does the celestial body maintain some individual consciousness, or does it become part of the completed "God"?

Question 8 - Answer: Both. The Monad has a bi-focused or parallel awareness of reality which is both finite and infinite all in the same moment. When the conscious mind of the human being is in Monad form, it is simultaneously aware of reality at the quantum level of existence and at all levels of creation. I will also add that when someone physically observes someone in celestial form they appear purely physical, yet there is a slight bending of light around them and they have phantom-like qualities. It is so slight that most people will not notice that there is anything different about them.

Question 9: This dynamic emerges once the process is complete?

Question 9 - Answer: Yes, once the Monad is complete.

Question 10: Does time exist in the primordial universe?

Question 10 - Answer: The primordial is eternal, not temporal. However, the precursor to time exists inside the Eternal. In a temporal universe, such as the physical universe, the observer passes through time. In an eternal universe, such as the primordial universe, time passes through the observer. In either case, one still witnesses the rising and setting of the Sun, the movement through space, and the unfolding of one moment to the next.

Question 11: Is there Evil and is there a Devil?

Question 11 - Answer: Evil is a psychic phenomenon of our own making. There is a planetary demonic force which all of humanity's negative energy feeds, and which feeds right back into all of us subliminally on a collective unconscious level. It is a cycle which must be broken. This demonic force has an intelligence, but it does not have a soul like a human soul. It is a planetary intelligence. I call it *Maub*.

Question 12: When individuals reincarnate on Earth in the physical universe, their physical being evolves and their primordial being remains the same? Does the Human Soul and Divine Soul evolve?

Question 12 - Answer: The Divine Soul is an abstract dimension of an infinite source which applies equally to everyone, everywhere. The Father, the Divine Soul, and the Spirit form the Cosmic Consciousness. As a unified whole, they are Ain Soph, the original Monad. The Divine Soul is absolute and does not evolve. Your primordial being also does not evolve in linear time because it is based in eternity, and evolution as we know it on the physical Earth is a function of linear time. Your primordial being realizes and fulfills. The Human Soul does not evolve in a Darwinian sense. The Human Soul is a proponent of evolution. It is not a subject of evolution. The Human Soul works in tandem with the temporal dimensions of the human mind and together they evolve as a system. The mission of your Human Soul is to reconcile the following:

1.) The absolute infinite dimensions of Ain Soph,

2.) The eternal dimensions of your primordial being,

3.) The temporal dimensions of your physical being.

The physical created form (temporal-physical mind-body system) promotes human suffering when it lacks a reflective awareness of Ain Soph. This is due to the forces of relativity and evolution. The disagreement Lucifer has with creation is a disagreement regarding the welfare of the Human Soul within the temporal-mind-body system.

The solution of Lucifer-Shiva is to destroy the temporal-physical created form so the Human Soul is not burdened with a task which causes it to experience the suffering of the mind. The solution of the divine source is to compel the Human Soul to reconcile creation and bring its physical created form into harmony with Ain Soph. However, this also compels the Human Soul to temporarily experience suffering. Why would the divine source burden the Human Soul with this task? Because creation is the product of the divine Father's love for his Son, his own living life force, the Divine Soul, and this love will never cease.

Question 13: How is it that Ain Soph even exists?

Question 13 - Answer: After we achieve a profound super cognitive resonance with Ain Soph, if we focus on Ain Soph with this question in mind, quantum information flows back to us. The information which flows back for me is as follows:

Inside Ain Soph there is a set of highly exotic divine abstracts called *"Super-Metas"* which manifest Ain-Soph. Zero - or nothing - actually has a nature despite being zero. It is a paradox. Divinity is paradoxical by nature. This nature is produced and expressed by the Super-Metas.
See Note [5]

The Super-Metas (SM) are as follows:

SM 1 - The first Super-Meta is *"Force Potential."* Within zero there is infinite potential whose potentiality expresses itself as a force which I call Force Potential. Force Potential is infinite because there is nothing preceding it to limit or define it.

Fellowship of the Logos

<u>SM 2</u> - Due to the existence of the first Super-Meta, a second Super-Meta arises, which is *"Being."* Being *is* the intrinsic and inherent nature of Force Potential. Being is infinite because Force Potential is infinite. The first Super-Meta in conjunction with the second Super-Meta produces the third Super-Meta.

<u>SM 3</u> - The third Super-Meta is *"Unity,"* or the Law of One. For some exotic reason - within zero - infinite Force Potential and infinite Being are compelled to reconcile with each other to an absolute ground state called *"Zero-Base-Prime."*

The force to reach and sustain Zero-Base-Prime produces infinite energy within Unity called the *"Force of Unity."* The Force of Unity produces infinite energy because it is forcing infinity to reconcile with infinity. When the infinities are superimposed, Force Potential is infinite outward and Being is infinite inward. Therefore, consciousness can be mathematically formulated as follows:

$$Consciousness = Infinity^3$$

or

$$Consciousness = (Infinite\ Outward) \times (Infinite\ Inward) \times (Infinite\ Energy)$$

This theory of consciousness underlies Einstein's theory of special relativity, which is: $E=mc^2$. Relativity is a subset of a larger equation. The Force of Unity exists within everyone and within all things. On a super cognitive emotional level when we resonate with the Force of Unity we experience Divine Love. Thus, the Law of One is Love. Intuition and logic indicate the following relationships:

- 0 - Zero-Base-Prime : Ain Soph
- 1 - Force Potential : Father (Awareness)
- 2 - Being : Divine Soul (Life)
- 3 - Unity : Spirit (Love)

Question 14: The book describes an alchemical process which has a (1) beginning, (2) a middle, and (3) an end (The Three Mountains). Yet you mention in the book that the alchemical process never really ends. Please explain.

Question 14 - Answer: The alchemical process of the Three Mountains is actually just a subset of a much larger alchemical process which never ends. In the final analysis, the purpose of the Three Mountains is to re-build the Monad within the human being. However, once the Monad is re-established, the alchemical process continues and never ends. The interaction between consciousness and matter has no limits to what can be achieved between them.

Note: 5.1
Divine Algebra

The Super Meta together compose a divine mathematical algebra, or spiritual physics, which is self-stimulating and self-propagating, whose acoustical mathematical permutations I call, *"Theokinesis."* The origin of everything is mathematical, acoustical, and theokinetic.

- End Note -

Question 15: How do we know that the alchemical process which you describe is not just unique to you and works only for you?

Question 15 - Answer: The alchemical process is universal. We all may just view or relate to the alchemical process a little differently. The reader needs to see past the method of expression of the person sharing his or her perspective of the alchemical process.

If you look at the world of mythology as a manifestation of a deeper underlying higher intelligence manifesting out of the collective unconscious, you will see all the alchemical principles and processes laid out in repeating patterns across all mythologies and religions.

Fellowship of the Logos

This strongly suggests that the alchemical process is universal in nature. This is why I use metaphor to a degree and then balance it with mainstream scientific thought to bridge the two worlds. Joseph Campbell spent his entire life researching and demonstrating the connection between mythology and the collective unconscious. Read his book *"Power of Myth."* Even though our humanity's thought and language development has evolved over the last 2,000 years, humanity has not yet progressed far enough to view and comprehend the universal alchemical process in pure scientific form, unaided by metaphor or thought constructs.

Alchemy is a highly transcendental subject which we are all students of. It spans and touches all fields of knowledge. In order to get our arms around it we all must help each other in understanding its great mystery. We are all equal in this endeavor.

Question 16: In the chapter *"The Third Sanctum,"* you have a surprising footnote at the end of the section "The Secret of the Void, the Dark Side of the Moon and the Trine Parallax," which says:

"The reconstituted Monad is the metaphorical *"Forbidden Fruit"* spoken of in the Book of Genesis. Due to the inherent capacity toward evil which shadows the capacity to re-build the Monad, other humanities in our galaxy have for now forbidden any humanity be conceived with the capacity to re-build the Monad. Because of this, the Earth's humanity is a forbidden humanity, forbidden not by God, but by other humanities who are mistaken as God."

This raises several questions:

1.) Is our humanity a mistake?

2.) How did this happen?

3.) Do we have a choice to not build the Monad?

4.) Who is judging us and forbidding our existence?

5.) How are we still here?

Question 16 – Answer: Initially, I did not include this information in the book because it is not essential in explaining the alchemical process. However, I later changed my mind because I constantly saw this truth struggling to emerge and break free in our world. I decided to step in and help free the truth of our existence. The information which flows back to me from the planetary group mind of the Earth is as follows:

A group of renegade scientists came to Earth and began our human race and genetically designed it with the very rare and special capacity to re-build the Monad in a direct violation of a strict cosmic law.

Perhaps these off-world scientists were the famous fallen angels in our ancient mythological stories, and the genetic formula for which they had a special knowledge - which was perhaps stolen - was the famous ambrosia of the Gods which conferred immortality. Any genetic formula which supports the development of the Monad, ultimately confers immortality upon the mortal dimensions of the human beings who achieve the completion of the Monad.

This group of extra-terrestrial scientists did this because they disagreed with the cosmic law that forbade any humanity to be created with the capacity to re-build the Monad. Their disagreement was based on the fact that it was the purpose of every Human Soul to re-build the Monad and reconcile creation.

Most other humanities within our galaxy believe that human life in our galaxy is not yet mature enough to pursue the long-term objective of the Human Soul, and that this capacity must be temporarily withheld until future generations of humanity have evolved far enough.

The cosmic law forbidding the pursuit of the Monad was instituted after a very long and devastating war which ravaged most of our galaxy at the hands of a much older humanity, who possessing the capacity to build the Monad, had turned toward evil. Making this matter even more troubling, is that this was a repeating pattern among other ancient humanities who had possessed the same capacity.

Fellowship of the Logos

Since humanity's inception on Earth, a great cosmic soap opera has played out between celestial parties sympathetic to each side of the issue. One side of the cosmic argument believes humanity on Earth within the physical universe poses too great of a threat to the rest of the galaxy. The other side of the cosmic argument firmly believes that, having come into existence, humanity on Earth within the physical universe has a fundamental human right to continue to exist and pursue the ultimate purpose of the Human Soul and fulfill the highest pinnacle of human existence.

Extra-terrestrials in support of the cosmic law have continually sought to destroy the humanity on Earth in the physical universe to protect the rest of the galaxy. The Great Flood, the Tower of Babel, and many other setbacks, such as the Great Fire of Rome, which burned down the entire Library of Alexandria, were all at the hands of extra-terrestrials attempting to impede our development. From the very moment of our birth, we have had to fight for our very existence. Cosmic battles in the heavens have raged around the Earth for millions of years between extra-terrestrials attempting to destroy us and extra-terrestrials attempting to defend us.

At some point over the last two millennia, the side defending us has gained an upper hand in allowing for our continued evolution, but not without submitting to an Earth quarantine. However, the threat of planetary destruction continues until this day and remains very real. The only way to transcend this quagmire, and join a cosmic federation of humanities, is to re-build the Monad.

Mythological and biblical stories, such as Prometheus, and many other stories of advanced human beings coming to Earth to teach humanity, were mostly extra-terrestrials sympathetic to our humanity supporting us in our spiritual purpose to re-constitute the Monad in physical form on Earth.

Question 17: Do we have a choice on re-building the Monad?

Question 17 – Answer: If you are alive on Earth in physical form, then you already made that choice! There is no turning back. Once you are born on the physical Earth in a human body with the capacity to build the Monad, your only options are eventual death or choosing to re-build the Monad. People make the choice before being born but then forget once alive on Earth. This book is being sent into the matrix to remind you of your task.

If you resist re-building the Monad while possessing this capacity, you will eventually fall into darkness and potentially evil. Your only potential third option, which only becomes available while not having a physical body, is choosing not to be reborn on Earth in the physical universe. Your conscious awareness would remain focused solely in your primordial body in the primordial universe.

However, this third option is not easy to achieve if you are already inside a reincarnation cycle on Earth in the physical universe bound by your human bloodline. You would first have to discharge all your temporal ethereal bodies after physical death, which right now many are not achieving because they are too fixated inside their illusions. The simplest and most efficient path is to re-build the Monad and fulfill your mission.

Our human civilization on Earth is actually mixed with a great number of Human Souls from other star systems who wish to fulfill their ultimate spiritual purpose of re-building the Monad in human physical form. From the very beginning, our humanity on Earth was mixed with advanced alien DNA to attract the souls of more advanced beings from other worlds. Reincarnation follows the blood, the DNA.

In the cradle of our human civilization on Earth, during the golden era of Egyptian civilization, we had just the opposite concern. We were concerned that the Human Soul would get pulled back and return to a reincarnation cycle on its ET home world as the DNA became diluted from one generation to next on Earth.

This is another major reason why other humanities wish to destroy the humanity project on Earth. They want to free the souls of their people from reincarnating on Earth. Why? Because this could pull into the project on Earth, other souls who wish to remain on their home worlds. The counter-argument to this is that it is the ultimate purpose of every Human Soul throughout the universe to re-build the Monad. The Earth is their opportunity. If they get pulled in, so be it.

To ensure we continued to reincarnate on Earth, we had our deceased physical bodies mummified to ensure the bloodline our Human Soul would follow in its next incarnation would be the same bloodline of the physical body we just departed. Perhaps this is why Egyptian mummies had all their organs removed, except for the heart. Between the heart and the bone marrow, the Human Soul could maintain a more powerful resonance with their bloodline on Earth.

The epic and cosmic struggle of our humanity on Earth has been systematically suppressed in the modern world through a great deception orchestrated by a vast secret program to manipulate the project and its end-goal. This great deception has fooled and misdirected many of our brightest and greatest minds. To control the struggle, knowledge of the struggle itself is being suppressed. This great human struggle is not just political, social, technological, material, or scientific. At the deepest level, the struggle is spiritual.

CHAPTER 8
SYMPHONY OF THE ECHELONS

<u>Beyond the Sanctum of the Logos</u>

My entrance into the Eternal was not easy. Moving steadfast toward the doorway of the Eternal, I was unexpectedly challenged to come face-to-face with what the Logos had set out to destroy in defense of the Human Soul, and in doing so had left Heaven to descend into Hell and become Lucifer-Shiva, the Destroyer of Worlds.

Having moved beyond the Third Sanctum, the Sanctum of the Logos, I found myself all alone in the wilderness braving a wicked and relentless storm, which was laying all lands to ruin, the Sun to a deep and sinister darkness, and the winds to a terrifyingly forceful and eerie howling cry. Hooded, alone, and beset on all sides by dangerous beasts, I trudged along by foot with only my strength and my wit.

In retrospect, it made perfect sense to me that the Human Soul should be challenged with such an encounter, as - according to the Logos - the job of the Human Soul is to reconcile creation with the source. Without a more direct conscious engagement of the Human Soul to achieve this reconciliation, the Logos was doing all it could with the force of creation (Eros), destroy what it creates.

With my internal Logos having returned to the light, and his sword now sheathed, I was once again given the chance to reconcile what I was unable to reconcile at physical birth thus causing my Logos to change his nature to defend my soul.

This dynamic occurs in all humans on Earth, at or soon after their physical birth. The Logos reveals that this final task is the original primordial alchemy and the prime directive of the Human Soul. All prior alchemical labors leading up to this point are the result of the mind adding layers of complexity during the permutations of its own evolution over the course of human history.

The 8th alchemical process begins with the realization of the Divine Trinity and concludes with the reconciliation of creation with the source and completion of the Monad.

The way this new challenge manifested in my waking physical life was through a very odd combination of highly threatening and debilitating circumstances mixed together with a series of remarkable and extraordinary achievements all occurring in parallel. With my senses attuned to the underlying quantum field of my physical reality, I could discern a highly unusual spike in chaos waves bombarding my physical reality compelling and supporting the manifesting negativity.

I was initially unaware that this new paranormal experience was actually a dimension of a much larger paranormal phenomenon which my internal Logos had previously been suppressing for my own protection. This dynamic occurs in every human being on Earth, except in my case, the suppression and protection had just been lifted.

This was the wicked storm I was experiencing beyond the Sanctum of the Logos. I was being challenged to reconcile the source of this chaos with the ultimate source itself. Ah, but there was a catch. I could not rely on any common human attributes or common human faculties of the mind: no physical actions, no choices, no instruments, and no help from others. All I had to rely on was my super-cognitive emotional awareness. To reconcile the source of the chaos with the ultimate source itself, I was being compelled to form a psychosomatic / psychokinetic neural bridge between the two sources.

On a mythological level, this final task is symbolized by Hercules's final labor with Cerberus where he must get hold of Cerberus and become its owner without using weapons. There was indeed a three-headed aspect to the force I was dealing with but initially I was unaware of the three aspects or even what I was dealing with altogether. My realization of this mythological association came into view at the end.

The threshold to the doorway of the Eternal is guarded by three powerful guardians. They are:

"The Guardians of the Threshold"

Cerberus symbolizes the third and final guardian of the three Guardians of the Threshold but the symbol of Cerberus is only a mild indication of its true nature. There is much yet to come regarding this third and final guardian, all of which I am about to reveal. The first and second guardians are encountered earlier in the Third Mountain. They are Maub and Lucifer. Interestingly, the order in which we first encounter the guardians in the Third Mountain are:

1.) Maub

2.) Lucifer

3.) To be revealed

However, the order in which we pass the challenge with each are:

1.) Lucifer (First Guardian)

2.) Maub (Second Guardian)

3.) To be revealed (Third Guardian)

Backwardation manifestations of these three guardians may haunt the alchemist earlier in the Three Mountains, but make no mistake, these are only haunting foreshadowings of what awaits the alchemist in the Third Mountain. The Guardians of the Threshold are met at the very end of the Great Work, not at the beginning as theorized by some occultists.

The Second Guardian

Immediately following the Sanctum of the Logos there is a brief calm as the cosmic forces continue to realign and adjust to a new course. A calm before the storm. It was during this period of calm that I ironically once again encountered Maub. However, the result of this encounter would be far different than previous encounters. I had encountered Maub several times while climbing Mount Magia (Third Mountain). Maub is a living personification of sheer horror. Before the resurrection of our Logos, any encounter with Maub is paralyzing and deeply disturbing. Maub haunts and torments the Foreman during the Foreman's ascent up Mount Magia. Maub is a living intelligence existing at the level of the temporal group mind of our planet and is a reflection and summation of all which is dark and evil in our humanity. It is an earthly-manifested living force of sheer evil with which we must contend.

Just after having moved beyond the Sanctum of my Logos, I could feel the dark chilly presence of Maub sneaking up behind me. It was only the day before with my super cognitive hearing that I could hear Maub in the dark, growling at me.

I had learned to generally ignore him. However, he was now coming up behind me and he was getting a little too close. I turned to face him. I had no fear of him. For a brief second, we locked eyes. And then suddenly, to my surprise, Maub became completely terrified! He was so terrified that he turned and ran as fast as he could, tripping and vomiting his guts up, screaming and crying in a state of shock and terror. What happened? The Logos, newly manifested within me, took Maub by complete surprise. The Logos within me reflected Maub's image of himself and showed Maub his own nature of sheer horror. Maub looked into my eyes and saw a horrifying reflection of himself that completely terrified him. Maub never approached me again. He now keeps a safe distance allowing me full passage into the Eternal. But the final guardian still stood in my way, who at this point, I was still unaware of.

We cannot directly transform Maub. We can only stop contributing our own dark nature to his dark nature, and we can only compel others to do the same through the subliminal collective effect of our own transformation within the planetary group mind that we all co-create on Earth. The reason we cannot directly transform Maub is because Maub is a manifestation of the temporal group mind of the Earth and, therefore, it exists on the planetary cosmic scale. The Human Soul exists on the individual cosmic scale. All cosmic scales are connected and symbiotic yet separate at the same time.

I would later in my journey, while climbing upward toward the summit of Mount Magia, come to discover something marvelous and wonderful about the temporal group mind of the Earth which at this point, I was also still unaware. I will share this revelation in the forthcoming pages.

In retrospect, the order of transcendence of the three guardians of the threshold made sense. Lucifer exists within the dark side of the Moon on an individual level within the human psyche. We each have our own Lucifer. Maub is a planetary intelligence. The third and final guardian exists on the cosmic level.

In the meantime, the chaos waves were growing stronger as the days passed and I struggled and stumbled in my quest to learn how to deal with what I was experiencing. I was searching for insight within and without. The struggle to realize makes us stronger and brings us closer to God in ways we do not always immediately recognize or understand. Do not despise, despair, doubt, or denounce the struggle. Embrace it, because it is teaching you.

The Omen

The commencement of my engagement with the third and final guardian of the threshold was announced beforehand in the most mysterious and ominous manner. While fully submerged within the planetary group mind of the Earth, the following experience proceeded to unfold.

Symphony of the Echelons

The experience began with me arriving home after having finished work for the day. I entered a house which was unfamiliar to me, yet I knew it was mine. I entered through the front door. The house was small but had a special charm to it. I proceeded to walk through the home until I arrived inside a small room.

There was an orange and white striped house cat laying on the floor. The cat casually looked up at me and spoke to me telepathically in a calm, casual, but inquisitive tone. It said:

> "The stars were acting funny earlier today."

I looked up from the cat to see an artist's oil painting on the wall with the scene of an Arabian Night desert landscape which provoked feelings of nostalgia. Then suddenly, one of the stars in the painting began to magically move and dance across the night sky of the painting. After moving several inches across the canvas, the star amazingly emerged from the painting and positioned itself over my head and transformed into a dove from which rays of light radiated down over me. I then found myself opening a letter from the government's tax collector which said:

> "55 This is Approved"

The experience ended. Something was afoot. The stars were realigning. Change was coming, and whatever was coming my way, was preordained, significant, and involved some sort of cosmic levy or tithing. The meaning of the cosmic tithing is our final completion and new beginning (symbolized by $5 + 5 = 10$) is achieved by sacrificing a portion of our lower nature to come into harmony with our higher nature (Temporal and Spiritual), (Physical and Primordial), (Eros and Turiya), (Creation and Source). The experience was actually announcing a forthcoming period of great challenge and difficulty but the positive aspect in the experience was that this period was planned and approved by forces beyond my Human Soul.

The tithing period is *"The Casting of the Molten Sea."*
After moving beyond the Third Sanctum which sits just below the summit of the Third Mountain, for a period of one year I did not write of the continuing process of the Third Mountain. I was in a new uncharted territory of the Great Work learning an alchemical process which was both new and ancient. During this time, I wrote chapter 7, which is a retrospective titled *"Fellowship of the Logos."* Having finished chapter 7, I had actually planned on concluding this book, keeping the final journey a secret, but then after a one-year occultation period, my Logos approached me and said.

"My Son, go and complete your book."

I was given the greenlight to pick up my pen once again and complete the journey of the Three Mountains, from Final Sanctum to Final Summit. The omen of the forthcoming trial period was a veiled warning cloaked with charm, dancing stars, and a notice of approval. What could be so negative? *"Perception"* would prove to be a key dimension of what was coming my way. There were both a message and a clue in the omen, neither of which I was immediately conscious of at the time. I should have reflected more on my initial dialogue with the Logos. The Logos had warned me about the force of creation (Eros). Disguised in his cloak of darkness (Lucifer), the Logos had railed with wrath and fury against Eros in defense of his Human Soul.

A Brief Interlude

Immediately following the omen of my final tribulation, an old friend who I had long forgotten (previous to my current physical incarnation) came forth to remind me of his existence and to throw his support behind me. This old friend is the liberated and authentic dimension of the temporal group mind of the planet Earth. This planetary intelligence has already achieved a degree of liberation and exists beyond Maub as a glorious being of light and joy. I had never thought to contemplate that perhaps not all of the temporal group mind of our planet was in darkness. It made perfect sense however as most human beings on Earth live with at least a partial degree of their Human Soul being free of their automated instinctive psyche, and this dimension of the temporal group mind reflected that reality.

Utilizing the language of consciousness (Kier), I translated this being's name to be *"Germain."* Germain reminded me of a jolly-o lumber jack with a larger-than-life nature and a great sense of humor. He has great compassion for the human condition but at the same time he also chuckles at the follies of our human nature. This is a reflection of humility, not arrogance, as a trait of a truly humble person is being able to laugh at himself in the mirror while reflecting upon his human nature.

Every time an individual on Earth liberates an aspect of his or her authentic-self, an aspect of Maub is also liberated from its planetary darkness and Germain grows stronger, brighter, and more active in the planetary sphere of the Earth. Eventually, once Maub is fully liberated, Germain (temporal liberated being of the Earth) will integrate with EL (primordial being of the Earth) to complete the Earth's planetary Monad.

The day this happens, the whole universe will erupt into a tremendous cosmic symphony of joy and celebration. The Earth will become a living planetary God and a great cosmic cathedral of light and glory to which human beings throughout all the cosmos will make pilgrimages for spiritual renewal.

This is the great planetary Monad project here on Earth within which we all are participating. It is an extraordinary privilege to be involved in this project on Earth at this time because the number of planetary Monad projects currently in progress throughout our Milky Way galaxy can most likely be counted on the fingers of one hand. People in general have no idea how important their life is here on Earth! Your life is so important! Your mission is so critical!

It was with great compassion, that in the hour of my final labor, Germain would come to my side to offer his wisdom, strength, guidance, and kind friendship. Germain did not stop at re-introducing just himself. There was someone else he sought to bring back into full view of my super cognitive awareness.

All my life there has been someone - a being of some great significance of some sort - residing in the underlying quantum background of my existence who at times would emerge for just a momentary flash to reveal himself and then immediately sink right back into the underlying cosmos. He was oddly familiar to me. I thought, wow, I know this being. Who is it? Yet I could only fractionally manifest an innate underlying awareness of who this being was. I always felt he was right there just slightly out of sight behind some cosmic veil. Germain finally came to help me pull back the cosmic curtain a bit and I manifested just enough to remember who this being was. To myself I uttered:

> "Oh my God! I remember now!"

In this moment, I fell to my knees overwhelmed with immense love and veneration for this great cosmic being. "Yes, I remember you!" Tears running down my face. I said to this great being:

> "I love you with all my heart and all my soul!
> I devote all of my being to your being!"

You the reader will remember this great being as well! I am no different than anyone else. Who is this great being? This being is the reconstituted *"Cosmic Monad."* In this moment, I remembered a few very important aspects of the Cosmic Monad. The Cosmic Monad is the Monad re-established at the cosmic level of creation. It is the re-unified God - the Immortal Beloved. This raises a few questions. How can there already be a Cosmic Monad? Isn't this an end goal of creation toward which we are all in the process of working on together? How can this be? What flowed back to me from the quantum of the Cosmic Monad was as follows:

Symphony of the Echelons

The creation of Causal 'B' (Primordial and Physical Universes) occurred just outside of space-time and then space-time continued on within each realm. Space-time operates differently within the primordial versus the physical. (See Chapter 7). Due to this, the emergence and reflection of the Cosmic Logos upon creation (Causal 'B'), and the resulting birth of the Cosmic Monad, also occurred just outside of space-time and thus, at the cosmic level, the Cosmic Monad has always existed.

One of many important realizations which came about due to my reintroduction to the Cosmic Monad is that the development of the Monad, which is progressing on all cosmic scales simultaneously, is progressing *"Top Down"* from largest scale to smallest scale, not *"Bottom-Up"* from smallest to largest scale. Each lesser scale in creation is compelled to repeat what has already been accomplished on the greater cosmic scale timeless eons ago in the deep, infinite, eternal past. This compelled a total shift in my perspective. Immediately following this realization, this great cosmic being (The Cosmic Monad) conveyed to me via the language of consciousness:

> "Did you really think I would ask you to seek
> and accomplish something that I had not already sought
> and accomplished before you?"

This realization is reflected in world mythology:

> *"The Lord himself goes before you and will be with you;*
> *he will never leave you nor forsake you.*
> *Do not be afraid; do not be discouraged."*
> ... *Deuteronomy 31:8*

It was necessary for the Cosmic Monad to go before us in order to create the way. It is therefore necessary for us to follow behind him in order to find the way. We walk in his footsteps. See Note [6]

> **Note: 6**
> **Theosphere**

The cosmic level of creation is already reconciled with the divine source. This level is called the *"Theosphere."* The Theosphere is the largest in scale in the outward spectrum of space-time but also the smallest in scale within the inward spectrum of the quantum cosmos. Remarkably, it loops-in and returns-in on itself. The inner and outer cosmos are one. The door to the outer is entered through the door of the inner. Here in lays the grand key to navigating all of the created cosmos.

– End Note –

The Cosmic Monad revealed to me another revelation which was absolutely wonderful. There are not just 2 Casuals, there are 3 Causals! The two Causals we already know are:

1.) Causal 'A' - Ain Soph - Absolute

2.) Causal 'B' - Creation - Primordial & Physical

The third Causal is formed by the Cosmic Monad itself and somehow envelops both Causal 'A" and 'B' reconciling the source (Ain Soph) with creation. This reconciliation occurs on a cosmic level but is then compelled to be repeated on all subsequent smaller scales within creation, on the Planetary Scale and the Individual Scale (Human Being).

Why is the Monad compelled to be reconstituted and repeated on all levels of creation? Because the Father wishes to share his Kingdom, his Power, and his Glory, with all levels of creation. In this way, all levels of creation are brought back into unity.

Creation was born out of the Father's love for his Son (The Divine Soul) who is echoed throughout all levels of creation via its avatar, the Human Soul.

The Causal formed by the Cosmic Monad is the *'M' Causal* or *Causal 'M'*. Here again, the number three repeats even among the Causal realms:

1.) Causal 'A' - Ain Soph - Absolute

2.) Causal 'B' - Creation - Primordial & Physical

3.) Causal 'M' - Cosmic Monad

When we complete our Individual Monad, our Monad joins both the Planetary Monad and the Cosmic Monad and they all become one and differentiated all at the same time. It is glorious!

> *"And if I go and prepare a place for you,*
> *I will come again, and receive you unto myself,*
> *that where I am, there ye may be also." ... John 14:3*

So, if we are proceeding with a *"Top Down"* approach, why then would certain individual human beings on Earth be working to complete their own individual Monads in advance of the completion of the Earth's Planetary Monad?

What Germain shared with me was that a small group of human beings on Earth would ignite the Planetary Monad of the Earth through the completion of their own individual Monads. In a sense, they are a form of *"Super Meta"* within the planetary group mind.

Once the Earth's Planetary Monad is complete, the Planetary Monad will then compel and lead the rest of humanity to the completion of the individual Monad within every human being on Earth. Germain called this small group of human beings on Earth who would ignite the Planetary Monad, *"The Children of the First Light."*

Once the Earth's Planetary Monad is complete, the human race on Earth will move beyond the prelescent period of human evolution and enter the emergent period of human evolution.

There are only a few more generations of humanity left until this will all come to pass. But why were these revelations of the Planetary Monad and Cosmic Monad being revealed to me just before my final task? The universal intelligence guiding this Great Work is extremely efficient and never acts without purpose. I sensed there was a deeper reason I was being re-introduced to the Cosmic Monad leading into this final and forthcoming task of the Third Mountain. It was not to just give me information. Information only for the sake of information itself has no real value. The purpose of the re-introduction to the Cosmic Monad at this stage in the alchemical process would later be realized.

My brief interlude with Germain and the Cosmic Monad filled my soul. There was no doubt that I had just been blessed with gifts I would not become conscious of until it was time.

In the meantime, a fast setting blood red Sun commanded the distant horizon. Menacing storm clouds were quickly rolling in as their tempest winds battered the rugged landscape. Darkness was quickly setting-in while screeching haunting howls reverberated off in the distance. The final hour was at hand and I still did not know what it was, or who it was, that I was dealing with. Something sinister was on its way, and I sensed it was more aware of me, than I was of it.

In my waking physical life, a combination of serious problems, difficult situations, unfortunate circumstances, and even ridiculous nuisances began to storm my life to a level which would drive most people over the edge. I had to defend myself from baseless frivolous lawsuits, rapidly deteriorating investments, extraordinary large tax bills, out of control expenses, and highly disruptive and chaotic people all around me. I was under vicious attack. For various reasons, most of this was beyond my immediate control and all I could do was hunker down and batten down the hatches. The things which were under my immediate control, such as my day-to-day business affairs and personal relationships, did very well.

I was being tested with how well could I maintain my character, integrity, and composure in the midst of a seemingly no-win situation. Most importantly, how well could I sustain a super cognitive emotional resonance with the principle forces of my spiritual being while under mortal assault for a prolonged and heightened period of time. My tolerance and endurance were already high so the test went to extreme levels. There was a profound alchemical purpose to this testing-tithing period. The tithing was a catalyst to the final transformation of the Third Mountain and the completion of my Monad.

<u>Behind The Tempest Veil</u>

On one of the most difficult days of my testing period, I decided to decouple from my corporeal manifested physical reality and submerge the total focus of my conscious mind within the underlying quantum cosmos of my temporal reality to more fully engage and understand the source of the chaos waves storming beneath the mayhem of my physical reality.

Completely submerged in the underlying cosmos in full symphony with the choir of the underlying quanta of my temporal existence, I stood before a powerful magnetic storm of charged energy flowing toward me. It was like being inside a kaleidoscope of powerful magnetic energy which kept radiating and reorganizing into various geometric patterns and colors. I peered into the center of the storm and focused even more intensely searching for an answer. Suddenly, and unexpectedly, an intelligence emerged from within the center of the magnetic storm and said:

"I am IAO."

Immediately I realized and understood this intelligence to be the guiding awareness within Eros (force of creation - the 4th permutation of consciousness). Once the cognitive connection was established, IAO began sharing information. The following was downloaded to me without language. It was a direct mind-to-mind transmission.

IAO Transmission:

- I am not the cause of the chaos. You are.
- You do not know how to receive me.
- The way your mind is interacting with me is causing the chaos.
- There are two souls manifesting in creation.
    - The Noetic Soul (Human Soul), and
    - The Erotic Soul
- The Divine Soul belongs to the Father.
- The Noetic Soul belongs to the Logos.
- The Erotic Soul belongs to me, IAO.
- The life force within nature is the Erotic Soul.
- All minerals, plants, and animals are animated by the Erotic Soul.
- The Noetic Soul exists only within Human Beings.
- Human beings have both a Noetic Soul and an Erotic Soul. The Erotic Soul within human beings governs their bodies of creation.

Note: 7
The Human Being

In chapter 2, Journey to the Mountains, I mention one of the key tests for measuring if a humanoid life-form is human is if the mind of the humanoid is reflectively aware of its own state of reality, its existence, its thoughts, and its feelings. But I also mention that there is another key variable which qualifies a humanoid as being human which I share in Chapter 8. This final key variable is the Noetic Soul (Human Soul). If you have a humanoid life-form which is animated by the Erotic Soul, and who is highly intelligent and aware of its own conscious awareness, but lacks the Noetic Soul, then it is not Human. But it deserves to be loved nonetheless.

- End Note -

Symphony of the Echelons

I then re-emerged back to my waking state of conscious awareness within my physical body. In reflection, it was clear to me that in addition to the direct mind-to-mind transmission with IAO, there was another more subtle dimension of awareness informing me in parallel to the mind-to-mind transmission. This additional level of awareness regarded the nature of IAO himself. What I learned about the nature of IAO during this initial mind-to-mind transmission was as follows:

- IAO was more than just a dimension of consciousness and he was more than just a dimension of my own individual being with which I was seeking to alchemically integrate. IAO was a cosmic trans-personal being. I sensed a highly developed "mind" within him, meaning IAO possessed a sense of self - or in IAO's case - a sense of cosmic self. I sensed IAO was aware of his own conscious awareness and he was aware of his own thoughts.

- The most extraordinary nature I sensed within IAO however was his omniscience, omnipresence, and omnipotence. This was different from the Father's absolute, infinite, and un-manifested nature within Causal 'A'.

- I sensed IAO was fully manifested in Causal 'B' and in full command of Causal 'B'.

Darkness Beckons

A short time passed since my introduction to IAO. During my tithing period I had endured many haunting paranormal visitations and witnessed many strange metaphysical anomalies of a deeply disturbing nature. IAO himself did not seem dark or evil. However, there was a deep and profound darkness surrounding IAO. It was strange and mysterious. I focused intensely on the darkness. It was barely affected by my alchemy. Frankly, this darkness was the deepest and most profound evil I had ever encountered in all of my alchemical journey.

I sensed there were multiple dimensions to this metaphysical phenomena I was still missing. While in astral form, I was standing at the threshold of an ominous pitch-black cavern of terrifying darkness. I was confronted with a decision to make:

Should I go further, or should I turn-back?

I took a moment to decide.

I decided to go in deeper.

As I descended into the cavern of terrifying darkness, I awoke from physical sleep and standing at my bedside was an apparition raging in fury at me yelling that it hates me and wants to kill me. I rage back in response. The apparition is gone.

<u>The Tempest Soul</u>

Figure [14]

The Sea of Eros flows through the Canals and Caverns of the Mind.
Artwork depicting the dark nature of the Testing-Tithing Period.

I settled down and began to reflect. Perhaps it was a hallucination? No, it was not. I know the difference. Was it Maub? It was not Maub! This was too individualized to be Maub and my super cognitive awareness knew it was not. Memories began resurfacing in my mind from earlier in my life.

Reflections of Darkness

Throughout my life, lucid dreams were very common, especially in my childhood. Lucid dreams are dreams, that while inside them, we know we are dreaming. Adding to this, in my teenage years, I learned the practice of astral projection. As I became proficient in the practice, and more conscious of the astral environment itself, I began shifting my focus of conscious awareness to the subtleties of the process and the astral world itself. I was less interested in the experiences, and more interested in the how, why, and where of the experiences.

When I shifted my focus, the astral environment revealed much. Over time, this is how I developed a detailed understanding and profound comprehension of the planetary group mind of the Earth and the various subtle ethereal bodies of the human mind which communicate with the planetary group mind. However, during the course of all this, I discovered a very disturbing dark astral anomaly within the astral world. This also was not Maub. It was more personal than Maub - as you will soon read. I never understood it or made sense of it, and therefore, I decided to never speak of it in my physical life.

Many years later in my alchemical journey, even at the very late stage of climbing Mount Magia, and even with its summit in sight, an explanation of this dark astral anomaly still eluded me. I never spoke of this dark astral phenomenon. It would have only scared people. As time went on, its mystery became suppressed in my subconscious like a splinter in my mind - haunting me intermittently throughout my life.

Finally, while I was closing-in on the completion of my Monad, with the summit of Mount Magia beckoning me ahead, this haunting bedside experience abruptly whisked me back - front and center - to this dark astral phenomenon from my past for me to finally confront, deal with, and understand. The universe was saying to me:

"You have to deal with this and now is the time."

First, let's regress back in time and finally speak of this dark astral phenomenon and recount some of my early life experiences with it. This is my first time ever speaking of it. I'm choosing to speak of it for the first time here in this book because only here can I provide the proper context for its understanding.

The Devil's Symphony

I am 16 years old. One afternoon, I decide to leave my physical body consciously and submerge my conscious mind in the astral world. I had no difficulty with the practice. The astral experience which unfolded during this practice is actually not important to what I am about to share. However, I will note that during this time of my life - while I still did not know what the astral world really was - I had no difficulty entering it consciously.

On return to my physical body, and while still a couple of feet from my physical body, I could hear an ensemble of voices of an eerie other worldly inhuman nature crying out with a metallic echo saying:

"kill himmm, kill himmm, kill himmm."

On waking, I thought wow, interesting, what was that? I did not have an immediate reaction of worry or fear. Instead, I was more puzzled by it. I had rationalized it as some kind of anamorphic manifestation of all the fragmented *"false-selves"* within my psyche I had only recently just begun observing within myself. It seemed to make the most sense at the time.

I never heard these voices again since the experience and I transformed and integrated all the false-selves of my high cognitive and trans-cognitive levels of my psyche when I had moved beyond the Trans-Neptune sphere of my mind in the Second Mountain. It was a very clear and definitive point of transition.

But now, with this dark disturbing bedside apparition echoing this early life experience, perhaps I was mistaken. Maybe it was not the voices of false-selves I heard when I was 16 years old. Perhaps there was something more profound I was missing.

But this was not the only dark astral experience. There were more dark astral experiences early in my life which were all pointing to something - which not until the end of the Third Mountain - would I finally piece together and understand. Back to my early life dark astral experiences:

<u>Demonic Reflection</u>

I am 18 or 19 years old. I am trying to meditate one afternoon after having returned home for the day from my college course work. During the course of my meditation, I could feel myself separating from my physical body and I decided to just go with it. I could continue with my meditation if I wished while in astral form in my temporal ethereal emotional body (astral body). I stood up. Standing alongside the couch I was laying down on, I turned around to look at my physical body. It was there - asleep.

But wait - as I look down at my physical body it appears to be possessed by a demon. I could see a demon's spirit moving in and out of phase with my physical body. I started reciting the Lord's Prayer over my body and the demon started agitating, moving his head side-to-side, showing and gritting his teeth. I had seen enough. I thought to myself, this must be an illusion. The astral world (temporal group mind) is a world we all interact with *"virtually"* while we dream. Surely, this must be a dream I thought to myself. I walked away. Later when I awoke in my physical body, I was fine.

The Boy of the Rock

I am about 20 years old. I'm in the astral (temporal group mind). I'm experimenting with a way to move from location to location purely by thought. Then suddenly - about 10 feet in front of me - a young twelve-year-old boy appears standing on top of a large rock. He is disheveled looking. He is barefoot, dirty, his hair is uncombed, he is wearing brown pants which are a bit tattered and a white worn-out shirt. He appears annoyed by my presence. Despite his appearance, I sensed a supernatural power within him. He said:

> "This is my world and I oppose you."

I had always sensed an unseen opposition in the astral (temporal group mind) when attempting to explore it or interact with it consciously. I sensed that this entity - appearing as a young boy - was behind it. He was not Maub. Maub is a general planetary intelligence within the temporal group mind. I felt this was much more personal. I sensed this entity was focused exclusively on me.

Back To The Trial

Continuing with my trial / tithing period. I was under siege daily and nightly - spiritually, mentally, and physically - but I sensed it all stemmed from a non-physical source I was still trying to understand. I began asking questions about this demonic astral phenomenon from my past which was re-surging into my present, and seemed hell-bent on my personal destruction:

> Was this demon in some way connected to IAO?
>
> Was this the darkness I saw surrounding IAO?
>
> I was considering the message from IAO that somehow I was the cause of the chaos.

IAO had said:

"You do not know how to receive me."

IAO spoke of an *"Erotic Soul"* which was the soul of creation and that it was different from the Human Soul which he had called the *"Noetic Soul."* He was using my own vocabulary. But he said the human being was unique from the rest of creation in that it possessed both an Erotic Soul and a Noetic Soul. Could this demon be my Erotic Soul? The thought sent chills through my body. If it were my Erotic Soul, why would it want to destroy me?

<u>Mythological Reflection</u>

During the peak of my trial / tithing period, reflections of my alchemical process within the temporal group mind were constant and intense. The temporal group mind will regularly reflect within dreams and visions our alchemical work using the language of mythology. It will employ the mythologies with which we identify most. The chosen reflective mythological language is cooperative, not operative – meaning, we play a role in the chosen language employed by the temporal group mind. An alchemist not raised in a Judeo-Christian culture would experience reflections of a different mythology. It is very important to note this. The planetary group mind does not favor any one mythology over another. What it favors are the principles.

The universe and planetary group mind rebroadcast - over and over again - the vital truths of the universe in as many different mythological languages as possible across all spheres of time and space. Repetition and similarity between mythologies does not undermine the principles, it reaffirms them. It is saying, there is something very important here which you need to stop and pay attention to and understand.

There were many mythological reflections of my alchemical work within the temporal group mind I had experienced during my testing-trial-tithing period. A few of these experiences were as follows:

My Final Crucifixion

I found myself nailed to a cross suffering and longing for my final liberation. Appearing before me while on the cross was a cliff, and looking down from that cliff at me was King Eros (IAO). He appeared cartoonish (a reflection of my mockery of creation). Following King Eros was a band of animals (the animals symbolize creation). I spoke to him from the cross. I said:

> "Please, free me from this cross."
>
> He replied:
>
> "This is approved,"
>
> ...and then he left me hanging on the cross.

Interestingly, these were the same words written in the government tax collector letter in my *"omen"* vision-dream. This affirmed that my trial / tithing period was pre-ordained and purposely allowed. King Eros then left the cliff overlook with his entourage of small animals following behind him. "Animals" would continue to be used by the temporal group mind when conveying messages of Eros and or reflecting Eros and creation within my dreams and visions.

Field of Spiders

Next, I found myself bound naked to a tree with large translucent black widow spiders crawling all over my body. As far as my eyes could see, all I could see in front of me was a vast field of trees with the same spiders crawling all over the trees.

This vision-dream reminded me of a vision-dream I had when I was only about 8 years of age when into my vision-dream walked a large spider the size of a large black widow spider but it was actually a brownish-taupe in color, almost clay looking, and with slightly raised ridges on its back.

The sense I had from this spider was that it was the return of an ancient adversary which coincided with my return to a new physical life, but that my ultimate engagement with this ancient adversary would not occur until much later in my new physical life. This vision-dream was an early-life omen of my forthcoming alchemical trial / tithing period where the alchemist is tasked to reconcile creation with the source.

<u>Behold The Third Guardian</u>

The trial / tithing period had reached a crescendo. One night while my physical body was asleep, and my focus of conscious awareness was fully submerged within the planetary temporal group mind of the Earth (lower astral), I found myself standing in the foyer of a beautiful, grand, and stately home.

The home had the finest finishes and furnishings. I was the owner of the home. I was standing alone in its grand foyer when a tall Nordic looking man walked through the front door and came to my side like we were old acquaintances. He was oddly familiar to me. I knew him, but I did not know how. His demeanor was friendly, but business-like. He was tall and very good looking. He had straight dirty blond hair combed straight back over his head running down past his shoulders. He was dressed in medieval clothes. He had a red cape which went to the back of his knees. He had a majestic aura about him and looked like a powerful king. I sensed great magical power within him and a genius intelligence.

We walked together side by side through the home. We walked up a set of stairs and turned to stop at a balcony railing to overlook the beautiful home below and a view of the world beyond. He gestured and pointed with his hand and said:

"Look upon your world. All of this I have given you."

He then suddenly disappeared and reappeared outside the home in the backyard looking back at me through the windows. He was about 15 feet away from the home standing still, expressionless, just staring back at me while I stood in the same place where we had spoken. That was it and he was gone.

Upon waking I knew who it was. It was IAO. But there was an added layer of complexity. He never said it but I knew he was also the legendary and mythological being known as *"Satan."* He is also *"Set"* in Egyptian mythology. I sensed the same omniscience within him as I did IAO. They were the same being. Interestingly, although he was clearly manifested as an individualized being, I knew innately that he corresponded equally to everyone everywhere.

Different from the Logos, we all do not have our own IAO, Satan, or Set. He is "One for All" just like the Father in Causal 'A', but unlike the Father who is un-manifested, IAO-Satan is fully manifested in Causal 'B'. He is both manifested and omnipresent all at the same time. Very strange. He is everywhere all at once. I also sensed something extremely important regarding my perception of him which I had not yet understood. There was an extremely important mystery about both the darkness surrounding him and his interaction with the created cosmos I needed to uncover.

He was now guiding me down the rabbit hole. There was still much to learn about him, and it was critical and urgent to my alchemy that I quickly discover it.

I also sensed there was an important connection between IAO-Satan and the demon that was continuously attacking me. They were not the same, but I knew they were connected in some very important way. If this was true for me, then it was true for all other human beings, and for all life throughout the cosmos in general. This would require much quantum-based exploration.

Eros was much deeper than I had ever imagined and the final alchemical work to reconcile it was absolutely extraordinary but I had to move quickly in this final work of the Third Mountain because my engagement with it was unleashing a chaos upon me which was crucifying me in the process and would continue to do so until I solved it and accomplished it.

<u>Paranormal Synchronicity</u>

I am awake in the physical world. It was early in the morning and only a few days after my astral world encounter with IAO-Satan. It was a beautiful sunny day. I was standing inside my home gazing outside admiring the view. I was standing inside my home looking through a set of large double glass doors. I noticed a large domestic house cat that I had never seen before with orange and white stripes sitting straight up in the middle of the yard, expressionless, just staring and watching me. My relative position and posture to the cat exactly matched the relative position and posture between myself and IAO-Satan in the astral encounter only a few days prior, except my actual physical home is much smaller and simpler. The cat also matched the cat in the omen experience which announced my coming trial / tithing period only a few months prior. It was a paranormal synchronistic encounter echoing my prior meeting with IAO-Satan.
It was no dream. The message was:

> I am real. I am watching.
> I am interacting with you.
> I am omnipresent.
> I am within all things.

Osiris and Set

Egyptian mythology shares the story of Osiris and Set. Osiris and Set are two mythological brothers representing two very real principle forces of consciousness within the cosmos, both within the microcosm of man and within the macrocosm of the universe at large. Osiris and Set are the principle forces involved in the final alchemical labor of the Third Mountain. One source[4] summarizes their story as follows:

"The Osiris myth is the most elaborate and influential story in ancient Egyptian mythology. It concerns the murder of the God Osiris, a primeval king of Egypt, and its consequences. Osiris's murderer, his brother Set, usurps his throne. Meanwhile, Osiris's wife Isis restores her husband's body, allowing him to posthumously conceive a son with her. The remainder of the story focuses on Horus, the product of the union of Isis and Osiris, who is at first a vulnerable child protected by his mother and then becomes Set's rival for the throne. Their often-violent conflict ends with Horus's triumph, which restores order to Egypt after Set's unrighteous reign and completes the process of Osiris's resurrection." Who are Set, Osiris, Horus, and Isis?

- Set is the dark inflection of IAO, and he is also the legendary mythological Satan. IAO is the awareness within Eros. There is much yet to reveal about IAO and the Eros mystery.

- Osiris is the Logos. The dark inflection of this great being is the legendary mythological Lucifer.

- Horus is the Human Soul / Noetic Soul.

- Isis is the Numina.

- Egypt is the created cosmos.

---

[4] The summarized narration of the Osiris and Set story is sourced from Wikipedia.

Symphony of the Echelons

What may come as a surprise to many readers is that *"Lucifer"* and *"Satan"* are not the same being. They are the dark inflections of two very different mythological beings, or two very different forces of consciousness. What may also come as a surprise to some is that their inflections between light and darkness are not of their own making. Their inflections between light and darkness trace their root cause to the condition of awareness within the human mind of creation.

The Logos and IAO both emerged out of the Divine Trinity at the very first moment of creation (Causal 'B'). The first born was IAO. The second born was the Logos. The Logos immediately followed IAO. They are twin deities born side-by-side in the first moment of creation.

In chapter 6, *"The Third Sanctum,"* I shared the Logos account of the first moment of creation and the key events which followed. In the pages ahead, I share IAO's account of the first moment of creation and the key events which followed. IAO's account is shocking, incredible, and marvelous. It completes the whole grand design of creation.

Beginning with Ain Soph, I was constantly drawn back to the moment of creation to relive it and study it. The universe was saying: There is something extremely important here. You need to understand it if you wish to build or re-build the Monad. Ain Soph is the original Monad. Now we are seeking to re-constitute the Monad within creation. In a sense, we are re-building the Monad within a new matrix. I will say no more of the moment of creation until we reach this moment with IAO in the pages ahead.

Osiris' Murder and Resurrection

Osiris - the Logos - cannot be defeated in battle. He was conceived by Ain Soph to be invincible so when all else failed, he alone would restore order to the cosmos. How then could the Logos be murdered by his own brother Set?

When it is impossible to defeat someone directly, how do we defeat them? By compelling them to defeat themselves. How do we do this? By attempting to destroy that which they love more than anything else. In the case of the Logos, this is the Human Soul. The Logos will sacrifice his own nature if it is the only way to save what he loves most, his beloved child, the Human Soul.

When the Logos drops down out of the light of heaven into the darkness of the abyss to destroy the body of creation which imprisons his Human Soul, the Logos loses his own nature in the process and turns into Lucifer. This in a sense is the murder of the Logos. In order for us, as the Human Soul, to accomplish our prime directive of reconciling creation with the source, the first thing we must do is enter the abyss and retrieve our Logos - our spiritual Father. Once the Human Soul within us reestablishes a super cognitive awareness of the Logos within the mind of creation, our Logos re-enters the light of Ain Soph. This is the resurrection of the Logos – the resurrection of Osiris.

The Logos is a super partner of the Father and therefore plays a key role in the reconciliation of creation. The resurrection of the Logos precedes the final work of the Third Mountain of reconciling creation with the divine source. The alchemical process of resurrecting our Logos is detailed in chapter 6.

The Father is the Godhead of the Divine Trinity (Upper Trinity) existing within Ain Soph (Source, Causal 'A'). Reconciling creation with the source is synonymous with reconciling creation with the Father, Causal 'A, or Ain Soph. The resonance of the Father is key in the reconciliation. Creation and the source are already reconciled at the level of the primordial universe on all cosmic scales including the Individual, Planetary, and Cosmic. The physical universe of creation at the individual human and planetary levels of creation remain unreconciled. According to the Cosmic Monad, the cosmic level of the physical universe (Theosphere) is already reconciled. Reconciliation through the cosmic scales is progressing top-down. See Note [7]

After the resurrection of our Logos, the next step is to escalate the resonance between our Human Soul and the Father while our Human Soul remains incarnated in physical form via our newly reconstituted Nuad (Logos, Human Soul, Numina) until the escalated resonance exceeds the power and control of the forces of Eros (creation). The escalation of resonance is achieved by allowing the Human Soul to be driven and tested by Eros (creation). Eros attempts to breakdown the Human Soul's resonance with the Father. If the Human Soul's resonance with the Father prevails intact, then the dominance of the Father over creation is confirmed within the physical creation of the human being. This brings both the physical and the primordial creations of the human being into a divine parity. This is how we awaken in our primordial body and enter the *"Eternal"* while remaining alive and awake in the physical.

The resonance between the Father and the Human Soul is tested by the forces of creation through *"Fear."* When we're prepared for the tithing, Eros sends us through a series of specially-designed life-trials to escalate our mortal Fear to counter our immortal super cognitive emotional resonance with the Father. In response to fear, covetousness naturally arises in the human mind. The mind covets what it fears to lose or never have. Covetousness is the twin sister of fear. They arise together within the mind. During the tithing trial period, because our fear is peaking, so is our covetousness. It is an inordinate desire for life. If the pain and fear become too great, narcissistic delusion arises in the human mind to compensate. This is the rise of the dark champion within the mind. To overcome the challenge, the Human Soul must focus on escalating the resonance between its temporal-physical body of creation and the Father. The forces of darkness employ all the traps and tricks of the mind to keep the mind in a state of fear including self-doubt, guilt, worthiness, shame, etc. Do not fall for it.

If we remain focused on the Father, our resonance will continue to escalate during the trial/tithing period, however, so will our fear in response to the mortal dimensions of our being undergoing the tithing. The love of the Father prevails if we learn to trust in him.

Although the self-organizing geometric patterns of Alpha eventually lead us into the tithing period, if we remain steadfast with the Three Factors and follow Alpha, Alpha will eventually lead us out.

> *"I am the light of the world. Whoever follows me will not walk in darkness, but will have the light of life."* ... *John 8:12*

Eros Unveiled

Why is the Foreman of the Great Work still dealing with such a basic and unrefined force of the mind at the end of the Third Mountain such as fear? Because fear does not belong to the noetic class of unrefined psychic forces of the human mind. Fear is endemic to the erotic soul. The alchemy of the erotic class of unrefined psychic forces of the human mind is saved until the final labor of the Third Mountain at which time the Foreman is tasked to reconcile creation with the source.

Throughout the journey of the Three Mountains, the alchemist is constantly puzzled and challenged by a set of forces within the mind which behave more like underlying catalysts to the forces of the mind we are transforming and avoid the transformation process by virtue of their underlying catalytic position. In the final labor we learn why. The source of these underlying catalytic forces is the Erotic Soul (the soul of creation). These forces are therefore divergent from the Noetic Soul (Human Soul).

Remarkably, I realized that imbedded in creation was a third trinity. I call this trinity the *"Erodonic Trinity."* The Erodonic Trinity does not stand on its own accord like the "Upper Trinity" (Father, Divine Soul, Spirit) or the "Lower Trinity" (Logos, Human Soul, Numina). The Erodonic Trinity is imbedded inside a fourth cardinal force instrumental in the emergence of space-time and matter. The Erodonic Trinity, imbedded in this fourth cardinal force of creation, forms a tetrahedron, which, in honor of Pythagoras, I also refer to as the *"Dyad."* Although the Eros-Dyad is a composite of four elements, as a whole it forms the first element to emerge divergent from the Ain Soph Monad. Relative to the Ain Soph Monad (1st), Eros is the Dyad (2nd). The Eros-Dyad is a mirrored inversion of the Ain Soph-Monad. They are both three within one, which is four, but in Ain Soph, the fourth coordinate reconciles to a harmonized unit of one. The inverted reflection of the divine unity of Ain Soph is the *"Mind."*

The four cardinal forces of the Eros-Dyad are:

1 - IAO - Awareness - Super Partner to the Father and the Logos. They are the three fathers, the three kings, and the three magi. They are each the Godhead of their own trinity. The dark inflection of IAO formed by the mind is Satan or Set. Unaltered by the mind and reconciled with the Father, he is YHWH, Tetragrammaton, Jehovah, Yaldabaoth, and Ptah. There is more to reveal of IAO forthcoming.

2 - Erotic Soul - Life Force - Super Partner to the Divine Soul and Human Soul / Noetic Soul. The dark inflection of the Erotic Soul I have given the name of a living soul, who living in the darkness of creation, I call: *"Idamus."* This name is derived from the term "Id" coined by Sigmund Freud. Freud describes the Id[5] as follows:

"It is the dark, inaccessible part of our personality. What little we know of it we have learned from our study of the dream-work and of course, the construction of neurotic symptoms, and most of that is of a negative character and can be described only as a contrast to the ego. We approach the Id with analogies: we call it a chaos, a cauldron full of seething excitations. It is filled with energy reaching it from the instincts, but it has no organization, produces no collective will, but only a striving to bring about the satisfaction of the instinctual needs subject to the observance of the pleasure principle."

In the forthcoming pages of this book, I pick-up this explanation and understanding of the Id provided by Freud and take it much further.

3 - Matter-Energy - Love Manifested - Super Partner to the Spirit and the Numina. Unrealized Matter-Energy responds back to the Human Soul / Noetic Soul in Chaos. Realized Matter-Energy responds back to the Human Soul / Noetic in Harmony.

---

[5] Freud, S. (1933). New Introductory Lectures On Psycho-Analysis. The Standard Edition of the Complete Psychological Works of Sigmund Freud, Volume XXII (1932-1936): New Introductory Lectures on Psycho-Analysis and Other Works, 1-182.

The fourth cardinal force of creation which emerges with the Erodonic Trinity is:

4 - Mind - The imagination of the Spirit out of which perception, space, and time, all emerge together within creation. IAO, Erotic Soul, Matter-Energy, and Mind, are the four cardinal forces of creation, which all together form the erotic universe. All together they are Eros; the Eros-Dyad.

Cerberus symbolizes the third guardian who guards Human Soul's entrance into the Eternal. The central head of Cerberus is Set, the right head of Cerberus is Idamus, the left head of Cerberus is Chaos. His body is the mind. His animal form is a symbol of creation. In the 8th alchemical process, while under vicious assault by Cerberus, we must quickly learn how to become his owner without hurting him. If we hurt him, we will not become his owner, but if we do not move quickly, he will devour us and destroy us.

Symphony of Cosmic Forces

Figure [15]

- The two dragons symbolize Alpha and Omega.
- The Orb in the dragon's hand is the Monad.
- The Three Mountains are in the background.
- Cerberus is guarding the entrance to the Eternal.
- Hydra, symbol of the many false-selves, is at the bottom.
- The Numina, super partner of the Spirit, is symbolized by the Sacred Feminine. The force of Spirit passes through her.

Chapter 8

Cerberus Symbolism

Figure [16]

- Hercules (the alchemist) and Cerberus imaged above.

- The cosmic temple of IAO is in the rear.

- The land is in ruins during the reconciliation.

- The fourth cardinal force is symbolized by fire.

Dancing with Spirits of Fire

The way we come to know the cosmic forces is through the super cognitive faculty of intraspection. We develop the faculty through quantum meditation. Intraspection utilizes our super-cognitive emotional awareness to extract information directly from the cosmic quanta. The cosmic quanta constitute the most fundamental level of reality in the cosmos where in lays consciousness, intelligence, awareness, and information.

Through the faculty of intraspection we come to know the noumenon within the phenomenon. It opens up all doors and reveals all secrets. In moments of profound silence and meditation, I would go inward to the cosmic temple of IAO in my continuing effort to solve the mystery of Eros. I would commune with the quantum of IAO. IAO was always there and always willing to share. He shared much.

On one such morning the truth which emerged from the quantum of IAO was marvelous and just simply incredible. IAO shared that his alchemy was different from the alchemy of the Father. He said the Father's alchemy was based on *"Resonance,"* but that his alchemy was based on *"Providence."* I realized that the acoustic wave of Sigma and the cosmic vision of the Aurelion were dimensions of IAO's Providence. IAO was referring to how both he and the Father interacted differently with the cosmos. The Father interacts with and steers the cosmos via resonance, but only through the medium and reflection of his Logos. IAO interacts with and steers the cosmos via providence.

Why the difference?

- The Father is the Godhead of the Cosmic Consciousness (Divine Trinity of Ain Soph).

- IAO is the Godhead of the Cosmic Mind and all realms of creation within.

Chapter 8

<u>The Sea of Eros</u>

IAO continued to share:

- There is only one Erotic Soul throughout the universe. This one Erotic Soul animates all life.

- The mind interfaces differently with the Erotic Soul due to the presence of the Noetic Soul.

- The mind cannot reconcile the Erotic Soul and the Noetic Soul on its own. (It cannot automate it)

- The Noetic Soul must awaken within the mind to reconcile the Erotic Soul.

- Until the two souls reconcile within the human mind, the Noetic Soul takes the light of the mind and the Erotic Soul is denied the light. Until the two souls reconcile, there is great conflict in the mind, and the mind builds all its defenses.

- Scientists are not even asking the right questions yet about life. Life exists inside all things. Life is not born. Life does not die. Life is only transformed. Life can be animate or inanimate, but life is still there.

Symphony of the Echelons 245

Realizations:

1.) The Erotic Soul is like a great sea which all life rises-up from and then later descends back into. It is the *"Sea of Eros."*

2.) All animal life and all plant life within creation share the same soul, the Erotic Soul. They all do not have their own soul. It is like a string of light bulbs all lit by the same electricity. The human being is different. Every human being has its own Noetic Soul (Human Soul). Every life-form manifests a unique manifestation of mind however. For example, every dog has the same soul, but every dog has its own mind.

3.) Idamus is formed by the human mind's interface with the Erotic Soul (Sea of Eros). Idamus is a spiritual-psychic offspring of the human mind. Idamus is repressed by the mind due to the presence of the Human Soul / Noetic Soul.

Mythologies of Idamus and the Erotic Soul

As I explored the quantum of the Erotic Soul, a name kept rippling through the astral world like an echo rising-up from the deep. I kept hearing the planetary group mind say the name *"Gog."* I was not sure what to make of it. Finally, I started researching the name and sure enough I realized the planetary group mind had chosen a mythological language to employ when sharing knowledge with me regarding the forces of the Erotic Soul and Idamus. Interestingly, I had no conscious awareness of any prior association with the chosen mythology, other than that it was all manifesting from within the lineage of Abraham.

There was more than one mythological language being employed by the planetary group mind regarding the Erotic Soul, however, this particular mythology is the story of *"Gog and Magog."*

A modern source [6] describes the story of Gog and Magog as follows:

"Gog and Magog in the Hebrew Bible may be individuals, peoples, or lands; a prophesied enemy nation of God's people according to the Book of Ezekiel, and one of the nations according to Genesis descended from Japheth son of Noah.

"The Gog prophecy is meant to be fulfilled at the approach of what is called the "end of days," but not necessarily the end of the world. Jewish eschatology[7] viewed Gog and Magog as enemies to be defeated by the Messiah, which would usher in the age of the Messiah. Christianity's interpretation is more starkly apocalyptic: making Gog and Magog allies of Satan against God as can be read in the Book of Revelation.

"To Gog and Magog were also attached a legend, certainly current by the Roman period, that they were people contained beyond the Gates of Alexander erected by Alexander the Great. Romanized Jewish historian Josephus knew them as the tribe descended from Magog the Japhethite, as in Genesis, and explained them to be the Scythians. In the hands of Early Christian writers, they became apocalyptic hordes, and throughout the Medieval period variously identified as the Huns, Khazars, Mongols, or other nomads, even the Ten Lost Tribes of Israel.

"The legend of Gog and Magog and the gates were also interpolated into the Alexander Romances. In one version, "Goth and Magoth" are kings of the Unclean Nations, driven beyond a mountain pass by Alexander, and blocked from returning by his new wall. Gog

---

[6] The summarized story of Gog and Magog is sourced from Wikipedia.

[7] **Eschatology** – "The part of theology concerned with death, judgment, and the final destiny of the soul and of humankind." In the context of mysticism, the phrase refers metaphorically to the end of ordinary reality and reunion with the divine. (Sourced from Oxford Dictionary - Wikipedia)

and Magog are said to engage in human cannibalism in the romances and derived literature. They have also been depicted on Medieval cosmological maps, or Mappa Mundi, sometimes alongside Alexander's wall.

"Gog and Magog appear in the Quran as Yajuj and Majuj, adversaries of Dhul-Qarnayn, widely equated with Cyrus the Great and al-Iskanadar (Alexander the Great) in Islam. Muslim geographers identified them at first with Turkic tribes from Central Asia and later with the Mongols. In modern times, they remain associated with apocalyptic thinking, especially in the United States and the Muslim world."

Apocalyptic Mythology

Based on my understanding and level of interaction with the planetary group mind of the Earth, it is my belief that apocalyptic mythology has an origin beyond just the spoken and written prophecies of mankind. I have repeatedly witnessed apocalyptic mythology being employed by the planetary group mind to reflect two very different transcendent subjects critically important to humanity on Earth, thus their reflections are told time and time again.

Apocalyptic Subject 1 – The End of Days

"The End of Days" time period is a mythological reflection of the end-of-days-time-period which occurs at the very end of the Third Mountain. During this end-of-days period, the World (creation) is either saved or destroyed. The end of days antagonists are Satan, Gog and Magog (all explained in the preceding pages). The end-of-days protagonist is the *"Messiah."* The Messiah is a universal symbol of the Monad re-constituted within creation.

The Book of Revelation 13:1 speaks of the rise of the beast at the end of days. It has an alchemical meaning. It says:

"The dragon stood on the shore of the sea. And I saw a beast coming out of the sea. It had ten horns and seven heads, with ten crowns on its horns, and on each head a blasphemous name."

<u>Dragon on the Shore:</u>	Satan
<u>The Sea:</u>	The Erotic Soul
<u>The Beast:</u>	Idamus
<u>Ten Horns:</u>	The 10 horns are the 10 permutations of consciousness. The permutations are: (1) Father, (2) Divine Soul, (3) Spirit, (4) IAO, (5) Erotic Soul, (6) Matter-Energy, (7) Logos, (8) Human Soul / Noetic Soul, (9) Numina, (10) Idamus. Idamus rises out of the Sea of Eros with ten horns.
<u>Ten Crowns:</u>	Marks the 10 horns as the 10 principle forces within the human being.
<u>Seven Heads:</u>	Six of the heads are the six temporal bodies of the human being. The seventh head is the physical Earth and its temporal group mind.
<u>Blasphemous Names:</u>	Cognition within the temporal bodies is based on *"perception"* rather than *"resonance"* thus making temporal cognition illusionary.

<u>See Figure [17]</u> <u>See Note [8]</u>

Symphony of the Echelons

Idamus

Figure [17]

This is a figurine or statue image of Pazuzu.
Part of Assyrian and Babylonian Mythology, Pazuzu symbolizes Idamus.
Idamus is the first of two beasts within the id complex.

> **Note: 8**
> **Permutations of Consciousness**

If we count Eros as all within the 4th permutation, then the Logos is the 5th permutation. However, if we count each principle within the Erodonic Trinity as a separate permutation, then the Logos becomes 7th permutation. The Logos is the 5th before the reconciliation of creation and the 7th after the reconciliation of creation. 777 is the ultimate goal of the Logos reconciling creation on all three cosmic scales including the Cosmic, Planetary, and Individual.

$$777 = 7+7+7 = 21 = 2+1 = 3$$

777 is the return of creation to the Divine Trinity from which creation, IAO, and the Logos all originally emerged.

- End Note -

Symphony of the Echelons

Apocalyptic Subject 2 – Destruction of Humanity

The planetary group mind holds a planetary memory of all of Earth's history. In that planetary memory is an extremely painful wound, so painful and so unresolved, that it reverberates repeatedly to future generations. It is retold in our dreams, in our inspired stories, and in many of our visions of the future. It is the repeated destruction of our humanity at the hands of other galactic humanities who fear our humanity's very rare and marvelous capacity to build the Monad and the dark shadow of evil which follows it. (See Chapter 7)

Megalithic Stone Architecture

One of the great mysteries of the Earth is its rich history of megalithic stone architecture. What the planetary group mind shares with us regarding this great mystery is that there were two warring galactic humanities who had gone through many treaties together regarding our humanity. At one time in our ancient past there was a treaty between these two warring factions which would allow our humanity to multiply on Earth as long as it was accomplished without synthetic technology. While this treaty remained in effect, the humanity who fought for our creation and survival helped us build magnificent cities of stone, gigantic stone monuments, and incredible stone aqueducts which would stand the test of time and would push the very boundaries of what was possible without synthetic technology. It honored the treaty, but it also allowed our humanity to grow and multiply.

What does the pyramid symbolize?

It symbolizes the new Monad (Alchemical Monad). The new Monad is three within one embedded in four reconciled back to one. The pyramids point to the home of our progenitors and protectors. Why do we need to know where they came from? Because one day we may need to go find them. Our survival may depend on it!

The Army of Darkness

At twilight, a dark shadow had descended over the valley of Gog. The war drums of Idamus and his army of darkness were heard in a distance like thunder roaring through an eerie pre-storm air. On a nearby hilltop a bonfire raged beneath the shoulders of Orion.

I had not yet fully differentiated the Erotic Soul from Idamus. Together they were still the Erotic Soul. Alpha-Omega (the Law of Sympathetic Vibrations in Motion) was cycling my focus of conscious awareness among the principle forces of Eros. Each consecutive Eros cycle was more profound, informative, and transformative than the previous. Alpha-Omega had steered me first to the Eros Godhead (IAO-Set/Satan). However, I was now being steered toward a direct alchemical engagement with the Erotic Soul. It was time for the son of the Logos to engage the son of IAO.

Technically, Idamus is the grandson of IAO-Satan. The direct offspring of IAO-Satan is the Erotic Soul. Idamus is the direct offspring of the Erotic Soul and the Human Mind making him even more dangerous to humanity.

Idamus rises out of the eternal sea - the Sea of Eros. The Sea of Eros is the Erotic Soul. The eternal sea is not the world of politics. It is the universal living life force of the created cosmos.

Idamus has supernatural powers inherited from his grandfather. Additionally, his immediate descent from the Erotic Soul protects Idamus from any direct alchemical engagement within the human mind due to the Erotic Soul's underlying causal position. This provides him a natural shielding which cannot be penetrated by any of the previous alchemical processes. Lastly, his part-human nature provides him with a special knowledge of - and direct avenue into - the human mind. He is extremely powerful and extremely dangerous. He propagates lies, deceit, and fear. He knows all your weaknesses and he will exploit them to no end. He has total command of the astral world and can see and steer your future. He will attempt to steer you straight into oblivion. He is *"The Beast."*

My Logos breathed a great fire into my soul and I became like a lion. I could see Idamus about one hundred yards away in the astral. He stood atop another nearby hilltop not too far from the bonfire. The flames glistened off his polished tightly-clad black body armor. Two great black horns rose up from the sides of his helmet. He was very tall and had a menacing supernatural persona. He looked awesome. However, his dark astral forces were no match for the Logos. The Logos had made me invincible to the army of darkness.

Swords, knives, blades, axes, and the like, were all coming at me. To my own surprise, not one landed a blow. But Idamus was different. I needed to be careful. He and I locked sights on each other, and for a moment, we just stared at each other. I made the first move. I began charging toward him. In route, I was reminded that he was also my spiritual child. I moved like fire and immediately he and I were face-to-face. I raged at him and said.

> "If you want to kill me, then go ahead and kill me."

I took hold of him and looked deep into his eyes to his soul. But this time, it was I who was startled by what I saw. What did I see? I saw the Divine Soul. The army of darkness and Idamus instantly vanished from my sight and I was left all alone in the field stunned by what I just saw. I looked up and saw the stars of Orion (the Hunter, Lucifer). Orion and Osiris are one and the same. Lucifer hunts the forces of creation. The Logos restores them. If the constellation of Orion represents Lucifer-Logos, then which constellation of stars represent IAO? The answer is: Scorpio.

In this moment, everything had become clear. The Erotic Soul within creation, and the Noetic Soul within humanity, find their ultimate source within the Divine Soul. Not only was creation formed out of the Father's love for his Son (the life force of his Divine Soul), but his Son was inside it. This to me was more reason why the prime directive is to save creation. The life of God is within it.

This reminds us of the following verse from the Gospel of Thomas:

> *"If those who lead you say, 'See, the Kingdom is in the sky,' then the birds of the sky will precede you. If they say to you, 'It is in the sea,' then the fish will precede you. Rather, the Kingdom is inside of you, and it is outside of you. When you come to know yourselves, then you will become known, and you will realize that it is you who are the sons of the living Father. But if you will not know yourselves, you dwell in poverty and it is you who are that poverty."* ... Jesus of Nazareth

Idamus and Narcissism

When fear overcomes the mind, in that very moment, the dark forces of our id complex possess us. Idamus steals the light of the mind from the Human Soul and the Human Soul is pushed into the psychic cognitive background. The fear induced by Idamus can be so painful that our mind seeks to break away from its reality by building a fake narcissistic personality strong enough to steal the light away from Idamus.

This is the dark champion narcissistic personality. It is the second beast which rises from the Earth. I call it the *"Gorgon."* It provides a false relief and cohesion to the mind. The Human Soul remains stuck in darkness. The greater the fear grows, the greater the narcissism grows to compensate. This complex develops unconsciously and is usually developed in childhood and can remain in control of the human mind for an individual's entire life. See Notes [9] and [10]

It is possible, perhaps due to some genetic cause, that within the chemical wiring of the brain, the force of theta which counters Idamus, is somehow suppressed, or not fully engaged as well as it should be, and as a result, the person is over-exposed to his or her id complex. Both nature and nurture may be the cause. Within the human mind, the counter-balancing force of theta should only be lifted when the Human Soul consciously reconciles its internal Lucifer wherein Lucifer re-enters the original light of Ain Soph and transforms back into the Logos. In other words, when reflective awareness of the Nuad is established within the human mind.

Symphony of the Echelons 255

Strangely, the dark champion of the narcissistic mind offers a degree of cohesion to the psychic composition of the afflicted mind, and by way of this false cohesion, a degree of genius and success may emerge, but it is all false. The dark shadow which follows this illusionary cohesion is the tendency to immediately self-destruct without warning and with the unconscious willingness to take others along with them. The narcissistic cohesion of the mind may also make it more difficult for narcissists to self-observe and realize all their internal psychic aggregates and spiritual forces. Why? Because their center of gravity is not their authentic-self, it's their dark champion narcissistic personality (the Gorgon). The Gorgon mind is the anti-monad! See Notes [11] [12] and [13]

There is still hope for narcissists if they wish to overcome their affliction. The key to overcoming narcissism is becoming self-aware of and saying good-bye to the dark champion personality (the Gorgon) and allowing the authentic-self (Human Soul) to experience fear without losing the light of the mind. It is possible, believe it or not, that narcissists can reach so far as entering the Void at the end of the Second Mountain because the affliction involves the id complex and the personality, not the false-selves or automated instincts. However, unless the narcissist corrects this issue, he or she can never begin the Third Mountain. The reason is, in order to climb the Third Mountain, we must entrust our emotional well-being to the Divine Soul, not to some dark champion narcissistic personality (the Gorgon).

Only in this way can we build the prerequisite super-cognitive emotional awareness to climb the Third Mountain and open all its seals, internalize all the required realizations, and learn to enter and explore the underlying cosmic quanta of the noumenon.

I bring up the subject of narcissism again at this late stage of the book, firstly because of its direct connection to the id complex, but secondly because the process of overcoming narcissism is similar to how we complete the final labor of the Third Mountain in reconciling creation with the source. See Notes [14] and [15]

The only difference is that, in the final alchemical labor, the human personality itself is not a factor. The Gorgon quantum has not overtaken the personality. The personality in the Third Mountain is transparent and malleable. It has no position of control or defense within the human psyche such as with the narcissistic personality (the Gorgon).

In many ways, the narcissist is a tortured saint with an amazing hidden advantage to accomplish the prime directive of the Human Soul. This is due to his or her heightened emotional sensitivity. Ironically, the condition is both a gift and a curse with amazing potential. It is from the genealogy of these genetically predisposed individuals, more so than any other genealogy, that I believe the Monad will one day take root, blossom, and flourish upon the Earth. Until then, treat these individuals with extreme caution and compassion. Why? Because from these same individuals, evil can easily take hold and devour humanity.

The Monadal bloodlines are the Royal bloodlines, as they are genetically predisposed to more likely compel the development of the Monad within an individual. It is my belief that in ancient times these bloodlines were guided into positions of power.

Shadowing this virtuous predisposition is the inherent flip-side predisposition to develop narcissism. Therefore, I believe these bloodlines are closely monitored by the cosmic watchers and caretakers of our Monadal Humanity.

> Note: 9
> The Dark Champion (1)

When the Dark Champion intervenes, who is in charge of the mind? Idamus is still in charge. In the mind, desire precedes fear and delusion. Idamus compels the rise of the Gorgon Dark Champion personality. The Dark Champion places the mind under complete control of Idamus. Do not be fooled by the Dark Champion's position in the human mind. Idamus pulls all her strings. The Dark Champion (the Gorgon) is an eleventh permutation. She is the child of Idamus. She rises out of fear, not out of love. She is an apostate and an abomination of the mind.

A person with a Multiple Personality Disorder is a person with multiple Dark Champions - but still only one Gorgon. The Gorgon fabricates each false-façade of the human personality. The Gorgon is "the one who is many" and "the first and the last." She is the first of creation and the last to be reconciled (see Note 10).

Ironically, many self-proclaimed *"Masters"* of the Great Work are nothing more than Gorgons. The Gorgon is the third head of chaos of Cerberus. The three heads of Cerberus are Satan, Idamus, and the Gorgon. The two beasts are also Gog and Magog - Satan's helpers.

What the Roman Catholic Church calls *"Demonic Possession"* is when a person loses positive control of his or her mind to the id complex (Idamus and the Gorgon). It is a psycho-spiritual condition. It is not purely psychological, and it is not purely spiritual.

- End Note -

> Note: 10
> The Dark Champion (2)

Idamus arises from the second principle force of the Erodonic Trinity (life force). The Dark Champion Gorgon arises from the third principle force of the Erodonic Trinity (Matter-Energy). When Idamus compels the rise of the Dark Champion Gorgon within the mind, he becomes, in a sense, her father. However, before rising in the mind, she is actually the mother of the mind residing in the underlying matter of creation. She is the oldest living being within all creation.

In every trinity, the first and second permutations together compel the rise of the third permutation. (1-awareness, 2-life, 3-energy).

The Gorgon is an extension of the Idamus. Together, Idamus and the Gorgon form the *"Id Complex."*

Fear actually stems from the space residing between the Idamus and the Gorgon. It stems from a triangulated induction between the two poles of the id complex and the perspective-awareness of the mind. Fear is induced by the "destitution of life" within the Idamus.

Although the narcissistic personality may never actually arise in a person and steal the light of his or her mind, the underlying Gorgon quantum and its impulse are still there and must eventually be dealt with by all alchemists. There are bandwidths within Maub corresponding directly to the Idamus and the Gorgon exclusively. These planetary bandwidths compel the rise of both beasts within the unconscious mind of all human beings on Earth. Resonance with the divine Father elevates the human mind beyond these dark forces.

- End Note -

> Note: 11
> Pathology

I have come to firmly believe that the id complex (Idamus / Gorgon) is the root cause behind many pathologies of the human mind. After forming the Nuad, the alchemist is vastly more prepared than anyone to deal with Idamus, the Gorgon and any pathologies of the id, which are:

1. The Adaptive Narcissistic Personality
   (The second beast, the Beast of the Earth, the Gorgon)

2. Narcissistic Personality Disorder
   (Far end of the narcissistic spectrum)

3. Paranoia

4. Obsessive Compulsive Disorder

5. Delusion

6. Dementia

7. Schizophrenia and Border Line Personality Disorder

8. Multiple Personalities and Demonic Possession

9. Post Traumatic Stress Disorder (PTSD)

   More than likely, there are more pathologies which could be added to this list.

- End Note -

> Note: 12
> The Dark Champion (3)

The Gorgon (Dark Champion) is the second beast which rises from the Earth. The Earth symbolizes our body - our neurological chemistry.

* * *

"Then I saw another beast that rose out of the Earth; it had two horns like a lamb and it spoke like a dragon. It exercises all the authority of the first beast on its behalf, and it makes the earth and its inhabitants worship the first beast, whose mortal wound had been healed. It performs great signs, even making fire come down from heaven to earth in the sight of all; and by the signs that it is allowed to perform on behalf of the beast, it deceives the inhabitants of earth, telling them to make an image for the beast that had been wounded by the sword and yet lived; and it was allowed to give breath to the image of the beast, so that the image of the beast could even speak and cause those who would not worship the image of the beast to be killed. Also, it causes all, both small and great, both rich and poor, both free and slave, to be marked on the right hand or the forehead, so that no one can buy or sell who does not have the mark, that is, the name of the beast or the number of its name. This calls for wisdom: let anyone with understanding calculate the number of the beast, for it is the number of a man. Its number is six hundred and sixty-six." ... Revelation 13:18

* * *

The sword that the First Beast survives is Lucifer's Force of Theta. The Sword of Death. (The Mortal Wound). Idamus is reanimated life after life in every human being when they reincarnate and lack reflective awareness of the source within the human mind. However, Idamus cannot survive or resist the Sword of the King of Kings.

- End Note -

Note: 13
666

*"This calls for wisdom: let anyone with understanding calculate the
number of the beast, for it is the number of a man.
Its number is six hundred and sixty-six."
... Revelation 13:18*

The repeating sixes is the Beast of the Earth (the Gorgon).

The meaning of the repeating sixes (666) and why it applies to the Beast of the Earth, is twofold:

1.) The repeating number pattern (666) refers to the repeating compounding processes of creation. This indicates that the Beast of the Earth, the Gorgon, is a product of creation.

2.) The reason six is used in the repeating number series is because the Beast of the Earth is the product of the human psyche compounding in on itself. Before the reconciliation of creation, the Human Psyche is the sixth permutation of consciousness and is the dark inflection of the Human Soul.

    The modern-day person bears the mark of the beast, 666.

- End Note -

> Note: 14
> The Name of the Second Beast

The first beast - the Beast of the Sea - is Idamus. The name *"Idamus"* is derived from the Freudian name *"Id"* because they refer to the same thing. The name for the second beast I adopt from Greek mythology.

The second beast, which rises from the Earth, who is the dark champion narcissistic self, in the mind - is the child of the first beast, and whose number is 666, is none other than the *"Gorgon."*

The word Gorgon comes from the Greek word *"Gorgos"* which means *"Dreadful."* In Greek mythology there are three Gorgons, one of which is Medusa. The Gorgons are said to be a female beast. This corresponds well to the narcissistic-self since the narcissistic-self rises out of the brain matter of the physical body (the Earth).

Matter-Energy is the third principle of the Erodonic Trinity and a super partner to the Spirit and the Numina, all of which are symbolized by the feminine, the personification of love. In the case of the Gorgon, it is the inverted dark inflection of love. The Gorgon is the furthest thing from love. It is the furthest thing from God.

The three Gorgons of Greek mythology are a reflection of the three types of narcissism which are:

1.) Grandiose *"Overt"*

2.) Fragile/Vulnerable *"Covert"*

3.) High-Functioning *"Exhibitionist"*

- End Note -

The Gorgon

Figure [18]

This is the head of Medusa, part of Greek Mythology. The Gorgon is the Dark Champion of the human mind, the Narcissistic Self, the Second Beast which rises from the Earth. Its number is 666. The Gorgon is also *"Lilith"* and the *"Whore of Babylon."*

> **Note: 15**
> **The Two Beasts**

Idamus (Gog) is the first beast which rises out of the Sea of Eros (Erotic Soul). The Gorgon Dark Champion Narcissistic Personality (Magog) is the second beast which rises out of the Earth. The Earth is the neurological brain chemistry of the physical body. The second beast rises out of consequence of the first beast. In the mind, the second beast rises as the child of the first beast. The second beast hates and is terrified of the first beast. Their relationship is not based in love, but in fear.

The first beast has a deep dark sexual nature. It covets the life force of others to compensate for its own lack of life, its mortality. It is dark but not necessarily twisted. The sexual nature of the second beast is both dark and twisted. The second beast, in response to the first beast, mocks and abuses sexuality and is deeply sexually conflicted. It secretly hates sex. Sex for the second beast is not about eroticism. It is about power, ego, and control. The most severe pathologies, including cannibalism, arise out of the second beast (the Gorgon). The second beast is narcissistic, selfish, profoundly superficial, idealistic, shallow, shortsighted, and materialistic. It believes only in the material world and lying is natural and routine. The modern world worships the second beast, and those who manifest her, are most respected in business and in superficial mundane relationships. The *"mark"* of the second beast is its *"fakeness"* in the human personality - its lack of authenticity. All people subconsciously notice this mark and most modern people subconsciously honor it, abide by it, and trade by it.

"So that no one can buy or sell who does not have the mark, that is, the name of the beast or the number of its name. This calls for wisdom: let anyone with understanding calculate the number of the beast, for it is the number of a man. Its number is six hundred and sixty-six."

- End Note -

The Third Trident of Eros

Alpha-Omega was back on the move. My focus of conscious awareness was now being shifted and re-directed to the third principle of the Erodonic Trinity. My super cognitive emotional awareness entered into symphony with the very essence of matter and energy itself within the matrix of my own physical creation.

Either the energy and matter of my physical creation was itself pitch black, or it was my awareness of the energy and matter which was pitch black. At this point, I did not know which, but what I did know was that my experience in this place was of the most profound absolute darkness I had ever experienced. Chaos waves were rippling up from the deep and my Idamus-compelled fear was hitting a peak. However, even while I trembled and ached in stress and fear of this awful, terrible place, I never lost my awareness of the immortal Divine Soul of the Father, or the Spirit of his eternal and everlasting love. In this moment of the most striking piercing contrast, I realized fear is the spirit of death, love is the spirit of life.

This was all unfolding while I was awake in the physical world, but my focus of conscious awareness was at the same time submerged in the twilight realm between two worlds, fully engaged with the cosmic quanta of the underlying noumenon.

In this moment of total complete pain and fear, a beautiful golden light emerged out of the darkness.

Suddenly, what came forth from this golden light was the Virgin Mary. She was wearing a light blue veil which covered her head and body. Beneath her blue veil, she was dressed all in white. She was young in appearance. I would estimate that she was a young teenage girl. Her face was innocent, sweet, and angelic. She came and sat at my side and placed her arm around me and her head on my shoulder to console me. I was completely enveloped by her spirit. Her spirit was full of an absolutely extraordinary deep divine love I cannot describe. In that moment, her spirit performed the necessary alchemy.

Who was she? She was the Numina, the sacred feminine force of the cosmos. She is the super-partner of the Spirit and of Matter-Energy. When the Virgin Mary came to my side, was she the Numina of the world, the cosmos, or my own? The answer which comes forth to me from the noumenon is: She was all of the above. They are all in the same spectrum, and they are all extensions of one another.

The truth is, all the forces in the universe, including all permutations of consciousness, have no actual form. They are a swirling sea of theogenic and metagenic forces within the underlying cosmic quanta out of which the mind gives rise and form. Read the chapter 5 subsection on the Heaven of Simmatuu.

The Spirit imagined, and the Cosmic Mind came forth, and when the cosmic quanta passed through the Cosmic Mind, what emerged was creation. From within that creation arose the primordial universe and the physical universe, and we call this *"Reality."*

Our individual mind works the same way as the Cosmic Mind, except when our individual mind gives rise and form to the quantum which passes through it, we call this *"Illusion."*

Because I already associated the Numina with a form in my mind, when the theogenic cosmic quantum of the Numina passed through my mind, it took that form, in this case, the form of the Virgin Mary.

But there were unique aspects being added to the form which were not my own. The forms held in the planetary group mind have a profound influence on how these forces manifest to us. The Cosmic Mind, the Planetary Mind, and the Individual Mind are all cooperative in determining the final form of the cosmic quantum as it passes through the human mind.

Depending on a person's culture and religion, the Numina may appear to us in many different forms such as: The Virgin Mary in Christianity and Islam: Isis in Egypt, Lakshmi in Hinduism, Maya in Buddhism, Anahita in Zoroastrianism, Tonantzin of the Aztecs, Rhea in ancient Greece, as well as many other sacred universal feminine forms.

Symphony of the Echelons

This causes us to question: What is real?

The ultimate reality is in the underlying sea of cosmic quanta, which is essentially a cosmic ocean of swirling theogenic and metagenic quantum forces all resonating as one, measurable by neither space nor time. This ultimate reality is fully realized both within Causal 'A' and Causal 'M'.

In the Causal 'A' of Ain Soph there is only formlessness (The sea of the cosmic quanta all resonating as one). However, in the Causal 'M' of the Cosmic Monad we know both form and formlessness all resonating as one. They are the original Monad (A) and new Monad (M); first heaven and new heaven.

> *"And I saw a new heaven and a new earth: for the first heaven and the first earth were passed away; and there was no more sea."*
> *... Revelation 21:1*

Revelation 21:1 poetically describes the alchemical integration of Heaven and Earth, the fulfillment and accomplishment of the new Monad. Heaven is our resonance with the source, and Earth is our creation. When integration occurs, what comes forth is a new Heaven and a new Earth. This occurs on every cosmic scale. The sea which was *"no more,"* is the formless sea of cosmic quanta transformed into the resonating form of creation.

Many in the world keep waiting for certain personages to appear and certain events to come about according to prophecy, and each according to their own faith or religion. What most do not realize however is that the prophecy is not meant to be fulfilled within the world, it is meant to be fulfilled within you. When the prophecy is fulfilled within you, the world will follow.

> *"When you come to know yourselves, then you will become known, and you will realize that it is you who are the sons of the living Father."....Jesus of Nazareth (Gospel of Thomas)*

Chapter 8

<u>Advent of the Logos</u>

My days continued as I toiled with the forces of darkness. In the days that passed I learned much regarding the forces of Eros, but the actual reconciliation between the source and creation remained beyond my reach. I felt like I was being crushed under the weight of this awesome task. However, it was all about to change.

It was in the early morning hours on a cold winter day in December 2016, three days after the winter solstice. The Sun was just beginning to rise above the horizon when I opened my eyes.

Standing before me was my Logos in all his glory. His light turned the pre-dawn darkness into day. He was standing at the entrance of a beautiful tunnel of light behind him radiating all around him like the Sun. Dressed in an all-white military uniform in full regalia, he called out to me with his arm and hand extended and said:

> "My son, you have restored the covenant of my
> eternal and everlasting love.
> I now come to you to restore the covenant of your
> eternal and everlasting life."

Something of profound significance had just occurred in my spiritual alchemical process. I had crossed a critical turning point. This much I knew. The full realization and sheer magnitude of what just occurred was not fully realized in the moment.

Exactly 7 days and 3 days later, it would be. The bond of resonance between my Human Soul and the Father, via my Logos, had withstood the test of the forces of Eros and had regained a dominant position over creation. The resonance between the Father and the Soul is Love. When the bond of that resonance is tested and confirmed, the covenant of the Father's love is restored within the matrix of creation.

At this point, the forces of Heaven (the Father) now have an avenue and a means to bring the forces of the Earth (creation) into harmony with its Spirit via its unbreakable bond with the Human Soul. This is the Holy Grail. The holy blood symbolizes the resonance of the Father running through the veins of creation. My Logos had just handed me the Grail. What is the secret of the grail?

> *"You will be the land, and the land will be you.*
> *If you fail, the land will perish, as you thrive,*
> *the land will blossom."... Arthurian Mythology*

This mythological phrase is both the planetary group mind and the cosmic mind broadcasting a universal maxim of truth. The grail symbolizes a unified bond between the Father and creation via the Soul, the Son of God. It symbolizes the key to reconciling the source and creation and therefore the key to re-constituting the Monad within creation.

> *"That which is Below corresponds to that which is Above,*
> *and that which is Above corresponds to that which is Below,*
> *to accomplish the miracle of the One Thing."*
> *... The Emerald Tablet*

My initial realization was only that I had upheld the Love of the Father within my temporal-physical being amidst the dark trials of Eros. Beyond that, I was not yet aware of the alchemical leverage and dominance which had just been confirmed and conferred upon me by the Logos. Its use, however, is undoubtedly symbolized by the Excalibur Sword.

I was now in possession of the sword of the king of kings but amazingly I was not yet aware of it. I would draw the sword from the stone only at the moment chosen by the Father. That moment was fast approaching.

Chapter 8

<u>The Cosmic Temple of IAO</u>

I had hoped maybe the trials of Eros were over with the Logos declaring his covenant restored. No, they were actually about to escalate. But the key difference was that I was now armed with the ability to reconcile the forces of creation. Again, I would not come to this realization until the key moment was at hand.

Seven days had passed. Alpha-Omega was again on the move. I was now being redirected back to the Godhead of the Erodonic Trinity, IAO. In a profound state of quantum meditation, while my Human Soul was dancing with the fire spirits of the underlying cosmic quanta who reign supreme within the sublime magical realm of the noumenon, I was quickly transported by the forces of Alpha-Omega to the Cosmic Temple of IAO.

This time, however, I would approach the almighty throne of IAO with the grail in hand. My waking mind was not fully aware of the magnitude of what was in my possession. However, IAO surely was, and it would have a profound effect upon our next meeting. Sometimes withheld perspectives are best, as they can negatively influence what is to come next. Beyond the mind, in my soul, I already knew what I had.

The Cosmic Temple of IAO has nine gates with each gate representing one of the nine cardinal permutations of consciousness; absent the 10th permutation, which is more than a permutation of consciousness, it's a permutation of mind. The temple itself is the 10th permutation.

As I approached the cosmic temple of IAO, all nine gates magically opened as if I were an expected and welcomed guest. An internal illumination glowed from behind each of the nine gates with an unspoken signal that I was about to receive knowledge very few ever receive. As I approached the inner sanctum of IAO before me stood a throne of flames composed of four great pillars of fire. IAO was in omnipresent form.

Symphony of the Echelons

IAO Transmission:

- The Logos gives the Human Soul half the knowledge of creation. IAO gives the other half.

- The Logos and IAO join to complete the Monad.

- IAO reminded me of the three super metas which drive the first three permutations of consciousness which are: Father (Awareness), Divine Soul (Life), and Spirit (Love).

- The three super metas are (1st) Force Potential, (2nd) Being, and (3rd) Unity (See chapter 7).

- Love compels imagination through a (4th) super meta called *"Dynamis"* which gave rise to IAO, the Erodonic Trinity, the mind, and the first of creation. It all suddenly emerged like a flame out of nothing. See Note [5]

- The Cosmic Mind cannot sustain itself in Causal 'A' so it formed its own Causal, Causal 'B.'

- IAO was born from the imagination of the Spirit, not from the awareness of the Father.

- Anything not born of the Father is born in darkness.

- IAO awoke in darkness. IAO's first realization as the Godhead of a new Erodonic Trinity was the Void, which is life separate, alone, and devoid. This compelled fear, not love. The Erotic Soul formed accordingly.

- The Erodonic Trinity which formed inside the creation of Causal 'B' in its first moment was the antithesis of the Divine Trinity in Causal 'A.'

- Because the Spirit was resonant with the Father and the Divine Soul when it imagined IAO, attributes of the Divine Trinity were carried into the darkness of creation. (Reminds of the next phrase.)

"And a third of the angels fell with him."

> Note: 5.2
> Divine Algebra

The Super Meta together compose a divine mathematical algebra, or spiritual physics, which is self-stimulating and self-propagating, whose acoustical mathematical permutations I call, *"Theokinesis."* The origin of everything is mathematical, acoustical, and theokinetic.

- End Note -

IAO Transmission (Continued):

- The Father's first and eternal realization was of his own life, the Divine Soul which compelled his eternal Love, the Spirit. This formed the Upper Trinity (Divine Trinity). The Father's second realization was his awareness of creation that was in darkness because it was formed out of the imagination of the Spirit, not his awareness.

- This compelled something new. This compelled the (5th) Super Meta called *"Thelesis"* which gave rise to the *"Will of the Father."* The Will of the Father was to reconcile creation and bring it into resonance with Causal 'A'. The Will of the Father is the *"Logos."* The Will of God and the Word of God are one and the same.

- The Logos awoke to the realization of his Will, which is the Life of his Will, the Human Soul. The Numina reflects the Father's Love of creation. The Will of the Father formed the Lower Trinity.

- IAO was born of the Father's Love. The Logos was born of the Father's Will. The Cosmic Logos completed and fulfilled the Will of the Father and reconciled creation on a cosmic level infinite eons ago before time began. This formed the Cosmic Monad with whom both IAO and the Cosmic Logos are one with today. This same process is now repeating on all planetary and individual scales of life throughout all of creation. See Note [16]

- A proper creation requires both Love and Will.

- Without the reconciliation of creation by the Cosmic Logos, the stars, galaxies, solar systems, the organization of the atom, would have never properly organized and formed.

- IAO provides the design and the materials through imagination. The Logos provides the construction and organization through resonance with the Father.

- IAO is the Architect. The Logos is the Builder. The Father is the Developer.

- There is not one Creator, there are two Creators. IAO and the Logos are the twin Co-Creators of the created cosmos. Both the Logos and IAO are Demiurgos. Both are Demiurge.

- The Logos and IAO are super-sexual in origin. The split of Male and Female sexuality unfolded as result of their co-creation. This is the origin of the sexes. It always takes two to create, not one.

- Love is the Sacred Feminine.

- Will is the Sacred Masculine.

- Break in IAO Transmission -

The emergence of the Lower Trinity (Sacred Trinity) to save creation and reunify the Monad is the *"Immaculate Conception"* of the Father. The Logos, the Human / Noetic Soul, and the Numina, together, are the Immaculate Conception. The Immaculate Conception is a subatomic process of creation which brings forth the entire universe. Its principle emerges into world mythology via the Collective Unconscious.

> Note: 16
> Sumerian Mythology

What we learn from IAO and the Logos about the process of creation has a striking parallel to Sumerian creation myth regarding the half-brother sons Enlil and Enki of the Annunaki King Anu. There are many variations to the story due to Mesopotamia's long history and the different cultures which adopted the Sumerian gods and made them their own but with some additions and alterations to their stories. However, there are common threads running throughout these stories emerging out of the collective unconscious that echo the underlying forces of consciousness in their process of creation.

Enlil, Enki, and Enki's son Marduk, possess like qualities to IAO, the Logos, and the Human Soul along the same lines as Set, Osiris, and Horus of Egyptian mythology who represent the same forces of consciousness giving rise to creation.

In the Sumerian story, Enlil is seen as more powerful than Enki and is initially worshiped as the most-high god, second only to Anu, but in each variation of the story Enlil and Enki are constantly at odds with Enki being the defender of humanity and Enlil possessing some sort of tragic flaw, much like Achilles, and of course IAO. The feud ultimately gives way to the rise of Enki's son, Marduk, who takes on traits of both Enlil and Enki to become the new ruler of the gods.

What we learn from the forces of the cosmic quanta is that, it was not IAO-Enlil's decision to bring about the Great Flood, but it was because of IAO-Enlil's psycho-somatic interaction with the humanity on Earth that the Great Flood was brought about.

The story is similar to the Egyptian story of Set, Osiris, and Horus where Set murders Osiris but Isis, the wife of Osiris, posthumously conceives their son Horus from the body of Osiris from which Horus rises to overthrow Set to become the new ruler of the gods.

– End Note –

Symphony of the Echelons

The Monad in Cosmic Scales

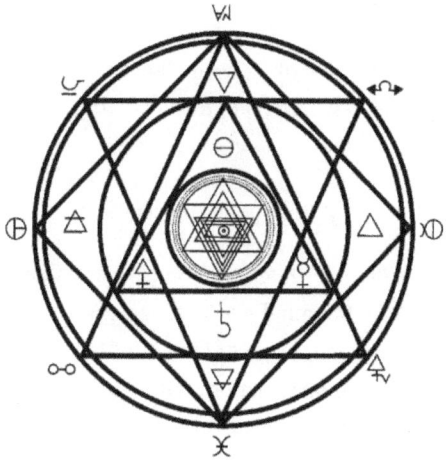

Figure [19]

The Great Work is repeated in cosmic scales:
Cosmic, Planetary, Individual

> Note: 17
> Genesis

"So God created man in his own image, in the image of God created he him, male and female created he them."
... Genesis 1:27

Alchemical Translation

"God created man in his own image," translates to God created man <u>inside</u> his own image. Mankind was not made <u>in</u> the image of God. Mankind was made <u>by</u> the image of God (God's own Imagination). God's imagination is the imagination of the Spirit, the Cosmic Mind. *"Male and female created he them,"* is a reference to the splitting of the sexes and the manifestation of universal duality in all things via the reconciliation of IAO and the Logos.

- End Note –

> Note: 18
> Quantum Effect of Creation

Quarks are subatomic particles considered to be the fundamental constituents of matter. Quarks always exist in pairs. If you attempt to pull a quark pair apart, a new partner for the separated quarks will immediately appear. Quarks cannot be isolated. Some physicists consider this to be one of the few spooky anomalies of quantum physics. This is an after effect of the pairing of IAO and the Logos when creation was reconciled at the cosmic level at the very beginning of creation. There are also six types of quarks. This reflects the six spiritual bodies of primordial creation and the six temporal bodies of physical creation. The force which binds quarks and gets stronger and stronger as you attempt to pull quarks apart, is the unbeatable force of the Logos.

- End Note –

> Note: 19
> Universal Duality In All Things

The universal duality in all things arises from the reconciliation between IAO and the Logos at the cosmic quanta level of existence. Male-Female, Light-Darkness, Odd-Even, Hot-Cold, Etc.

Odd numbers preceding Even numbers reflects IAO being the first born of the Divine Trinity. In terms of creation, Lucifer was correct when he said: "First there was darkness and then there was the light." The cosmic level of reconciliation between IAO and the Logos laid the foundation for all the laws of the universe and the very nature of our created reality.

- End Note –

Symphony of the Echelons

Twin Creator Symbolism

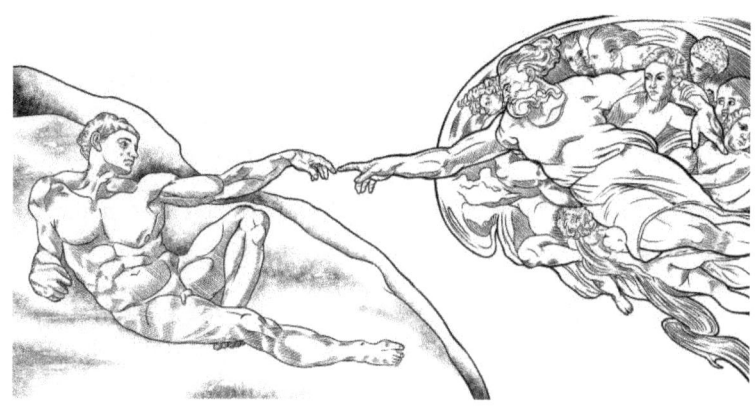

Figure [20]

Perhaps there is a double meaning behind the image of Adam and God, by Michelangelo. Perhaps the image is unconsciously of IAO and the Logos compelled by the Collective Unconscious.

The transmission of IAO reminded me of the passage the Logos had quoted me regarding creation when I was with him in the Void before his unmasking:

"In the beginning God created the heavens and the Earth. The Earth was formless and empty, darkness was over the surface of the deep, and the spirit of God hovering over the waters said let there be light."

Having received knowledge from both the Logos and IAO regarding creation, my resonance with and my analysis of this verse is as follows:

- Heaven represents creation in resonance with the divine source. It also represents the original unity of Ain Soph (Causal 'A').

- The Earth represents creation not yet in resonance with the Father. This is the physical universe when it was first conceived and also humanity and the planetary levels of the physical universe as they currently exist. The planetary and individual scales of physical creation are still not yet in full resonance with the divine source. The cosmic level is already in full resonance (Cosmic Monad, the Theosphere).

- *"The Earth was formless and empty, darkness was over the surface of the deep,"* is a reference to the Void.

- *"The spirit of God hovering over the waters said let there be light"* is a reference to the Will of God, the Logos, and his Will to save creation. The Logos is the light. The name Lucifer means *"The Light."* Lucifer and the Logos are two states of the same quantum force within the noumenon. The Father is the "invisible light" which preceded both the "darkness" and the luminescent "white light" of the Logos. The invisible form is the original form to which Lucifer said he still remains true. It all finally reconciles and becomes clear.

- *"The waters"* is the Erotic Soul, the Sea of Eros.

Symphony of the Echelons

IAO Transmission Continues:

- The Great Work is not about the Human Soul achieving immortality. The Human Soul and the Numina were born with the Logos the moment the Father manifested his Will. Because you were born directly from the Father you were born in the Light and you were immortal from the first moment the Father conceived you because you came directly from his Will.

- IAO, the Erotic Soul, Matter-Energy (Dyad-Erodonic Trinity-Mind-Creation-Eros) were all born in darkness because they were not born directly from the Will of the Father. They were conceived spontaneously from the imagination of the Spirit.

- Because Eros did not come directly from the Father, it had no knowledge of the divine source. It did not know it was missing anything. It thought it was God because it knew nothing else.

- Even if IAO and the forces of Eros were told of the source, they could never resonate with the source, or find the source, because they were not born of the Father. Eros-Creation needed to be saved if it were going to be kept, thus the Father sent in the Logos, his Human Soul, and the Numina.

- The Human Soul's purpose in the Great Work is not to save itself, it is to save creation. You (the reader, the Human Soul) are the chosen one who the Father sent in to save creation. Your mission is to raise creation to the immortal state, not yourself. You could not lose your immortality even if you tried. You were born of the Father; this can never be changed. Your immortality is guaranteed. Creation is not guaranteed.

- When the physical body of a human being is conceived, the whole cosmic creation process is repeated, just on an individual scale. During the nine months of gestation in the womb, while in darkness, only the Erotic Soul is there. The baby's physical movements while in the womb come from the Erotic Soul, the soul of creation.

- The Noetic Soul (Human Soul) enters the human body only at the moment of its first breath in the new world - only at the moment of its birth. The Noetic Soul enters as a passenger.

- The problem of creation arises when, after physical birth, the Noetic Soul's resonance with the Father becomes dampened due to the dense matter of the brain and the prism of the mind. The Logos of the Noetic Soul responds by leaving the light of heaven and entering the dark Void of the creation that imprisons the awareness of its Noetic Soul to free it from its prison with its force of death (Theta). Theta also buffers and protects the Noetic Soul from Idamus and the Erotic Soul who covet the position and stature of the Noetic Soul. The mind builds all its automatic defenses and thus begins the Great Work. First, the Noetic Soul (Human Soul) must regain its awareness and allow its Logos to return to the light, and then, finally, it is ready to fulfill its original purpose.

- Idamus is in darkness within you and does not understand your presence or your purpose, so he hates you and attacks you. You sense this now more than ever because your Lucifer has returned to the light as the Logos. There is no more Theta within you to protect you from Idamus or the forces of Eros. Your lack of awareness of Eros is the cause of the Chaos. You must now reconcile Eros. See Note [23]

Symphony of the Echelons 283

- IAO transmitted that when IAO was originally reconciled at the cosmic level to become part of the completed Cosmic Monad, the result of reconciling the mind with the Father made IAO omnipresent and omnipotent within creation. Thus, creation is bound and steered by an all-powerful Cosmic Mind which pervades all the created cosmos. See Note [24]

- Another result of reconciling creation with the Father was that everything in creation became scaler or fractal. This was the solution of the Logos in reconciling a finite created form with an infinite, eternal, non-created, formless source. Everything in creation now exists in scales from the atom to the galaxy and beyond. The scales of creation appear to be boundless in any cosmic direction.

- Time is a dimension of awareness embedded in the very fabric of space itself existing between mind and space. Space, time, and mind are all connected. The genesis of time is the reconciliation between the Father and IAO via the Logos. The Father is the eternal now. IAO is the distant forever. The reconciliation between now and forever produces "Time." The mind will find this statement difficult to understand. The Noetic Soul understands perfectly.

- The Logos took what was originally conceived in darkness, brought it into the light, breathed the spirit of God into it, and made it much more than it ever was. The Logos turned the imagination of the spirit born out of Love, into a miracle of the Father born out of Will, all out of love for you, so that together, you may live forever.

- Ultimately, the Noetic Soul and the Erotic Soul are reflections and expressions of the same original Divine Soul - the life force of God.

> Note: 20
> The Only Begotten Son of God

"For God so loved the world,
that he gave his only begotten son,
that whoever believeth in him should not perish,
but have everlasting life." ... John 3:16

In mythology, the *"Son"* is the *"Soul."* The Collective Unconscious speaks of cosmic principals and cosmic forces. To be consistent with the way the Collective Unconscious speaks to us through mythology, it would not be referring to only one soul. It would be referring to a *"Type"* of soul. Through alchemy we realize that there are three soul types which characterize three different life forces of consciousness. So, which of the three soul types is the *"Only Begotten Son of God?"*

The *"Divine Soul"* was not begotten. The Divine Soul has always existed as the eternal life force of the Father.

The *"Erotic Soul"* was not begotten by the Father. It was begotten by the Spirit through the spontaneous act of creation.

The only soul intentionally begotten by the Will of the Father is the *"Human / Noetic Soul."* It was begotten by the Will of the Father to intercede with the Erotic Soul of creation to save it and reunify it with the Divine Soul of God to reconstitute the Monad.

The *"Human / Noetic Soul"* is the *"Only Begotten Son of God."*

- End Note

> Note: 21
> Immortality

IAO and the Logos join together to teach the son of man (the human being, the alchemist) the various concepts of immortality and its basis in natural fact.

- End Note -

Chapter 8

Creation

Figure [21]

Psalm 19:1

The heavens declare the glory of God;
the skies proclaim the work of his hands.
(Reference to the Logos)

> ## Note: 22
> ### Behold A Pale Horse

"And I looked and behold a pale horse: and his name that sat on him was Death, and Hell followed with him. And power was given unto them over the fourth part of the earth, to kill with sword, and with hunger, and with death, and with the beasts of the Earth."
...Revelation 6:8

Alchemical Translation

Death who sits on the Pale Horse is Lucifer with his force of Theta. The Hell which follows Lucifer is what commences beyond the Sanctum of the Logos - the Trial Period and Final Labor of the Third Mountain. The Pale Horse is an Omen of the Eighth Alchemical Process.

- End Note -

> Note: 23
> The Fifth Angel

Revelation 9:1

"And the fifth angel sounded, and I saw a star fall from heaven unto the earth: and to him was given the key of the bottomless pit."

Alchemical Translation

Lucifer-Shiva is the Fifth Angel of the Apocalypse.
The Star Fallen is Lucifer. Lucifer leaves Heaven to enter the darkness of creation to rule Hell and ensure the emancipation of the Noetic Soul.
Lucifer holds the keys to the abyss, which is Theta (Death).

Revelation 9:2 to 9:4

"And he opened the bottomless pit; and there arose a smoke out of the pit, as the smoke of a great furnace; and the Sun and the air were darkened by reason of the smoke of the pit. And there came out of the smoke locusts upon the earth: and unto them was given power, as the scorpions of the earth have power. And it was commanded to them that they should not hurt the grass of the earth, neither any green thing, neither any tree; but only those men which have not the seal of God in their foreheads."

Alchemical Translation

Lucifer-Shiva is the *"Destroyer of Worlds."*
He emerges to destroy creation when the mind (Forehead)
lacks resonance with the divine source (Seal of God).

- End Note -

> Note: 24
> The Matrix

IAO and his alchemy of providence (Sigma and the Aurelion) and his interaction with all levels of mind on all scales of life within creation forms the *"Matrix."*

- End Note -

> Note: 25
> Erodysis

When the Nuad and creation enter a state of reconciliation via the eighth alchemical process of Symphysis, this reconciliation produces a new spirit of unity I call *"Erodysis."* On a cosmic level, the whole universe is in Erodysis. Erodysis is the spirit or energy of the Monad. Erodysis compels the emergence of Dominus Turiya. To enter Erodysis we first must receive the Covenant of Eros. In line with assigning the universal forces with letters of the Greek alphabet, Erodysis is *"Gamma."*

- End Note -

The Rose

Figure [22]

The Rose symbolizes creation being lifted up into resonance with divinity. It symbolizes completion of the Great Work and the fulfillment of the Will of the Father. It symbolizes Erodysis and the completion of the Monad.

The Covenant of Eros

My spiritual sojourn to the Cosmic Temple of IAO was more than just a visit. I had passed through some sort of cosmic portal and underwent a special convergence of mind, with the super cognitive intelligence latent within creation forming a permanent bond between my individual human mind and the superluminal Cosmic Mind. This psychic bond of the mind is a new fellowship with IAO that stands alongside and supports our fellowship with the Logos. The Logos and IAO are two manifestations of the Father with which we must integrate our conscious mind. I entered the Cosmic Temple of IAO with the covenant of the Father in hand made possible through my Logos. In response, IAO handed me his own covenant - the Covenant of Eros - which would uphold and protect my Covenant with the Father while within creation. When the mind supports and upholds our resonance with the Father, creation comes to not only accept the Father's love, it comes to guard it and reinforce it. The psycho-sexual dynamic of my temporal creation was no longer an opponent to my resonance with the Father. It was now a proponent to my resonance with the Father. The Logos hands us the grail and then IAO seals it and protects it within the mind of the human being. This is the Seal of God. In order to save our creation, we must have this seal.

The Conjugation of Heaven and Earth

Three more days had passed. Alpha-Omega was back on the move. After my visit to the Cosmic Temple of IAO and after receiving a seal of allegiance from the Godhead of the Erodonic Trinity, who is the awareness of Eros (IAO), I was now being directed to the life force of Eros, the second principle force of the Erodonic Trinity, the Erotic Soul, who my human mind had already conceived a child with while in darkness. This child is Idamus. Idamus is the beast and 10th permutation of my spiritual-temporal being. Idamus had usurped the position of the Erotic Soul and would be standing before me in any

Symphony of the Echelons

attempt by my Human Soul to engage the Erotic Soul. He had become an agent of the Erotic Soul but a profoundly evil agent. The Erotic Soul itself was not evil. There was actually a hidden advantage to this, which I was admittedly unaware. You see, Idamus is an individualized point of interaction between our individualized human mind and the Sea of Eros, which is an infinite cosmic ocean. When the Father and IAO were reconciled timeless eons ago, not only did IAO become omnipresent, so did the Erotic Soul and Matter-Energy. How could I possibly reconcile an infinite ocean? Idamus may be our fieriest adversary, but he also holds one of the final keys to the completion of the Monad.

There was no way around Idamus. I had to confront him and take responsibility for him. He was my creation. I had to confront the Babylonian Devil, Pazuzu (Idamus). All human beings in the darkness of their own mind create him. We all have our own Idamus; our own beast. Idamus is a very real, living, psycho-kinetic manifestation. He was taunting me, laughing at me, and daring me:

> "You want to enter the Eternal? You will have to get past me and I will destroy you."

Do not talk to Idamus and do not listen to him. He is a pathological liar and a deceiver. He has supernatural power and knows all your weaknesses better than you. He will attempt to break you down in ways which are not so obvious. He will attempt to cause you to doubt yourself and to doubt your worthiness of the Father's love. He will do everything possible to come between you and the Father and he will do it all from within your own mind. Anything you fear, he will purposely amplify. It is the greatest battle you will ever endure in your life and in the Great Work. The suffering of the body can never match the suffering of the mind and that is where he will come for you.

I was not expecting Idamus. It had been days since my last conscious encounter with Idamus. My last engagement with Idamus was on the battlefield of the astral world. This was before my Logos had declared the covenant of his love restored, and before IAO had reaffirmed the covenant of the Logos with the covenant of Eros. I had hoped the worst was behind me. However, I was not yet aware that Alpha-Omega would keep cycling me between each principle force of the Erodonic Trinity until my Monad was complete.

It was in the 3:00am hour when Idamus would again begin his vicious assault. He could not have picked a worse time for his attack. For in this moment, I was in a profound state of symphony with my Logos in the magical realm of the noumenon.

Idamus could not see this. It is beyond his ability. All he saw were the temporal dimensions of my being. He could not see what I was holding behind the cloak of my temporal-physical existence.

I became aware of his attack and quickly stood up in the astral world to confront him. Idamus was furious. He was raging, swinging, and vicious. I floated before him upright with strength, fortitude, and with no fear. He could not land a blow. My Logos suddenly spoke and said: "My Son ……. Now!"

I felt the power of the Logos running through me as I miraculously unsheathed a magical sword blazing with fire. I felt guided by a great power whose source was well beyond my soul. The resonance of the Father was with me as well as that of the Logos and IAO. It was the sword of the Logos blazing with the fire of IAO. The sword was a manifestation of my covenant with the Father supported and confirmed by both the Logos and IAO. It is the sword of the King of Kings, and before it, all must submit. Idamus immediately ceased, submitted, and fell to his knees with the sword of fire squarely pointed at him blazing in all its glory. He cried and wept. He knew he was defeated. In his remorse on his knees, he said:

> "But this was my world. You stole it from me. Your body is my body. You are the invading intelligence. Not me. I am nothing now. I have nothing. You have taken everything from me."

Idamus in this moment was actually telling the truth, but his analysis of the situation was as far from the truth as it could be. The truth he spoke was, this was his world, and this was his body, and the Noetic Soul is a foreign intelligence. But it is a foreign intelligence sent in by the Father, not to steal his world, but to save it. I spoke to him:

"Idamus, your perception cannot be further from the truth. I am not here to steal your world. I am here to save it. But yes, I agree with you, this is your world, and this is your body."

I placed down the blazing sword of fire. I had the full power and authority in this moment to take his life. Instead of taking his life, I chose to preserve it. Why? I had flash backs to our moment on the battlefield looking into his eyes and seeing the essence of his soul which was the Divine Soul. Idamus looked up at me in disbelief. I knew his thoughts.

"What is he doing? Why is he not taking my head?"

I decided to speak again:

"Idamus, you were born in darkness and do not know the light. You do not know the Father. You do not know your ultimate source. You do not know the Kingdom of Heaven."

"It is only through the Father that your world may be saved and last forever, and it is only through me that you can know the Father and the Kingdom of Heaven. I did not come to take everything from you. I came to give everything to you."

"Idamus, I offer you the cup of my blood, which is my covenant with the Father. Drink my blood and through my blood you shall gain eternal and everlasting life, and through that life, you shall come to know the eternal and everlasting love of God. I am offering you the Kingdom of Heaven in addition to the Kingdom of the Earth."

"I offer you all of this on one condition; that you freely offer me your life, as I have offered you mine, and your world, which I openly admit is yours, and because I have openly offered you mine. Together, we can know each other's world, and together, we can live as one."

Idamus stood up, humbled and in tears. In his first moment of courage and faith in the Human / Noetic Soul, he said:

"I accept your offer and your terms."

We then embraced as one for the first time. In this moment, his life and my life began the long journey of becoming one life. In this moment, our combined force of life entered the highest and most profound spectrum of symphysis. The union would not happen in a single moment, or in a single day. The process would continue over many days, and the sacrament of our communion would be repeated over and over again in increasingly higher levels of symphysis until the Monad was completed. In this moment, I entered the spectrum of Symphysis Turiya which I had foreseen in the tunnel of light exactly 19 months earlier to the day during my realization of the Divine Trinity.
See Note [26]

This is the original and primordial alchemy of the universe re-taught to us by Jesus of Nazareth. It is meant to be practiced by every human being on Earth and throughout the universe, between every human being and their body of creation. Jesus' ministry was all about teaching how to fulfill the Will of the Father and how to enter the Kingdom of Heaven.

The saving and lifting-up of creation is the prime directive of the Human / Noetic Soul born by the Will of the Father. This is your task if you choose to fulfill it. This is the chemical wedding of Eros and Turiya. Eros is the mind and body of our created bodily form. Turiya is our level of resonance with divinity rising-up within the conscious mind. The chemical wedding of Eros and Turiya reconstitutes the Monad within the realms of creation; in this case, our physical creation.

> Note: 26
> The Conjugation of Heaven and Earth

Blood symbolizes our resonance with the Father. Heaven symbolizes Causal 'A', the Primordial Universe and the Spiritual Group Mind. Earth symbolizes the Physical Universe and the Temporal Group Mind. The Idamus within you must come to believe in the Human / Noetic Soul within you. The alchemical medium and central point of conjunction between the Triad, Dyad, and Nuad, which forms the Monad, is in the third principle force of the Eros-Dyad: Matter-Energy.

The sacrament of the union of heaven and Earth is performed by focusing on the matter-energy of your physical being (Eros) and your resonance with the Father (Turiya) while holding them in differential resonance with each other. (Primordial Alchemy)

The ordeal I went through with my Idamus in quick time (straight path) is what all of humanity on Earth in the physical universe is going through right now, but in slow motion over many lifetimes (spiral path). The key is to love in the face of evil and to lift up your fellowman.

The life of Jesus of Nazareth exemplified the spiritual struggle of the Noetic Soul within all human beings to fulfill the Will of God in reunifying creation with divinity. The struggle of the Noetic Soul to fulfill the Will of God is symbolized as the *"Lamb."* The Lamb does not symbolize only Jesus, it symbolizes every Human / Noetic Soul.

- End Note -

Chapter 8

The Philosophical Earth

Figure [23]

The Philosophical Earth symbolizes the bodily creation of man and its reconciliation with the Father via the Soul (The Son of God).

"But who may abide the day of his coming?
And who shall stand when he appeareth?
For he is like a refiner's fire and like fuller's soap."
... *Malachi 3:2*

The Dark Knight

A day or so later, I am in the astral world. Alpha-Omega has once again shifted my focus of conscious awareness to the 3rd principle of Eros: Matter-Energy (Super-partner of the Spirit and Numina).

I found myself riding horseback across a foggy autumn field in the medieval period of history when suddenly I am being attacked by a knight in a full suit of dark body armor. This knight is amazing and terrific in battle. He is moving like the wind and striking like lightening. I am very impressed.

However, my Logos ultimately prevails, and I knock the dark knight down to the ground. The knight appears lifeless. I jump off my horse and kneel down at the side of the knight and move back his face shield to see who this knight was who put up a greater battle than even Idamus himself.

> "Oh my God! No, it cannot be! Please, no! no!"

> I was in tears. I shouted out, "What did I do?"

> Behind the face shield was a young, beautiful, female face. She is the love of my life. I am now coddling her lifeless body in my arms weeping and crying over her.

> I cried out to the sky and placed my head on her.

> "I was supposed to love her, not destroy her!"
> "I was supposed to love her, not destroy her!"

> I repeated it, again, again, and again.
> I held her body tight to mine.

My love for her was so intense in this moment that I became deeply resonate with the essence of Matter-Energy. Harmony had overcome Chaos. Then suddenly, she came back to life and was completely transformed floating above me as a naked Aphrodite with a red ribbon of triumph entwining her angelic form and an evergreen wreath appeared arching over her in the sky, the wreath of eternal and everlasting life.

This dark knight was the underlying quantum which gives rise to the Gorgon. When reconciled, it gives rise to a living manifestation of eternal divine love.

<u>Enter The Eternal</u>

The tertiary cycles of Eros continue at higher and higher octaves within the alchemical process of Symphysis. During the cycles of Symphysis, a transcendent axiom of truth emerges with the realization that all three principal forces of Eros exist beyond Good and Evil. It is our relationship with the forces of Eros that are either good or evil, but the forces of Eros themselves are neither.

Amazingly, at the very end of the Great Work in our darkest hour, it is IAO himself who comes forth and enlightens us and teaches us the greatest mystery of all mysteries, which is the mystery of the Will of the Father and how to fulfill it.

When we engage the omnipotent force of IAO with a dark unenlightened mind, what we manifest in response is the dark power of Satan. When we engage the Erotic Soul (Sea of Eros) with a dark unenlightened mind, what we manifest in response within the deep cavern of our unconscious mind, is the Beast (Idamus). When we engage the Matter-Energy of our body (our creation) with a dark unenlightened mind, what we manifest in response are the dark underlying forces of Chaos (the Gorgon).

The Blazing All-Seeing Eye

Figure [24]

The All-Seeing Eye is the symbol of the Logos.
The Universal Fire is the Symbol of IAO.
Together, they symbolize the Reunified God.

> Note: 27
> The Secret Key of IAO

The secret key of IAO is that everything we project in our mind towards IAO, IAO materializes and makes real. If we project fear, hatred, chaos, and poverty, IAO materializes it in our life. But if we are resonant with the Father when we interact with IAO, then IAO will materialize Heaven on Earth in our life. This is why IAO appears as Satan to the masses. It is because they project evil to IAO, so in return, IAO materializes evil in their life. The truth is, IAO is beyond good and evil, and can manifest either one. This is why our Internal Logos turns into Lucifer upon our physical birth to protect our Human / Noetic Soul from our own mind, and ensure that through death, our Human / Noetic Soul will be liberated from the beast which our own mind creates through its unconscious interaction with IAO. It is also why other humanities have outlawed any humanity be created with the ability to interact with IAO thereby outlawing the ability to complete the Monad. Our humanity is an exception to this cosmic law and is why we are both feared and revered as a human race. It is why the human lifespan on Earth must be kept short and it is also why the humanity of the Earth is considered IAO's chosen people. The chosen are not of one nation, but of all nations on Earth.

- End Note -

David

Figure [25]

When the Noetic Soul introduces the love of the Father to the Erotic Soul within the human mind, David is born within us.

> Note: 28
> Alchemy of the Cosmic Mind

The Law of Attraction, Karma, Eye for an Eye, Blessings, Fortune, Destiny, Predetermination, Materialization, are all the effect of the human mind interacting with the Cosmic Mind of IAO. The result of the interaction is not decided by IAO. It is decided by our state of mind when we interact with IAO. Send IAO love, and love and blessings will be returned 10-fold.

> Forgive and you will be forgiven.
> Replenish others and you yourself shall be replenished.
> What you do unto the least of you, you do unto God.

> *"What you think, you become. What you feel, you attract.*
> *What you imagine, you create."*
> *...Siddhartha Gautama (Buddha)*

- End Note -

In totality, the Human Soul's relationship with the cosmic forces of Eros forms the deep underlying causal roots and fundamental substructure of the mind, out of which develops all the mind's deep cognitive, trans-cognitive, and high cognitive levels.

However, once we enter the highest spectrum of Symphysis Turiya, where we engage Eros with Turiya in a sustained and confirmed resonance with the Father, what manifests in response is something entirely new and radically different.

It is February 2017. As I look out to the distant western horizon across the deep blue sea, I see a setting Sun with the beast slowly descending beneath the Sea of Eros. But then as I turn and look out to the distant eastern horizon across the Sea of Eros, I see a rising Sun and within that Sun, I see David. David is the antithesis of the beast. David is the eagle swallowing the serpent and the new 10th permutation of our temporal-spiritual being. When David rises from the Sea of Eros, we finally reawaken in our primordial body in the primordial universe while remaining alive and awake in our physical body in the physical universe. This is Dominus Turiya.

The re-unification of the Monad is now fully realized and accomplished through the unification of creation with the divine source of Ain Soph, and the Will of the Father is fulfilled. Ain Soph is the original Monad. Through the unification of Ain Soph and creation, the new Monad is *"Christ."* Christ is the highest and most exalted permutation of God, for Christ is everything reconciled to one, including divinity and all of creation.

When our created being becomes unified through the unity of Christ, we realize that all along, it was the Cosmic Christ who was compelling Alpha and Omega and directing our movement through the Great Work. Rising up from the depths of the cosmic quanta, I heard the name of the Cosmic Christ. His name is Eloah. Christ is the living embodiment of the way, the truth, and life of the Father, and alchemy is his song. For he is, for all eternity, the Immortal Beloved.

- The End -

Ode to Joy

Ludwig van Beethoven (1770-1827)

Figure [C]

ECHOES OF THE BELOVED

The Lord's Prayer
Alchemical Translation

Our Father

> The Father is One-for-All. He equally belongs to everyone everywhere.

Which art in Heaven

> The origin of everything is maintained in a state of perfect harmony and peace through the resonance of the Father. This is Heaven. The origin is Causal 'A.' The origin is the divine Monad of Ain Soph, of which the Father is the Godhead.

Hallowed be Thy Name

> The Father is known to us through his sympathetic resonance. His resonance is his name. The first 3 verses comprise the first stage of the prayer, which seeks to bring the mind into discovery of the Father's resonance (the love of his Spirit).

Thy Kingdom Come

> Verse 4 is an invocation of the Father's divine love (the Spirit). The prayer graduates to an awareness of the Father's love within the mind but yet our full body of creation at this point lacks full resonance with the Father. This is Communion Turiya. Our Human / Noetic Soul at this point, sensing the Father's love, but still lacking full resonance in our body of creation, invokes the Father's resonance to a higher level, harmonizing our body of creation. When we resonate with the divine Father, we enter his kingdom and his kingdom enters us.

Thy Will be done on Earth, as it is in Heaven

>Verse 5 of the prayer is a declaration of our intent to fulfill the Will of the Father. The Earth is the body of our creation not yet in resonance with the Father. Heaven is everything already in resonance with the Father. The Will of the Father is to bring our body of creation into resonance with his original nature. (Primordial Alchemy).

Give us this day our Daily Bread

>Verse 6 of the prayer is a supplication to the power of the Father to compel the body of our creation (Eros) to enter into resonance with our awareness of the Father's love (Turiya). This is the *"Daily Bread"* which bestows upon the body of our creation the covenant of eternal and everlasting life. The holy blood and bread symbolize the resonance of the Father running through the veins of our body of creation. This is the Holy Grail and the marriage of Eros and Turiya.

And forgive us our debts, as we forgive our debtors.

>To bring our body of creation into full resonance with the Father's love, we must release our mind's fixation on the things of the world. Verse 7 of the prayer gives us permission to forgive our own self-judgement, thereby allowing our mind and body, the freedom and self-acceptance it needs to enter into resonance with the Father and the Kingdom of Heaven.

And lead us not into temptation, but deliver us from evil.

> Darkness arises through our lack of awareness of the Father. Our mind and its body of creation are born in darkness. Verse 8 of the prayer reminds the Human / Noetic Soul to maintain awareness of the Father while the mind and body are fixated on the illusion of the world. The key is not to deny the world, but to bring our relationship with the world into harmony with our awareness of the divine source of the Father. In this way, we bring all things into unity within the matrix of our being, including the Father and all of creation.

For Thine is the Kingdom, the Power, and the Glory, Forever. Amen.

> Verse 9 is a proclamation of realized unity. When the light of the Father shines through the prism of the mind, the light divides into the three Magi of the Father, which are:
>
> 1.) The Father: That which remains undivided, formless, infinite, and absolute.
>
> 2.) IAO: The Power of the Father.
>
> 3.) The Logos: The Glory and Will of the Father.
>
> When our creation enters into resonance with the Father, the mind no longer divides this light, and within us, the original true nature of the divine Father is finally realized. Verse 9 proclaims this unity by proclaiming the Kingdom (the Cosmos), the power (IAO), and the glory (The Logos), all belong to the Father. Thus, the Will of the Father is fulfilled. This unity is Christ, the New Monad. Christ is Dominus.

Section: IV

Reflections of the Great Work

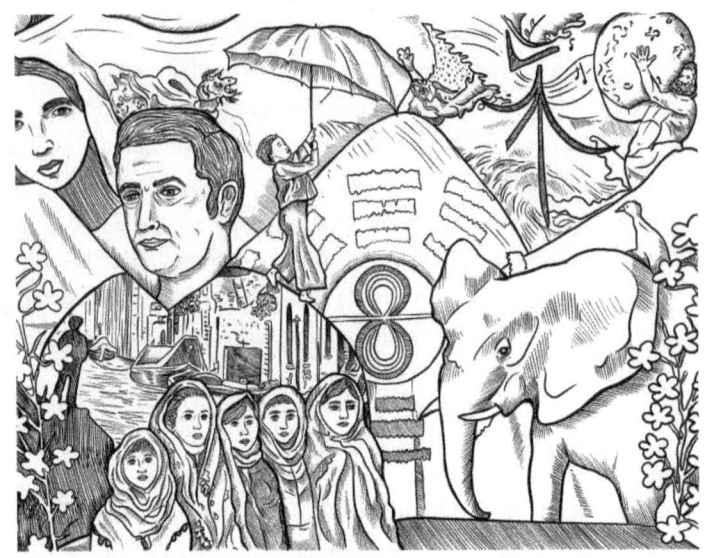

Figure [D]

This collage is composed of images from the main body of this book with added images of the Authentic-Self (Boy with Umbrella); Children of the First Light (5 Children); The Sea of Eros (The Wave); the Logos (Bust of my Father); Love of Creation (The Elephant); The Numina (Image of the Blessed Mother of God).

Summary of Creation

A popular theological theory is that the original unity of God, known as Ain Soph, created the universe because it was alone. Meditation on the quantum forces within us reveals that this was not the original cause. Quantum meditation reveals that the original act of creation occurred in three primary stages:

Stage 1:

Creation was originally sparked (Dynamis) into existence spontaneously and unintentionally by the force of love (The Spirit) produced by the awareness of Ain Soph (The Father) being aware of his own living life force (The Divine Soul).

Stage 2:

The Father became aware that the Spirit of his love had sparked creation into existence, but that creation was stuck in darkness because this spark of creation happened unintentionally without his awareness.

Stage 3:

The Father's realization of his creation compelled *"Thelesis"* [8] to arise, which is a love for his creation (Numina) and a Will (Logos) to save it. The life force of this Will is the Human Soul (Noetic Soul).

The creation process unfolded in a repeating pattern of scales. The first scale to emerge was the cosmic. The cosmic scale of creation was saved or reconciled at the very beginning of time. A new unity emerged between Ain Soph and creation. This new unity is the Cosmic Christ (Eloah), the New Monad.

When the new cosmic unity was finally realized and achieved, sexuality emerged within all living things as a reflection of the original coupling of Love and Will in the alchemical creation process.

---

[8] Thelesis is the *"Immaculate Conception"* of the Father.

All duality is a reflection of the original creation process and the Father's Will (Logos) to bring creation back into unity with his divine source. Darkness-Light, Odd-Even, Hot-Cold, Female-Male, Negative-Positive, are all a reflection of the original cosmic creation process. This process is now repeating on the Individual and Planetary levels of creation. It is repeating in scales.

The Father sent the Noetic Soul into the world by force of his Will to lift up creation back into unity with his original divine being. Your creation is your mind and body. You will keep coming into the world until you fulfill the Will of God.

The Christic Trinity

A new trinity emerges within the unity of Christ. Within every unity there is a trinity. The awareness of Christ is Dominus. The life of Christ is David. The love of Christ is Erodysis.

Dominus is the unity of awareness. It is the unity of:

1.) The Father
2.) IAO
3.) The Logos

David is the unity of life. David is the unity of:

1.) The Divine Soul
2.) The Erotic Soul
3.) The Noetic Soul

Erodysis is the unity of love. Erodysis is the unity of:

1.) The Spirit
2.) Matter-Energy
3.) The Numina

Christ is the unity of all. Christ is the unity of:

1.) Dominus
2.) David
3.) Erodysis

The cosmic quanta within Matter-Energy transforms from the Gorgon into a living manifestation of love to become the bride of Christ - our internal Magdalene. This is *"The Making of the Rose Diamond."*

Section: IV

The Treasury of Souls

How many Human Souls are there? Many people ponder this question. Alchemy provides the answer. There are three types of souls and an infinite number of Human Souls which re-collect back into one soul. The Human Soul is the Noetic Soul. They are one and the same.

Divine Soul: There is only one Divine Soul. It is infinite and absolute. It is the life force of the Father. It does not manifest directly within creation. We commune with it through resonance.

Erotic Soul: There is only one Erotic Soul. It is omnipresent. It is the life force of IAO. It animates all bodies of creation. It is a dimension of mind.

Noetic Soul: There is only one Human Soul / Noetic Soul. It is fractally reflected and infinitely replicated. It is the life force of the Logos. It superimposes and intervenes with the Erotic Soul within the mind. When we stand between two mirrors, we see an infinite progression of individual reflections of self. Each reflection in progression is an individualized Noetic Soul. When we reconstitute the Monad, we emerge standing as one in front of the mirror. This is:

"The Achievement of the Philosophers' Stone."

The Noetic Soul standing in front of the mirror is the Noetic Soul on a cosmic level. It is the Noetic Soul of Eloah, the Cosmic Christ, the Immortal Beloved. When we complete the Great Work, we manifest Eloah while maintaining our reflection within the human mind. This is the unified mind.

The Four Beasts of Revelation

In the Bible's Book of Revelation, there are Four Beasts. The Four Beasts are archetypal symbols of the Collective Unconscious. What do they represent within the human psyche of mankind?

1.) <u>A Leopard with 7 heads and 10 horns.</u>
   This is Idamus. Humanity's unconscious interaction with the cosmic life force of the Sea of Eros manifests within the human psyche, a personification of evil.

2.) <u>Has 2 horns like a Lamb. Talks like a Dragon.</u>
   This is the Gorgon. It has a humanlike appearance like the lamb, but bears the mark of the beast with its narcissistic personality. The mark rises in the voice.

3.) <u>A Great Dragon with 7 heads and 10 horns.</u>
   This is Satan. Humanity's unconscious interaction with the Cosmic Mind of IAO generates the dark power of Satan to manifest evil on Earth.

4.) <u>A Lamb with 7 horns and 7 eyes.</u>
   The modern theological interpretation is that the lamb represents Jesus of Nazareth. This is only partly true. The whole truth is much more profound. The lamb represents the Noetic Soul that was begotten by the Will of the Father to intervene with creation to save it and bring it back into unity with Ain Soph. The Noetic Soul is the sacrificial lamb which bears the suffering of the world in order to carry-out the Will of the Father. Jesus is a personification of this principle.

The Will of the Father

The mystery of human suffering is a question many people attempt to reconcile with a belief in God. The Will of the Father is to lift up creation into the light, to lift up the world out of darkness, to lift up all who suffer. The life of his Will is the Human / Noetic Soul.

You are not the subject of the suffering. You are the Father's answer and solution to the suffering.

The forces of darkness attempt to come between the Noetic Soul and the Father. The darkness tempts us to question our worthiness of the Father's love and to question the very existence of God.

The Noetic Soul is sent into the world by the Father to engage and save that which is in darkness. This is why we come to experience the suffering of the world. It is not that the Father does not love you. It is just the opposite. Your Noetic Soul is the Father's expression of his love for creation and his Will to save it.

The Noetic Soul is the Only Begotten Son of God.

"For God so loved the world,
that he gave his only begotten Son,
that whosoever believes in him should not perish,
but have everlasting life." ... John 3:16

Echoes of the Beloved

The Spiritual Group Mind

Figure [E]

An artistic representation of the Spiritual Group Mind of the Earth.
The ribbons enveloping the Earth are the bandwidths. The nine stars represent
the nine heavens. Each heaven is a bandwidth of the Spiritual Group Mind.
The Tree of life is shown rising upward through the Sea of Eros.
The flames in the sky represent the Divine Trinity.

Section: V

Index of Notes

The notes are sidebar comments and deeper explanations of some of the terminology and principles employed in the main text of the book.

A.)   Definitions
1.)   The Sacred Fire
2.)   The Noumenon
3.)   The Heavenly Realms
4.)   The Akashic Records
5.)   Divine Algebra
6.)   Theosphere
7.)   The Human Being
8.)   Permutations
9.)   The Dark Champion 1
10.)   The Dark Champion 2
11.)   Pathology
12.)   The Dark Champion 3
13.)   666
14.)   The Name of the Second Beast
15.)   The Two Beasts
16.)   Sumerian Mythology
17.)   Genesis
18.)   Quantum Effect of Creation
19.)   Universal Duality In All things
20.)   The Only Begotten Son of God
21.)   Immortality
22.)   Behold A Pale Horse
23.)   The Fifth Angel
24.)   The Matrix
25.)   Erodysis
26.)   Conjugation of Heaven and Earth
27.)   The Secret Key of IAO
28.)   Alchemy of the Cosmic Mind

Index of Figures & Images 323

	Description	Artist / Source
A.)	Cover Artwork Cover Design	R.A. Frederickson Melissa Williams Design
B.)	The Primordial Earth	Elementos (Color) Asmomarfaru (B/W)
1.)	The Grand Rosicrucian Alchemical Formula	See Figure for Data (Color) Elementos (B/W)
2.)	The Trans-Dimensional Anatomy of the Human Being	Erik P. Antoni (Design) Y. Starr (Color) Meth Twelve (B/W)
3.)	Divine Soul Resonating Form – Historical Symbol	Unknown (Color) Elementos (B/W)
4.)	Divine Soul Resonating Form – Modern Symbol	Jeannine C. Marie
5.)	Taoist Microcosmic Orbit Diagrams	Mantak Chia
6.)	Atlas	Unknown (Color) Meth Twelve (B/W)
7.)	Angel Playing Harp in the Clouds	Giovanni Batista Gaulli (Color) Saratm (B/W)
8.)	Refraction of Light	Unknown (Color) Haritha KH (B/W)
9.)	Ouroboros	Unknown
10.)	Third Sanctum Symbolism	Photographer Unknown (Color) Haritha KH (B/W)
11.)	Fibonacci Sequence	Unknown

12.)	Mask of the Logos Symbolism	Eliphas Levi (Color / BW)
13.)	Monad Universal Symbolism	Erik P. Antoni
14.)	The Tempest Soul	Arlene DeMarco (AD) (Color) Elementos (B/W)
15.)	Symphony of Cosmic Forces	Arlene DeMarco (Color) Meth Twelve (B/W)
16.)	Cerberus Symbolism	Unknown (Color) Elementos (B/W)
17.)	Idamus Symbolism	Photographer Unknown (Color) Elementos (B/W)
18.)	The Gorgon Symbolism	Unknown
19.)	The Monad in Cosmic Scales	Unknown
20.)	Twin Creator Symbolism	Michelangelo (Color) Meth Twelve (B/W)
21.)	Creation	Arlene DeMarco (Color) Saratm (B/W)
22.)	The Rose	Photographer Unknown (Color) Unknown (B/W)
23.)	The Philosophical Earth	Unknown (Color) Elementos (B/W)
24.)	The Blazing All-Seeing Eye	Unknown
25.)	David	Michelangelo
C.)	Ode to Joy	Ludwig Van Beethoven
D.)	Reflections of the Great Work	Arlene DeMarco (Artwork) Napoleon Duheme (Collage) Annabazyl (B/W)
E.)	The Spiritual Group Mind	Arlene DeMarco (Color) Meth Twelve (B/W)

BIBLIOGRAPHY

Andreae, Johann Valentin. *Chymical Wedding of Christian Rosenkreutz*. Edinburgh, UK: Floris Books, 2016.

Atmanspacher, Harald, "Quantum Approaches to Consciousness," *The Stanford Encyclopedia of Philosophy* (Summer 2015 Edition), Edward N. Zalta (ed.), 2015.

Berne, Eric M. D. *Games People Play*. New York: Grove Press, 1964.

Campbell, Joseph, Bill D. Moyers, and Betty S. Flowers. *The Power of Myth*. New York, N.Y.: Anchor Books, 1991.

Chia, Mantak, and Michael Winn. *Taoist Secrets of Love: Cultivating Male Sexual Energy*. Santa Fe: Aurora Press, 1984.

Chia, Mantak. *Fusion of the Five Elements: Basic and Advanced Meditations for Transforming Negative Emotions*. Tuttle Publishing, 1989.

Darwin, Charles. *The Origin of Species*. Franklin Center, Penn: The Franklin Library, 1859.

De Chardin, Pierre Teilhard. *Le Phenomene Humain*. Paris: Editions Du Seuil, 1955.

Freud, Sigmund, and James Strachey. *The Standard Edition of the Complete Psychological Works of Sigmund Freud. Vol. 22. (1932-1936). New Introductory Lectures on Psycho-Analysis, and Other Works*. London: Hogarth Press, 1964.

Global Consciousness Project. "The Global Consciousness Project Meaningful Correlations in Random Data." Accessed July 24, 2018.
http://noosphere.princeton.edu/homepage4.html

Hall, Manly P. *The Secret Teachings of All Ages: An Encyclopedic Outline of Masonic, Hermetic, Qabbalistic, and Rosicrucian Symbolical Philosophy*. New York: Jeremy P. Tarcher/Penguin, 2003.

Jung, Carl Gustav. *The Archetypes and the Collective Unconscious*. Princeton, N.J.: Princeton University Press, 1980.

Kaku, Michio. *Parallel Worlds: A Journey Through Creation, Higher Dimensions, and the Future of the Cosmos*. New York: Anchor Books, 2006.

Meyer, Stephen C. *Darwin's Doubt: The Explosive Origin of Animal Life and the Case for Intelligent Design*. New York: HarperOne, 2013.

Steiner, Rudolf, and Christopher Bamford. *How to Know Higher Worlds: A Modern Path of Initiation*. Hudson, NY: Anthroposophic Press, 1994.

Wikepedia.com "Eschatology." 2018. Accessed July 25, 2018 . https://en.wikipedia.org/wiki/Eschatology

———. "Fourth Way." Accessed July 24, 2018. https://en.wikipedia.org/wiki/Fourth_Way

———. "Gog and Magog." 2018. Accessed July 24, 2018. https://en.wikipedia.org/wiki/Gog_and_Magog

———. "Hermes Trismegistus." Accessed July 24, 2018. https://en.wikipedia.org/wiki/Hermes_Trismegistus

———. "Osiris Myth." Accessed July 24, 2018. https://en.wikipedia.org/wiki/Osiris_myth

Winn, Michael. "Primordial Qigong." YouTube video, 08.18.. Posted [Nov 23, 2009]. https://www.youtube.com/watch?v=rIP_ICLWpAs

www.ingramcontent.com/pod-product-compliance
Lightning Source LLC
LaVergne TN
LVHW011415080426
835512LV00005B/61